ARROWS OF FORTUNE

ARROWS OF FORTUNE

BY

ANTHONY DEANE-DRUMMOND

LEO COOPER
LONDON

To
Evie, Shirley, Angela, Anna and Celia,
and with the greatest respect and admiration
for all those soldiers and civilians
with whom I have worked
and played.

First published in Great Britain in 1992 by
LEO COOPER
190 Shaftesbury Avenue, London WC2H 8JL
an imprint of
Pen & Sword Books Ltd
47 Church Street, Barnsley, S. Yorks S70 2AS

A CIP catalogue record for this book is available
from the British Library

ISBN 0 85052 323 0

Typeset by Yorkshire Web, Barnsley, South Yorkshire
in Plantin Roman 10 point

Printed in Great Britain by
Redwood Press Limited
Melksham, Wiltshire

CONTENTS

FOREWORD

by Major-General John Frost

From the start, which is a description of the first British Parachute operation which had the object of blowing up an aqueduct in Southern Italy and ended disastrously for the participants, to the end, we have a story of a man of the utmost determination and courage.

After an amazing escape from the POW camp in Italy, we find him almost immediately back again with a Parachute unit, where he is involved with helping other British prisoners of war to escape. No sooner is this over than he is back in the thick of things with the Battle of Arnhem, from which he once again manages to make a fantastic escape from being a POW.

Despite fearsome medical setbacks, he is soon again involved with aircraft, to become a British Glider champion and to take command of 44 Parachute Brigade TA. His introduction to this was to be beguiled, by his predecessor, into the "This is your Life" programme on the BBC. However, it is as commader of the SAS, both in Malaya, where they become the most successful unit in the army, and in Oman where they have to take a major part in quelling a most dangerous rebellion, that he will be best remembered. Later he is selected as deputy commander at Sandhurst and finally to do a stint at the Ministry of Defence in the operations department, where he has to face all the frustrations which meet any active officer in such surroundings. Despite his formidable record, this is his last appointment in the army.

Undeterred, he launched into British industry in the shape of paper making, but, preferring to do his own thing, he was soon in the country again, very successfully supplying much-needed wood-burning stoves. One might regard this as yet another example of a man who was continually turning on the heat.

In all, this is a wonderful account of someone who constantly sets a really fine example. I feel proud and honoured to be asked to write this foreword.

ACKNOWLEDGEMENTS

About three-quarters of this book concerns my military service; the rest provide linking chapters and vignettes on gliding, the eight happy years I spent in the paper industry and my subsequent efforts as an entrepreneur exploring many avenues from selling to doing up houses.

My own book *Return Ticket,* now out of print for many years, was my main source for the wartime years. Raymond Foxhall's book, *The Guinea Pigs,* also provided some extra background to Operation Colossus, as did the Public Record Office at Kew. Much later on, the more I looked into what happened before Arnhem, the murkier the story became. I am most grateful for the assistance provided by Tony Hibbert who read the chapter and offered useful suggestions. Likewise, Lewis Golden's excellent and well-researched book, *Echoes from Arnhem,* and personal comment helped a great deal. Richard Moberly (Major-General R. Moberly), Brian Urquhart, Major-General R. Urquhart, Charles Mackenzie and Geoff Norton all wrote letters from which I have drawn in the narrative. Geoff Norton's account of his discussion with "Windy" (General Sir Richard) Gale was particularly useful and made me look a lot further.

The gliding chapter may bring to life the poetry of soaring flight, the sheer joy of using air currents to keep one aloft. My thanks go out to Rika Harwood and Wally Kahn for their many useful comments.

The chapters on the SAS try to explain a little about their fortitude, their intelligence and self-discipline against a background of fighting peculiarly nasty individuals in Malaya and later on a much better organized party of 500 rebels operating from their own Shangri La perched up at 7-8000 feet in the Oman. I am most grateful for helpful comments and suggestions from John (now Lieutenant-General Sir John) Watts and Malcolm Dennison.

Some people may think that my job in the paper industry was a far cry from my time in the Army. It wasn't. I was fascinated, and the more I became involved with the business world, the more I realized what needed to be done. The best companies were very, very good, but unfortunately the majority varied from below average to awful. With a few exceptions most of the employees could be trained up to do their job well. The trouble lay in management who had little idea how to manage. I am most grateful to Neville Whitehurst (onetime Chairman of Bowaters) who read the chapter and made useful suggestions.

My time as an entrepreneur stemmed directly from my experience in the paper industry and also the Army. I hope the last few pages will give encouragement to many and perhaps advice to a few.

Finally, my wife Evie has endured typing the whole book, first on a typewriter and latterly on an Amstrad Word Processor. I am most grateful for her help and many excellent suggestions.

* 1 *

INTRODUCTION

This is a story that my wife, my family and friends have been encouraging me to write for a long time.

I was 9 years old in 1926 when my mother had to divorce my father, and my mother was left to bring up my elder sister Ildica, myself and my younger sister Marigold. My father did, however, set up a trust allowing us to live reasonably well and to meet the usual school bills. This was not the end of my father's amorous adventures and, at the time I was married in 1944, my wife had the dubious advantage of having no less than three living mothers-in-law.

We grew up in the lovely little Cotswold village of Little Barrington, near Burford, where my mother had the Old Vicarage on a long lease. Her wealthy sister did not live too far away at Eastington Hall near Upton-on-Severn and she was able to provide us with some extras, like a horse for Ildica on which to go hunting with the Heythrop, and a second-hand Purdey shotgun for myself.

I had a rather inauspicious beginning at school as my mother considered me somewhat backward and delicate. She sent me to Summerfields (St Leonard's) preparatory school with all its output going to Eton or occasionally to Winchester. By this time my mother had decided that both Winchester and Eton were unhealthy places because they were low down by rivers. She selected Marlborough for my education – 'nice and high up and lots of fresh air'. It turned out to be probably one of the tougher educational establishments available in the early 30's, but a sound foundation was laid which no doubt did me good.

Quite early on in my school career I found myself in a class run by a quite remarkable and enthusiastic master. A. R. Pepin had wide outside interests which he managed to use as illustrations to emphasize anything from ancient history to mathematics. This caught my imagination and for the first time in my school career I worked hard. I was top of his form one term and was then moved up. I remember he drew me aside and said something like this: 'Well done, Deane-Drummond. Put your heart and soul – as well as brains – into anything you do at school or after you leave here, and you will get to the top.' I have never forgotten the encouragement this gave me.

After eighteen months as a cadet at the Royal Military Academy, Woolwich, I was commissioned into the Royal Signals in 1937. This choice was made partly because at Marlborough, in my last year, I had been a member of the signal platoon, also run by the now legendary A. R. Pepin, one of whose interests was in amateur radio. Our Officer Training Corps was certainly one up on other schools with our home-made field radios, which sometimes worked. It was also because of the three available choices, to join either Sappers, Gunners or Signals; only in Signals were two Army horses or 'chargers' automatically a 'right' of every officer. As a member of the saddle ride at Woolwich, I thought this to be a compelling attraction.

I was only one of many others from Marlborough who were attracted into the Royal Signals at this time. They were all due to become senior officers, some of them generals.

An 18-month course at Catterick provided a pleasant introduction to Army life in peacetime. Leave off to hunt was encouraged – it was said to improve an eye for country (although why this was thought to be important I never fathomed) – and I went out with the Bedale or Zetland hunts mounted on my Army charger. In the spring I had rides round several local Point-to-Points. No great results were achieved but they were great fun, which was perhaps why, in my first summer at Catterick in 1937, I also started gliding. I was keen on rugger but had never been much good at summer ball games, particularly cricket. On the other hand, I always had a yen to fly. This activity seemed acceptable to the powers at Catterick and I joined the Yorkshire Gliding Club, which was established on the top of the hill at Sutton Bank, a great natural bowl 1000 feet high, jutting out over the Yorkshire plain to the west. All training was done solo, using very basic gliders – 'kitchen chairs under wings' – which were either catapulted or winched up a few feet by an old Rolls Royce, jacked up on one side, with a steel drum full of cable bolted to one of the back wheels. The first few landings were always done straight ahead; turning came later. One of my friends from Catterick came over one day and found himself overshooting the edge of the bank on his third flight. He kept his head and continued to fly straight and level over the valley 1000 feet below. Fortunately he just happened to grind to a halt in the middle of a large grass field, with all of us watching from above with a mixture of anxiety, fascination and laughter. By the time we had retrieved him he owed us all a lot of drinks.

Somehow we learnt to fly, but it was not until a year later, in June, 1938, that I made a cross-country flight in a Kirby Kite glider from Sutton Bank to the beach just south of Scarborough, a distance of some 40 miles. This was the distance qualification for the Silver C badge, whose issue was controlled by the Germans, who were the acknowledged leaders of the sport. There followed height and duration qualifications of a 1000 metres' climb (about 3300 feet) and five hours' duration, which were soon done and I received the Silver C Badge, no 37 in the British register. I was hooked. Even during the war that soon followed, I dreamed of once again soaring over the lovely English countryside and perhaps doing better than my peers. The aim at this time was to go further, climb higher or stay up longer than anyone else. I was quite determined that one day I should do it. Little did I realize then that, twenty years later, I was to become the 1957 British National Gliding Champion.

My first real job in the Army was to command an Artillery Signal Section which was part of the 3rd Divisional Signals on Salisbury Plain and whose task was to provide communications for 3rd Medium Regiment RA, one of the medium gunner regiments allocated to 1st Corps. We all moved to France in September, 1939, and took up positions on the flat farms and fields between Douai and the Belgian border as part of the British Expeditionary Force. The task of looking after thirty men during that bitterly cold winter in France in 39/40 taught me responsibility and gave me real satisfaction. We usually managed to do things better and were more comfortable than our gunner friends with whom we lived. But a change was on the way and, soon after Christmas, Brigadier Ambrose Pratt moved me up to command the much larger Signal Section providing communications for all the Regiments in the Corps Medium Artillery. Ambrose Pratt was a wise and good soldier and gave me a great deal of encouragement. When the battles in Belgium and France started, he never failed to have a word with my soldiers on most evenings to put them in the wider picture and to encourage them. I learnt a lot about man management from him.

We all came back from Dunkirk on 3 June, 1940, and were based in Lincolnshire awaiting the German invasion. The media hype at the time painted the evacuation as a great success. It skated over what had happened and that the superb but tiny British Army had been defeated and flung off the Continent. Naturally I was glad to have survived, but stories in the newspapers and on the radio rankled. It was time to do something more active.

At about this period every Army unit was bombarded with letters asking for volunteers for special service or the Commandos. Commanding Officers were specifically instructed to send forward the names of all volunteers. But Ambrose Pratt did not agree. He let it be known that he would first select those officers he thought suitable and who would then be allowed to volunteer. Fortunately he chose me and two officers from the gunner regiments. We all went for interview, but I was the only one to be accepted. Two days later, in July, 1940, I joined no 2 Commando, later called 11 Special Air Service Battalion, and later still to become 1st Parachute Battalion. It was at the beginning of experimental parachuting in the British Army. We learnt from our experience and the occasional tragic failure when one man's parachute either failed or the procedure on the aircraft went wrong. After putting it right, we carried on. I do not think that these accidents much affected our morale. Statistics at the time clearly demonstrated that only about 1 in 5000 went wrong. Surely it would never happen to me.

I well remember my first jump. This was from a Bristol Bombay, a small troop-carrying aircraft of which there were only two or three in existence. It had a side-opening door which, when open, could be lifted off the two vertical pins on which the door swung. My static line cord, which automatically opened the parachute, was tied to one of the pins with two half-hitches. Such a procedure would horrify modern safety standards, but it shows how urgently everybody worked to produce an answer to Churchill's requirement of 22 June, 1940: 'We ought to have a corps of at least 5000 parachute troops.'

All was well, the parachute opened and I landed at Tatton Park, after a short flight from Ringway Airfield, (now Manchester Airport) which was our take-off airfield and base for parachute training.

In August, 1940, during a jump at Tatton Park, the static line cord wound itself round a man's leg and broke. It was replaced with a massive strap which has survived to this day. On another occasion, the dog clip used to fasten the static line to a bar in the plane became unfastened after a snap from the strap following an exit. Safety pins were inserted from that moment on. A further problem occurred very infrequently when the parachute failed to inflate and remained like a 'candle'. The design was changed by stiffening the edge of the canopy and changing the material to make this even less likely. We relied on our parachute and statistically it was still very safe. Or so we were all led to believe. Throughout the war we only had one parachute; no reserves were carried. This decision would save the Treasury a lot of money. We thought it rather sissy much later on when we saw American parachute troops with two parachutes.

The early chapters of this book go on to describe Operation Colossus, the first British parachute operation in Southern Italy and my subsequent efforts to escape from prisoner-of-war camps in Italy. These were followed by similar difficulties after the Arnhem operation in September, 1944.

★ ★ ★

On return from Holland at the end of 1944, I was sent on a Staff College course for the first six months of 1945. During this period the war was coming to an end and included the crossing of the Rhine and the advance up to the Elbe. Although I was to miss the great battles in Europe, it did allow me to live with my lovely and vivacious wife whom I had married in January, 1944, and also with our first child, born a year later. A whole year's course had been crammed into six months and we all worked very hard. The syndicate method of discussion and debate was a superb way of instructing students like myself who had all had plenty of experience and were able to contribute and occasionally disagree with the 'school' solutions. I think our instructors or directing staff must have had quite a difficult time but the method adopted allowed sensible answers to evolve.

A job on the staff automatically came after the Staff College Course, and I was posted as GS02 (Operations)* to Headquarters 6 Airborne Division, shortly to move to Cairo and then Palestine to help keep the King's Peace. Soon after arrival in Palestine my boss, Lieutenant-Colonel Willy Pike of the Grenadiers, developed typhoid and he never came back. I stepped into his shoes for the next three months. This was an interesting time with an ever-rising tempo of civil disturbance in the main cities of Tel Aviv, Haifa and Jerusalem. The pressure to increase the immigration into Palestine as a result of the horrific Nazi death camps was intense. Equally, the Arab population of Palestine was vociferous in saying that such a tiny country could not absorb the inflow of thousands of Jews into areas all owned by themselves and their forefathers for hundreds or thousands of years. It was a classic Catch 22 position in which the British Army had a near impossible task. The Jewish population was encouraged by various 'underground' organizations to keep the pot boiling and numerous outbreaks of violence arose in the area allotted to the Division. No doubt for good reasons, the General, Eric Bols, was invariably in Cairo whenever a flap started and our delightful chief gunner, Brigadier 'Chubby' Faithful, had made sure he was well clear if any trouble was likely. The senior Brigadier, then left in charge of the Division, preferred to stay with his Brigade. By the time Gerald Lathbury came in (he had been a brigade commander at Arnhem) all instructions were drafted, which he then altered or confirmed at his orders for the deployment of the troops. My procedures must have been reasonably clear and efficient because when the War Office eventually appointed a replacement for Willy Pike, Gerald Lathbury asked me to be his Brigade Major, (the senior staff officer in a brigade and also in charge of all headquarters troops). This was a top-rate job. All three battalions were commanded by superb officers; Napier Crookenden, Tubby Butler and George Hewetson were totally different characters but were great fun and outstanding commanding officers. We were all of us, except Hewetson, who returned to teaching English in Cumberland some years later, due to become generals in due course.

* A major's job under the GS01, a lieutenant-colonel, who was the senior operational advisor to the GOC and responsible for the production of all written orders.

On one occasion we were the reserve brigade for the whole of Palestine and based at the old disused airfield of Quastina. The Brigadier was away and I had decided that I would not, after all, go to the King David Hotel in Jerusalem for dinner, but for once have an early night. I had just gone to bed at about 11 pm when the telephone rang saying that the Hotel had been blown up that evening and the whole Brigade was required to cordon and search the old city of Jerusalem, starting by first light the next day. All the Divisional transport was located in Gaza about 30 miles away to the south. Phone calls were made to the transport and the three battalions from my bed and also to Napier who was now Acting Brigade Commander. The cordon was in position 30 minutes before first light after the 40-mile journey from Quastina to Jerusalem. Tubby's battalion was doing the search but found nothing all day. We thought we had drawn a blank and orders had just been issued to return to our camp when a report came in that, when searching a mortuary, a toe had twitched under a sheet. Two men were arrested and handed over to the police.

On another occasion the Brigade was based on Mount Carmel above Haifa. From time to time riots occurred all over Palestine and after one of them General Bubbles Barker, who was GOC Palestine, decreed that all nightclubs were out of bounds. There was a particularly well known one, the Piccadilly, further up Mount Carmel and our Military Police were told to visit all of them to see that the instructions were being carried out. Once again my Brigadier was away when a worried MP Sergeant came into our mess at 10 pm to say that a Guards brigadier was in the nightclub with a 'lady called Rachel' and he would not leave. I went back with the MPs and, leaving them outside, I told a rather merry Guards brigade commander, who was then dancing wrapped up with his attractive local lady, that either I should have to arrest him or he would have to leave immediately. He saw that I meant it and he left in high dudgeon muttering that this would never have happened if his Brigade had been at Haifa (as it had been before we had taken over). I retorted that we obeyed orders and he was lucky to get away with it. He also achieved high rank later on.

By this time General Jim Cassels had taken over as the new GOC. He was a proper soldier and also a tease with a twinkle in his eye. I had been in Palestine nearly two years and was due to return home on leave in a week's time to see my wife and two daughters. He came into our headquarters one morning when he was not expected and saw the Brigadier and myself. 'I am very sorry Tony,' he said, 'I have had to cancel your leave'. This was a bombshell and he paused to see my reaction. I was speechless. He went on, 'I have decided to send you on the one vacancy allotted to the Division on the ski mountain warfare course in Austria, which all brigades have just turned down, saying they could not spare anybody.' I was delighted. This was terrific news. The telephone had just been opened to UK and I was able to speak to my wife and give her the news, and suggest that she joined me in Austria, although technically no families were allowed for students.

About two weeks later I arrived in Mallnitz, the centre used for the ski course, and found an efficient organization run by Major Tony Rishworth-Hill. He had his wife there officially and he said that, if mine turned up, he would accommodate her somehow. There were no ski lifts at Mallnitz. All the instructors were well qualified ex-Wehrmacht Austrians who were glad of doing a job which gave them rations and which they enjoyed. After six weeks we were able to climb 4-5000 feet twice in a day on skis and ski down different paths. We became very fit and quite competent.

About two weeks before the end of my two-month course in April, Evie turned up. She had had quite a journey. She and a girlfriend had driven our car across France to Buchs in Switzerland, where the trains crossed into Austria. No unauthorized people were allowed on to the trains. Speaking fast but ungrammatical German to the station master, she was pushed on to the train with a wink and arrived in Innsbruck a few hours later. It was a Sunday, so she found her way to the UNRA displaced persons building and they agreed to find her a bed for the night. Next day she went to the British Army HQ and, after some discussion with the Colonel in charge, who could not understand how she had got there, she was given a grey pass entitling her to free travel on Austrian railways. She arrived at Mallnitz after a few more adventures and the Rishworth-Hills were charming hosts. Technically she was a 'displaced person' for rations, and she quickly found her feet again on skis before the end of the course. We had a few days' skiing together at the start of my month's leave and then we travelled slowly back to Switzerland to pick up the car, via Vienna and Venice, staying a few days in each place. In Venice we stayed at the best hotel, but the place was so dirty and smells of garbage floating in the canals so appalling that we left very rapidly.

In Switzerland I even had a few days Alpine gliding at Samadan near St Moritz. The dark rocks facing the sun appeared to have continuous up-currents of air rising up them and it was not difficult to climb quickly up above the mountain tops to nearly 13,000 feet, in one case passing a group roped together and climbing a minor peak. The crystal-clear view of mountains all round was fantastic, with a visibility of more than fifty miles. This was Elysium. The only noise came from a slight background whisper from the air flowing past the cockpit; truly a sight for the Gods. It was a shame that I was the only one to enjoy it.

We arrived back in England to discover that I was to do a staff job in the War Office, which would once again allow me to live with my wife and family. This only lasted a year and in September, 1948, I was sent on an 'advanced signal course' run by the US Army at Fort Monmouth in New

Jersey, and which allowed families as well. Rationing was still in force in the UK and this was a wonderful opportunity to see the USA and savour their way of life. On arrival I had to go to Washington to see the Senior British Officer, General Julian Gascoigne. Together with about a dozen other officers, all going on different US Army Courses, he told us that a cavalry officer had recently disgraced the Brits by failing his long course. He made it very clear that unless we all passed out in the top third of our courses, he would make sure that we would be graded 'adverse' on our annual confidential reports. As I was completely out of date from a signals point of view and because all the thirty other American officers on my course had good university degrees, I was going to be hard-pushed; that is until I became aware of the system followed throughout US education. Continuous assessment was used with short tests after each lecture. A good memory and a knack of selecting likely questions during the lecture led me to come out second in the course, although if I had not disagreed with their solutions on Airborne communications I would have been top.

We enjoyed every minute of our time in the States and met a lot of superb people. We travelled quite widely in a beat-up old car and certainly made use of their officers' clubs and PXs. Hopefully they also formed a good impression of the British Army, because my next job was instructor at RMA Sandhurst to find myself living next door to Lieutenant-Colonel Tag Pritchard, my boss on our first parachute operation into Italy. During the four years he had spent in prisoner-of-war camps, his girlfriend to whom he had been engaged gave him up. The horror of four years in a prison camp was compounded by this personal tragedy. Soon after he returned he married Pat on the rebound, although I had a small part in trying to prevent this happening. She did not like the Army and did her best to get him out. Unfortunately at the end of his time at Sandhurst, he developed TB and, after long spells at Midhurst, he had to leave the Army anyway. It was sad to see a man so wasted in body and spirit. After the divorce, he did, however, remarry (with me as best man) and they both lived on in London, blissfully happy until first his wife and then Tag died in 1982.

Martin Lindsay was staying with Tag Pritchard before his TB had been diagnosed and heard that I had written notes on my escapes from prisoner-of-war camps. We both knew him quite well because he had been on the staff at Ringway in 1940 and had made a name for himself pre-war in the arctic. He was now a Member of Parliament and had written several books. He was most complimentary about my notes and, after suggesting a few alterations, offered a covering letter to his publisher. I spent the next three weeks rewriting the manuscript and at last sent it off to Collins on a Thursday, together with Martin's covering letter. Billy Collins rang me up at 8 am the following Monday morning saying he would very much like to publish *Return*

Ticket. It came out about a year later with extracts published in three successive Sundays in the *Sunday Times.* It was to become a best-seller.

Towards the end of my time at Sandhurst in 1951, I heard that my next job was to be an instructor (or member of the Directing Staff) at the Staff College, which was located nearby in the same lovely grounds. The Commandant at the Staff College was now Gerald Lathbury and he had obviously asked for me to join him. This was great news and included my own promotion to Brevet Lieutenant-Colonel. This was a Treasury device, which gave me the rank of Lieutenant-Colonel, but the pay of a Major. I was also under Colonel Tubby Butler, who was in charge of one of the three divisions at the Staff College. This was even better; the Airborne machine was getting into jobs of real influence in the Army. Tubby had an incredible knack of seeing the wood for the trees and getting the right answers. I was delighted to be working for two people for whom I had enormous respect.

The first year at the Staff College in 1952 was hard work. Not only did we direct the discussions and arguments in a ten-man syndicate, but also had to correct and adjudicate on their written work. Overall it was great fun and we all enjoyed ourselves, although Evie had had her problems. Just before Christmas, 1953, when six months pregnant, she had to be rushed into hospital. A little girl was aborted and died soon after, to our very great sorrow. At this time it was the only cloud on our horizon, although there was more to come.

In my last year at the Staff College, I became conscious of a tiny lump in the centre of my neck above my Adam's apple. It had been there a long time and I thought it was part of my anatomy. However, Evie persuaded me to ask her father for his opinion. He had been an eminent London surgeon* and he said that it should be removed.

This was done in Aldershot and started a chain of events that was to lead once again to service in the Parachute Regiment, to give me time to practise and to win the British Gliding Championships (and selection for World Gliding Championships), to command of 22 SAS Regiment and later promotions. Perhaps this was all my good fortune, but, as a quirk of fate, what might have been a tragedy turned out to be much more rewarding. Perhaps the dreaded lump was indeed my philosopher's stone.

* Sidney Boyd, FRCS, MS

SWITZERLAND
AUSTRIA
FRANCE
YUGOSLAVIA
Varese
Como
Milan
Piacenza
Bologna
Marseilles
Pisa
CAMPO 27
Florence
Appennines
Adriatic Sea
Pescara
Popoli
ROME
Sulmona
Termoli
Foggia
Naples
Salerno
Bari
Brindisi
Taranto
Tyrrhenian Sea
SICILY
MALTA
Miles
0
50
100
Ofanto R.
Calitri
Tragino Bridge
Taora
Pescopegano
Appennines
Salerno
Sele R.
Appennines
Miles
0
10
20
Italy

* 2 *

OPERATION COLOSSUS – THE PLAN

'Rise and shine, Pommy. Breakfast's up and Portugal is on the port bow'.

For a moment I could not remember where I was. It gradually dawned on me that a penetrating Australian twang was shouting that breakfast was ready, and that we had just made landfall near the northern tip of Portugal. I was on my way to Malta in a Royal Australian Air Force Sunderland flying boat, on an enterprise the like of which had never before been attempted by the British Army.

As I lay on my bunk, still only half-awake, with the muffled roar of the Sunderland's four engines drowning everything, I drowsily reminded myself what I was now meant to be doing. I was the advance party going to our advanced base in Malta from where we would take off for Italy. Today was the 1st of February, 1941. Our task was to blow up an aqueduct in the heart of Southern Italy and then be taken off by submarine from the west coast. The aqueduct fed the naval ports of Bari, Brindisi and Taranto, which were being used to supply Mussolini's war in Albania, Greece and North Africa. But the main reason for our operation, cynically called Colossus, was to test out our ability to land in enemy territory by parachute and then successfully to carry out our mission. A British civil engineering company had assisted in building a 993-mile-long aqueduct in southern Italy to divert the water from the River Sele which flowed west into the Mediterranean, back through the mountains in a large underground culvert which then flowed east towards the ports on the south-east coast. In places this watercourse surfaced and then became a bridge, including one crossing the Tragino Torrent. Such a pinpoint target was not one that the Air Force could bomb successfully. The snag was that it was located in wild and mountainous country about 60 miles from the coast. The task of dropping a party accurately at night among these hills, some of which went up to 4 or 5000 feet, would have deterred even modern aeroplanes and sophisticated pathfinding equipment. Wing-Commander Tait and his crews, flying modified Whitley bombers, deserve great credit not only for finding the target but also dropping five out of six planeloads accurately on it. But that was all to come. My task on arriving in Malta was to brief the heads of the

Navy, Army and the Air Force on our task and to find accommodation for our party which was due to arrive any day.

Soon after landing at the seaplane base of Kalafrana towards dusk, I was whisked off to deliver up my documents and brief the Governor, General Dobbie, who was very much in control of the three services. General Dobbie was kind enough to put me up for the night in his house. Naturally I had only taken the minimum for the trip and so felt very unkempt when I came in to dinner in my battledress, whilst all the others were wearing starched shirts. I was soon put at my ease and I had my first wartime dinner in pre-war style.

In bed that night I thought about my mother in the Cotswolds. At that moment the news on the wireless would have just finished and she would be going up to bed. Later I heard that she thought that I was still training in the north of England as a Signals officer and had no idea that I had been in a parachute unit for eight months. I suddenly started laughing. What a shock she would have when she heard what I had been doing. She would hardly believe it.

The next day there followed a frantic rush around all the various Naval, Military and Air Force HQs in Malta, fixing up accommodation for the party which was due to arrive any day. The aircraft carrier *Illustrious* had been dive-bombed in Valletta harbour only about a month before and a suitable barracks which satisfied all the security requirements was difficult to locate. At length I found that the old quarantine hospital of Lazaretto, on Manoel Island, would fill the bill. It had just been taken over as a naval base and included the submarine *Triumph* which had been instructed to take us off from Italy.

The first warning of a possible operation had been given to No 2 Commando in December, 1940. This gave time to select an appropriate sized party, to extract out of the Air Ministry eight Whitley bombers with experienced air crews and to make up models of the target area. The second-in-command of the Commando, Major T.A.G. Pritchard, known as Tag, characteristically put himself in charge and selected five officers to go with him. Each in turn would choose a senior NCO and five men. I was fortunate to be on the list and Sergeant 'Taff' Lawley in my troop was a natural to come too. A superb soldier with a tangy wit, he had already served seven years in the South Wales Borderers in Egypt and Palestine. After leaving the Army he became a London bus driver but was recalled to the Colours soon after the war had started. Together we sorted out five junior NCOs and men. These were to join the others to make up the new 'X Troop'*. A total of six officers and twenty-eight men were found from the first four troops to be raised in No 2 Commando.

* Full list of X Troop at Appendix I, p.252.

Christopher Lea, myself and Geoff Jowett would provide protection for Gerry Daly and George Paterson who were sappers and would be responsible for blowing up the aqueduct.

Major Pritchard, Royal Welsh Fusiliers, was a regular soldier and had been a good heavyweight boxer in his younger days. In spite of a rather gruff and inarticulate manner, there could not have been a more effective commanding officer. Captain Christopher Lea, from the Lancashire Fusiliers, was a regular like me. On first impressions, he was both lanky and languid, but this concealed a highly professional and energetic person underneath. We were to become great friends in the next few months. Captain Gerry Daly was a regular Sapper. Short and studious, but very knowledgeable, he was teamed up with 2nd Lieutenant George Paterson from Canada, who was also a Sapper. George was tall and thin and had been studying forestry at Edinburgh University at the outbreak of war. 2nd Lieutenant Geoff Jowett, another Canadian, was small and stocky with a nearly bald head and a large moustache. More Sottish than the Scots, he wore his emotions on his sleeve and prided himself on being more aggressive and bloodthirsty than anyone else.

Early in January, we were joined by two Italian interpreters, Flight Lieutenant Lucky of the RAF and Sergeant Pichi. Both were about 45 and Lucky was wearing ribbons from the 14-18 War. Sergeant Pichi was perhaps the most surprising member of our party and certainly not the least courageous. In civilian life he had been banqueting manager at the Savoy Hotel. He had been interned as an alien at the beginning of the war, but, with many like him, he had volunteered for any job that the British Government might give him. He was fanatical both in his hatred of the Fascists and his love of Italy. Uniform did not change him much. He was still the suave polite little man, with a bald top to his head and slight middle-aged spread, who might be expected to be in charge of banquets at the Savoy.

Back in England, the whole party, including eight RAF Whitleys, were moved to RAF Mildenhall in Suffolk on 3 February, from which airfield they were to fly to Malta. On 7 February, 1941, Admiral Sir Roger Keyes, Chief of Combined Operations, came to see them off. They all paraded in a hangar together with the aircrew and some of the Whitleys. He spoke to everyone individually and ended with a short talk. 'You are setting off on a very important job, and I should like you to know that I have been assured that no better, fitter and braver men could have been selected than you to play this very vital role.

'I know that you will tackle this job with determination and enthusiasm, and with a bit of luck I am sure you will pull it off. We shall be waiting to hear how you have got on; waiting to learn what British paratroopers can do. I decided that I just couldn't let you go without coming here to say goodbye to you.'

He then drew himself up and saluted *them.* This dramatic gesture caught the troop unawares. They returned his salute, their arms going up in ones and twos until finally the whole parade was stiffly at the salute.* As the Admiral turned away, one trooper heard him whisper a remark to himself which he did not intend anyone else to hear. 'A pity,' he said softly, 'a damned pity.' He of all people realized that the chances of doing the job were good, but the prospect of getting back were very small.

At dawn on 8 February all eight Whitleys arrived in Malta, much to the surprise of the RAF who had expected one or two to fall by the wayside as had always happened on previous flights to the island. They had flown the 1400 miles from England with a following wind and they arrived in record time. The explosives had to be loaded up into the containers and the containers into the planes. Arms and ammunition had to be checked over and all rations for the operation had to be sorted out. In addition the men had to be rested. By 4 pm on the 10th all was ready and then for the first time Tag Pritchard spoke to everybody on the actual object and the hoped-for result of our operation. 'Only now can I let you into the big secret of this trip,' he told them. 'The job on which you are now embarking is an experiment to see what you can do. We are to jump right into the middle of Mussolini's Italy and blow up an aqueduct which takes water to a large military area.* After we have done the job – and we shall see to it that we do – the only way out will be across mountainous country to the coast.

'Quite simple and straightforward and I should like to wish you all the best of luck.'

Maps were issued and the whole plan gone over again and again. Although the blowing up of the bridge had been practised and rehearsed at Tatton Park in the minutest detail, the subsequent orders to get to the coast were necessarily vague. We would split up into several parties and rendezvous at the same spot on the coast five days later. Light signals were arranged to bring the submarine in, but routes were left to the individual groups to work out for themselves.

All we needed now was a favourable weather report and we would be off. So far so good, and we all prayed that our luck would hold. We would need it in large measure.

* *Guinea Pigs*, Raymond Foxall, p 47.

* *Guinea Pigs*, pp 48, 51.

* 3 *

OPERATION COLOSSUS – THE ACTION

The weather report looked good. We were given the off at 5 pm and gulped down some hot tea and hard boiled eggs, although none of us felt too hungry. As one of my men put it, 'These Maltese eggs seem coated with glue.' Our fingers twitched with nervous excitement as we dressed, ending with the parachute which we checked with each other. It would not be long now. A truck waiting outside took us to our plane and we squeezed laboriously down the narrow tunnel of the Whitley. We all had a Li-Lo air mattress to lie on to insulate us from the cold in the unheated plane.

We soon settled down and heard the engines start up. I was lucky because I had the earphones and could hear what was going on. Quite soon we were flying at 10,000 feet over Sicily and were rocked a little by anti-aircraft fire as we passed over the northern coastline. My word, it was cold. But soon after crossing the Italian coast which showed up clearly in the bright moonlight, the aircraft started a slow descent towards our target area. We had been in the air a little over three hours and were due to drop at 9.30 pm. We wanted to look down on Italy but we knew that as soon as we opened the doors covering the hole through which we had to drop, we would become even colder.

We had a good team. Sergeant Lawley was quietly confident, and, because I had decided that he would come last out of the plane, he would act as despatcher. I handed him the earphones. A large pair of plywood doors covered the four-foot-wide hole in the middle of the aircraft, which was only about six foot wide. Three of us were forward and three aft. Alternately each of us in turn would swing our legs over the edge and then straighten up to drop clear. Containers holding arms, ammunition and explosive were carried in the bomb racks and would be released in the middle of the 'stick' of six by the despatcher. The whole procedure should not take more than about fifteen seconds.

The aqueduct bridge was awkward to get at from the air. It was astride a tributary cascading into the main river flowing from the Apennines to the Adriatic. Little villages were perched on high ground each side of the valley and connected to each other by twisting roads which wound their way up in a series of hairpins. The plan was to fly low over the village of Calitri, turn half-right and drop us between the main river at the bottom of the valley and the line of the tributary leading up to the bridge. After dropping, the planes had to turn left to avoid hitting the mountain towards which they were flying. It was quite a challenge for a 'first' operation.

By now most of the men had settled down comfortably and were nicely asleep when Sergeant Lawley passed on the news 'fifteen minutes to target'. Everybody was immediately electrified into action. Equipment was checked over, parachute static lines sorted out and the exit doors unbolted.

After what seemed a very long fifteen minutes, we were astonished to see the rear gunner come through from his perch in the tail and shout out, 'You are due to drop in under a minute. Get cracking'. The intercom had failed at the last minute, and for about ten seconds there was pandemonium while we opened up the doors and the first two swung their legs over the edge of the hole.

Suddenly I saw the lights of Calitri flash by underneath not a hundred feet below. We knew that we might expect the red light in a few seconds. On it came and we braced ourselves waiting for the green. We knew we had five more seconds in the plane. Was I really going to parachute into Italy? I seemed to have time to think about everything. I glanced at the rest of my section, wondering what was passing through their minds. They looked cheerful but pale and they too were looking at each other. Through the hole, some houses and then a large river flashed by in the moonlight. It could not be long now.

'Green Light!' A sudden jolt into reality. I was number five. Sergeant Lawley started counting 'No 1' 'No 2' 'No 3' 'Containers.' (The containers' release switch was pressed and out dropped all the containers). Everybody had gone out superbly so far – and after a small interval for the containers, No 4 opposite me dropped out and I followed.

A tearing gale, a slight jerk and I found myself swinging gently in blissful silence a few hundred feet above the ground. The containers were bunched together, oscillating rhythmically under their coloured parachutes a few yards away, and beyond them were the first four parachutes swinging like myself in the light of the full moon.

We had been dropped rather low from not more than five hundred feet. I heard later that the rear gunner thought that the last two out would not be high enough to allow the parachutes to open. But we were all right and, from about two hundred feet at the most, I began to take a more intelligent interest in the few square yards of Italy on which I was going to land. It looked as though I was coming down near a small bridge with a few cottages nearby. Was this really our bridge? It stood out clearly, looking just as it did in the air photograph. 'Well done the pilot,' I thought to myself. The cottages were those that my section had to clear of all inhabitants to prevent them giving the alarm. I was drifting towards a ploughed field on the side of a hill about a hundred yards from the aqueduct. As my toes touched I pulled down hard on my rigging lines and the parachute slowly lost its shape and fell over me in the still air. It was the best landing I had ever made.

The arms and explosive containers were only a few yards away. By this time one or two of my section had joined me and we quickly opened up the containers for our weapons. As there was clearly no military in the area, I divided our section into two to clear the two lots of cottages and bring the inhabitants to me at the bridge. I would wait there for the others and could tell them what I had done.

I think we had all expected a country rather similar to Scotland and its moors but with rather higher mountains. What we found was a wild and precipitous hillside, covered with ravines and scattered farmhouses, where every square yard was cultivated but was also deep in mud.

Our plane had been due to drop third, but there was no sign of anybody else. What had happened to them? I had a funny feeling inside me that perhaps our planeload was the only one to arrive. I think we all had the same thought. If this happened, we could do our best with the explosives we had brought, but the chances of doing any serious damage would be small.

Forty minutes later, at 10.15 pm, we heard more planes overhead. I expect one of the pilots had spotted our white parachutes on the ground and he fired off two green very lights to attract the others. One by one they turned for a run in over Calitri and we saw the parachutes floating down in the silent night. We were all mighty relieved to see it happen in front of us, as were our Italian peasants who were grouped near the aqueduct. They also had front row seats and continually crossed themselves in amazement as they saw something they had never seen before. The Italian children jumped with excitement and clapped their hands.*

'*Angeli, angeli*' they shouted while their parents looked on in awe. No angels these, however, even though they were later to give part of their chocolate ration to the children.

There was a loud crashing through the bushes and thorn ash in the valley bottom. My men took the cue and prepared to fire, only waiting my signal in case it was one of us. But when the trees parted, out came old Tag by himself, a little out of breath, as his planeload had been put down about a mile away down by the river. Carrying up all the explosives was clearly going to be hell and we decided then and there to use all the able-bodied peasants to help us. They told us that it would give them enough to talk

* *Guinea Pigs,* p. 70

about for the rest of their lives. They were not so amused when each one was loaded up with two forty-pound packs of guncotton to carry up to the aqueduct.

One of the oldest and most wizened of the peasants suddenly exclaimed in a broad American accent, 'Are you guys English?' Quick as a flash one our Cockneys retorted, 'No, chum, we are Abyssinians on our way to Sunday School.'

It turned out that the old man had been a bellhop in the Waldorf-Astoria in New York for several years. He had returned to his humble cottage with no mains water, no electricity and no lavatory, as soon as he had saved up enough money to buy his passage home to 'his house in the country'.

My section was just below the bridge. Near it were the cottages into which we had put the women and children; Christopher Lea's was on either side of the bridge and Geoff Jowett was opposite me on the north side of the stream. Our orders were to give warning of anybody coming up the valley and, if necessary, to prevent interference with the parties carrying the explosive. There was to be no firing unless it was unavoidable. As it happened, the only man in uniform who appeared was the local station master from Calitri railway station. He was duly pressed into the labour gang and made a good porter – as was only proper. His biggest worry was that he would be late taking over from his relief and would get the sack. I told him that his skilled labour was required, but that, if he liked, I would give him a certificate to say he had been detained against his will. This cheered him up tremendously and from then on nobody could stop him talking.

All the time gangs of men had been passing up the track through our position loaded down with guncotton. Muffled swear words came from their lips as they sweated. This was the only noise to be heard apart from the occasional yapping of dogs and the tinkling from the stream nearby.

Word came back that enough explosive had been placed against the piers, so I stopped the last of the porters who was carrying two boxes on his shoulders. I put it under one end of a small bridge carrying the track which led to the main aqueduct. This would delay the repair work. Corporal Watson RE placed the charges and I sent a message to Tag to explain what was happening. The small bridge would be blown up as soon as I heard the warning bang. The explosion of a single slab of guncotton was the signal that the aqueduct was about to be blown up. This would act as a warning for all the defence sections. When they heard it everybody had to move to a safe position about two hundred yards to the west.

'Whoomf'! Our bridge went up in a cloud of flying concrete, iron rails and bits of masonry. I had never expected so much debris. The wretched people in the cottages set up a wail and a woman ran out of the house with a baby in her arms when the bits started thudding down on the roof. Not thirty seconds later up went the main bridge with a tremendous roar. About a third of a ton of guncotton had been carefully slung into place against one of the piers under George (Pat) Patterson's orders. The aqueduct was constructed with three concrete piers and we had planned to blow up all three. Back in England we had thought the piers were made of masonry; concrete was completely different and much stronger. Unfortunately Captain Gerry Daly had not turned up and we had to assume that his planeload was either lost or never took off. Pat took over and decided to concentrate all the explosives on one pier. Even so, the chance that it would break would be small.

Tag and Pat went back to see the results of the demolition. When they came back with not a smile on their faces, we wondered what had happened. Surely seven hundred pounds of guncotton had been enough? Tag put up his hand and everybody stopped talking. All he said was 'Listen'. We strained our ears and sure enough we heard the sound of a great waterfall. It was a success. How we cheered and cheered. Those British cheers must have been heard a good mile away or more.

All our inward hopes and fears about the success of the operation were now stilled and the reaction made us feel very tired. What was even more tiring was the thought of having to walk sixty or seventy miles across the mountains to the coast.

Tag had decided before we started that we would have the best chance of getting to our coastal rendezvous if we split into smaller parties and made our own way to the sea. Tag and myself were with the first party, Christopher Lea and Pat Patterson the second, and Flight Lieutenant Lucky and Geoff Jowett the third.

The barks of a dog pierced the night. It seemed impossible that we would not have all Italy on our heels by the morning. This was going to be no easy walk over the Scottish moors. We bent our backs and laboured slowly through the mud and up the hills.

* 4 *

MANHUNT

A manhunt is an unpleasant thing. If you are the man it is worse still. The bridge was blown up and we had achieved all we had set out to do. Now came the anticlimax; we had to get to the coast as quickly and secretly as possible. Tag had given orders to lighten our loads and so all our heavier weapons, which included Brens and tommy-guns, were taken to pieces and pushed into the mud soon after leaving the bridge. This still left each man carrying a thirty-pound pack containing five days' rations, mess tin, water bottle and miniature primus stove. For arms, we only retained our Colt automatic pistols.

Our plan was to climb the mountain behind the aqueduct and then follow the contours until we reached the highest point at the pass over the Apennines before moving down the north side of the Sele valley towards the Mediterranean.

One man had landed on rocks and had broken his ankle. Lance-Corporal Boulter was a good man but clearly he could not come with us. Tag spoke to him and so did I. He would have to be left behind. He not only knew he would soon be taken prisoner but that every effort would be made to find out from him more about us and what we were trying to do. I shook him by his hands and looked him straight in the eyes. I did not say anything; we both knew what the other was thinking.

'On your way, you lot,' he joked*, 'Don't waste time on me. I'm the lucky one. I've got out of that bloody long march over the mountains.'

Right from the start we met difficulties. Fields knee deep in mud, impassable little ravines, innumerable farm houses all with noisy dogs, were only a few of our obstacles. We soon learnt to disregard the dogs, as does everybody else in Italy. Their function in life was to yap for twenty-four hours a day if need be. Any excuse would do from the farmyard cat to people like ourselves moving close by.

Every three-quarters of an hour Tag stopped and we sat down, munching chocolate or sipping a little water until we were sufficiently recovered to

* *Guinea Pigs* p.86.

continue. On and on we tramped, pulling ourselves up the sides of the steep little gorges by our hands and then slithering down the other side on our seats. The moonlight exaggerated the rough nature of the route we had chosen and made every false crest appear to be far away until once again we breasted the obstacle to see yet another one beyond.

We had left the bridge at 1.30 am and we finally stopped at about 7 am. By that time we must have covered at least fifteen miles over the ground but had only done about six of the sixty we had to do before reaching the coast. This meant that on future nights we would have to double our mileage if we were to get there on time.

We found a nice, sheltered little ravine in which to lie up during the day. There was a stream nearby and plenty of cover. Off came our equipment and some of us attempted to sleep before cold made it impossible.

After a wonderful three hours' rest we were woken at 10 am by the noise from a low-flying aeroplane. It was obviously looking for us and was only about five hundred feet above where we were hiding. We kept our faces well down and remained quite still and soon it flew away and we did not see it again.

From our hiding place we could see peasants at work in the fields. Beyond them, on the other side of the valley we could still see Calitri perched on the side of the mountain. The brilliant sun and a light breeze brought the delicate smell of wild thyme, mint and rosemary wafting over us, although we were in no position to appreciate such muted pleasures. My main concern was to decide which way to lead the party that night. Straight in front of us, not more than a quarter of a mile away, rose a sheer cliff about 300 feet high, which we would have to scale that evening.

Night came at last and on went our packs, with our pistols on our belts. Tag had noticed a shepherd with a flock of goats come down a path in the cliff during the day while I had been asleep. He said he thought he could find it, so he started off by leading us across a small stream not more than ten yards wide but flowing fast between boulders with deep pools in between. We found a way across using stepping stones with a six-foot gap, across which we jumped. When we arrived at the cliff, it was not as steep as it had appeared from our hiding place. With some difficulty we pulled ourselves up the slope of mud and shingle using every bit of scrub or long grass as we scrambled up to the top. All our reserves of energy had been used up to climb that hill and we were to feel it later on.

I was leading now and slowly we crept on in single file with ears strained for any unusual sound. We could see a few cottages against the skyline and assumed that they must be the outskirts of Pescopegano. Dogs could be heard barking all over the village and farther up the valley. Perhaps it was one of the other parties that was causing the disturbance. I kept wondering how they were getting on.

The country looked wilder and more impassable than ever. The moonlight distorted every natural hummock and glade into grotesque and weird shapes. Before us stretched mile upon mile of the roughest country we had ever seen. Few landmarks could be picked out and so we decided to march by compass to a large crossroads near the source of the River Sele. We crossed countless small streams and stumbled through wild junipers and stunted oak thickets. We were always walking either up or down or along the side of a hill but we did manage to strike a small road which we were expecting to find.

At this stage we decided it was too risky to walk along the road, but preferred to use it as a guide, keeping it at about a quarter of a mile below us. There were many little farmhouses scattered on the hillside round which we moved in single file. Our mouths were dry with exhaustion and some of the men were completely worn out. Tag decided to stop and have a brew. The hot sweet tea was like nectar and gave us renewed energy. It was the best dixie of tea I've ever had. When we got up, a new briskness was obvious in all of us.

At about 1 am we had not seen anything on the road for some time past, so Tag very wisely decided to march straight along it and damn the risk. The change of walking along that road after trudging through the mud revived us both mentally and physically.

For five or six miles we marched along the road and eventually reached the big crossroads which was the highest point on our route to the coast. From now on the way ran downhill and our only worry before dawn was to find a safe hiding place for the following day. As we scurried over the crossroads, we looked down the valley. We could see it stretching for miles in the moonlight with rugged, cultivated and muddy sides interspersed with innumerable farmhouses.

A light clopping of hooves on the road ahead startled us out of our thoughts. We were too tired to move off, so Tag formed us into file and made Trooper Nastri, our interpreter, call the step in Italian. A pony cart laden with vegetables came into view, with its big hood pulled right down over the peasant woman driver. She was fast asleep and was probably taking her wares to the local village market.

Our maps showed trees covering the top of a nearby hill and we decided to try and lie up there. We climbed gradually now, hoping to strike the trees, but none could be found. Eventually we came up to the base of cloud which just covered the top of the hill. Unfortunately what the map indicated as trees turned out to be yet another farmhouse. Our sweat-soaked clothes quickly became ice-cold and in the raw mist we were soon shivering from cold and exhaustion. Tag and I decided to climb up a little higher to try and find a better hiding place. We knew we could not go much further and the men were in the same state. Less than fifty yards higher up cultivation ceased and we came upon boulders and juniper bushes, which we thought might do. It was not good but we had no alternative. At this point I had a funny feeling inside me that we were bound to be discovered on that hill. There were too many people about.

The time was about 5.30 am. We had been on the move for about ten hours and covered twenty miles in a straight line, but at least forty miles through the mud. We did not have much energy left.

The men soon curled up and fell asleep. I was not long following suit and did not wake up till dawn an hour later. Every bone in my body ached and shivered; my clothes were soured with sweat and my teeth could not stop chattering.

At first I could not believe my eyes, but it was unfortunately too true. A peasant was standing not a hundred yards away looking intently in our direction. He had obviously spotted us and started to walk away. Tag made a quick decision and sent Nastri after him to tell him we were a party of Italian and German troops on an exercise.

When Nastri returned, he was not too hopeful that he had convinced the man of our peaceful intentions. I knew in my heart that the game was up but I could not believe that this was the end. I was even more alarmed when Nastri said that quite a lot of women and children had seen him talking. He thought he also saw a few of them running off down the hill to a village beyond our hill. Tag decided that it was useless to try to move off as it would only attract even more attention. We sat where we were, feeling apprehensive about what was going to happen next.

Some rather scruffy Italian children with a few mongrel dogs were our first spectators. They sat down about a hundred yards away, sucking their thumbs and gazing at us as if we were men from the moon. A minute or two later a man came over the hill behind us with two pointers at his heel and carrying a shotgun. He pointed it straight at Tag and accompanied it with a voluble flow of Italian which none of us could understand. By this time quite a ring of spectators had collected, including a few peasant women in black dresses who seemed to be the mothers of the children. Nastri was now asking the man with the shotgun what it was all about. The man then gabbled something and ended by waving his gun around to emphasize his sentences. He wanted us to lay down our weapons. As these consisted only of .32 automatics, it seemed a lot of fuss to make about such singularly ineffective weapons.

The crowd surrounding our position had now become quite large and we were rather uncertain what to do. I remember telling Tag that I did not agree with him when he gave the order to lay down arms.

'All right, Tony,' he said, 'you throw a grenade at those people on the right and I will throw mine over there.'

At that moment I realized I could not do it. Women, children and unarmed peasants were everywhere. All we could achieve were a few extra hours of freedom at the price of a particularly inglorious action.

Disconsolately I agreed with Tag and he told the men. There was a dead silence for a moment and then one man asked in an incredulous voice,

'Aren't we going to make a fight for it, sir?'

I had never seen such a look of anguish on anybody's face as on Tag's at that moment. He just looked at the women and children and then at the man who had asked the question, and said that he was very sorry but they would have to give in. Our hearts ached as we put down our pistols and told Nastri to tell the Italian that we were giving in because of the women and children. As soon as the peasants saw that we had dropped our weapons, they came surging up to us and took all our equipment, much to our chagrin and disgust. I have never felt so ashamed before or since that we should have surrendered to a lot of practically unarmed Italian peasants. This was the morning of 13 February, 1941.

Our farmer captors were now grinning from ear to ear with justified self-congratulation. We heard later that the Italian local radio had just given out that enemy parachutists had landed in the area and had succeeded in sabotaging bridges. Everybody had been asked to keep a lookout for desperate men. The authorities were astonished that such a raid could have taken place in so isolated a spot. Unfortunately, so were we.

By this time we were surrounded by quite a big crowd. We could see winding up the hill below us a small section of Italian soldiers in dark green uniform wearing forage caps and carrying small rifles. They sweated as they climbed up and the crowd parted to let them through. We were going to be led off and handed over to the police in Teora. We were in no position to do anything else as the soldiers took us off.

We had not gone more than a few hundred yards down the hill when we were met by a posse of six, dressed in dark blue with red stripes on their breeches, white bandoliers over their shoulders and large blue hats badged with a silver flaming grenade. This was the Carabinieri, who combine the duties of civil and military police. The local bobby in Italy is a Carabinieri as well as being the military policeman in the army.

As they came up to us we could see they were all sweating profusely as they took over from the soldiers who were guarding us. After searching once again for arms, they took handcuffs and chains from small boxes riveted to their bandoliers. We were tied together in parties of three or four, although Tag was spared this ignominy.

Just before we started to move off again, Tag noticed that one of our grenades had a broken split pin. He told Nastri to tell the Carabinieri this and also to tell them that he should throw it away – without pulling the pin – as it was dangerous in its present condition. This caused a flap. The *Sergente di Carabinieri* in charge began talking and shouting and waving his arms. He eventually drew out his revolver and, cocking it, held its muzzle right against Tag's head. His finger was on the trigger and he was trembling so violently with rage that I expected to see it go off any minute. Tag lobbed the grenade into the mud where it stuck. The commotion over, the poor little *Sergente*, sweat pouring down his unshaven face, collapsed like a pricked balloon. He looked a bit ashamed of himself.

A narrow winding track led us down into the nearby village of Teora where a small crowd was out to meet us. A few shouts went up '*Viva Carabinieri Viva Duce*', as if the Carabinieri had had any part at all in our inglorious capture. We were led into the local police station which felt damp and cold after the warm sunshine outside. The room in which they locked us up had bare whitewashed walls and a cold red-tiled floor. Its window looked out through heavy one-inch bars on to the green hillside down which we had just come. Outwardly we tried to look cheerful but inside we were all mighty depressed.

* 5 *

IN JAIL

Once more we were thoroughly searched and each time one or more items of escape kit were discovered. These had been sewn into the battledress and included silk maps of Italy, money and miniature compasses. Fortunately, enough remained to give us a complete set when eventually we reached the prison camp.

The sight of this escape kit being discovered somehow encouraged me. All was not yet lost. Outwardly we had tried to look cheerful, whilst inside we had plumbed the depths of despair. I was an officer and must try to do better. None of us could do much without food. I asked Nastri to demand water and food in accordance with the Geneva Convention on prisoners of war. Eventually, and rather to our surprise, hunks of bread and a few tins of Italian bully beef were dumped on the floor. These we greedily devoured and immediately we felt new energy and hope surge through our veins.

Something then happened which I will never forget. A very small man, not much more than five feet tall and wearing a large hat, came into the room and started shouting. We continued to munch our hunks of bread until Nastri translated that he was a general and expected us to rise when he entered. After a little hesitation Tag told us to get up. He said, with a laugh, that it might get us some more food if we tickled his vanity.

The shouting went on and Nastri translated that we were to be treated like soldiers and heroes. All our needs would be granted, he said. The only thing he wanted to know was how many more of us there were and he received the usual answer 'I can't say.' At this he just shrugged his shoulders and went out. It was quite peaceful when the shouting stopped.

Nastri and Pichi were called out soon after the General's departure and were questioned by a Blackshirt officer. When they came back they said that he had told them that we were all going to be shot at dawn the next day, so that we might as well tell everything. This, of course, received the usual laughing reply which infuriated the Italian who then strode out of the room.

That evening we were all pushed into a lorry, driven to the railway station and hustled into an evil-smelling waiting room. The stench of our guards who reeked of garlic and spat every three or four minutes on the sawdust-covered floor, when combined with our own sour smell, would have been nauseating if we had not been so tired. Gradually we dozed off where we were sitting. All that could be heard was our own continuous heavy snoring, interspersed by the usual Italian throat-clearing followed by a spit. Throughout my time in Italy I could never accustom myself to this unattractive habit.

Morning came at last and brought with it the other two parties who had been captured not very far from where we had been taken. One of Geoff Jowett's party had fired a tommy gun that he had kept and killed an Italian officer and two peasants. When they were captured soon after, their clothes were ripped off and they were rather roughly handled until they arrived at the station.

Our train came in about 10 am. The men were put all together in a carriage like a dining saloon with a Carabinieri in every seat near a window. The officers were split into pairs and put in ordinary six-seater compartments with four Carabinieri who sat in each corner. It rather flattered us that the Italians thought we were such desperate characters.

We sat in the same seats all day and eventually arrived at Naples about an hour after sunset. Lorries were waiting to take us to the local military detention barracks, and ten minutes later we were all herded into Naples Military Prison. My cell was about ten feet long by five wide. Along one side was a concrete block about two feet off the ground on which had been scattered a little straw. This had obviously been used before and was damp with condensation. In the corner there was a smelly 'hole in the ground' lavatory that was blocked with newspaper and was damp all round with urine. A very small square pane of glass high up in the end of the cell gave the only light. The door was heavily barred, bolted and locked, with a small peephole for the sentry stationed outside.

Morning came at last after a night spent sleeping by fits and starts. A sentry banged open the door and plonked down a bowl of ersatz coffee with a small piece of dried fig. I heard that we were soon going to be interrogated and I think we rather looked forward to it. We were all quite confident that nothing would be got out of us, but we had heard so much about the questioning of prisoners of war that we were all curious to see what it was really like.

We were all lined up in the corridor outside our cells and brought in to be interrogated one by one. I saw Pichi looking very depressed and tried to cheer him up.

'It's no good,' said Pichi 'They'll find out who I am. I don't see how they can fail.'

'I don't see why they should,' I told him. 'Not if you stick like glue to the official story – that you are a Free Frenchman in the British Army. I really don't think they can prove a thing.' I am sure he did not take my advice when he went in to be questioned. We never saw him again.

Two months were to go by before we read in the Italian papers that he had been shot as a traitor on Palm Sunday. We all felt sad at his passing. The job he had been given had been so small compared with the risks he had taken. He was a great little man.

The men were being interrogated singly in one room while the officers were allotted another. The men had all been told individually that the next day at 6 am they would face the firing squad. The story being repeated to them was that 'they had been caught making war on the civilian population committing acts of sabotage, and in Italy that is punishable by death. But if you cooperate, you can avoid execution.'*

Although some of them may have half-believed this to be true, our very excellent sergeants soon spoke out. 'It's a farce,' they said. 'It's just a ploy to try and make us talk.'

A different and more sophisticated tack was adopted with the officers. A well-dressed man in civilian clothes was sitting behind a desk with two Black Shirt fascists standing behind.

'I am the Commandant of the camp you are going to,' he said, 'and all I want are a few details for the Red Cross.' This was a lie, of course, but it was a device designed to put us at ease. I then butted in on his smooth talking and told him, 'My number is 71076, my rank is Lieutenant and my name is Deane-Drummond and you can expect nothing else.' This did not put him off. He continued to ask details of my next of kin etc. To all these questions I told him, 'I can't say.' Eventually he gave up and I was sent out. Heaving a sigh of relief at finishing something unpleasant, I went out and rejoined Tag and Christopher who had already been through. They told much the same story, but the questioner had used the line that all he wanted to do was establish who was 'guilty of shooting the three men'. This was absurd because they already knew the answer, and anyhow we were quite within out rights to shoot anybody who attempted to interfere with us while we were getting to the coast.

Back we went to our cells and found a tolerably good lunch waiting for us. Afterwards we had a shave by a barber who had come in from the town. We now felt immeasurably better and ready to face anything. In the meantime Lucky, as an Air Force officer, had been taken off for separate questioning by the Italian Air Force. He managed to persuade them that all the officers should be moved to the aerodrome where there was much better accommodation and food. We were all very grateful.

We stayed on the aerodrome nearly two weeks and watched it being used to ferry German fighters to North Africa. We ate too much, took too little

* *Guinea Pigs,* p 58

exercise but could see no way out. While we were there, Gerry Daly turned up. He had managed to stay out five days after being dropped two miles north of the correct bridge. His plane had lost the way and his drop took place two hours late. He had not been on the ground more than forty minutes when he heard the bridge go up. With his party, he managed to get to within fifteen miles of the coast and had been caught trying to get a truck. Eventually he was taken to Naples jail, from which he escaped the first night. He had noticed that the lock to his door was rotten. Sure enough it broke open to quite a small push when he tried it at 11 pm. With his rubber-soled boots he slipped past three sentries and wandered round Naples all night. Unfortunately he slipped and fell down when trying to board a train the next morning at 11 am. Once more he was a prisoner. The Naples Carabinieri were the laughing stock of all Naples when the news of Gerry's escape spread around.

We were moved by train, guarded by no less than one colonel, one captain, one subaltern and thirty-five Carabinieri for the thirty-five of us. I think we were all regarded as desperadoes; they certainly did not want a repeat of Gerry Daly's efforts on the train.

The train wound its way through the mountains to Sulmona all day. At times we were perched on the sides of precipices and at others we clattered through evil-smelling tunnels. The scenery grew wilder and more desolate as we neared Sulmona, the birthplace of Ovid. As each barren and deserted scene moved past the train's windows, our depression increased. Our chances of escaping from a country with so many natural obstacles looked slim.

About four o'clock in the afternoon we burst out of a tunnel and found ourselves rattling along a hillside high above a green and beautiful valley, sparkling in the sunshine with little streams and red-roofed, whitewashed farmhouses. After the desolate country we had come through, it was like looking down into a real promised land. Before many months were out, we were to hate that little valley, surrounded as it was on all sides by five-thousand-foot mountains.

We were met at the station by an Italian officer who could speak English. He told us we had a five-mile walk to the camp, which cheered us up enormously because we had not had any real exercise in the last fortnight. The Carabinieri guard were not at all pleased and when it started to spit with rain they looked far more depressed than their prisoners.

After a most enjoyable walk we arrived at the camp. We had visions of Red Cross parcels and plenty of company from the others. We were soon to realize what a mistaken idea we all had of prison camps. On arrival we were led in through tall barbed-wire gates and then through a door in a brick wall about ten feet high leading into a hut devoid of any furniture. One by one we were searched. Nothing was found on us and soon we were led off through a maze of walls and passages to be shown our homes for the next two months. The Italians had gone to the trouble of building a small walled-off compound in the middle of the camp especially for our benefit. The officers were put in this and the men were led off by themselves and locked up in another one which again had been specially constructed in their honour.

All the view we could see from outside our hut was the sky and a sheer mountainside. Half-way up, an old hermit's house had been built into the side of the rock and was the only sign of habitation that was visible from our prison. We had to feed, sleep and exercise ourselves all in a little courtyard thirty yards long by three yards broad.

The next two months were hell. It hurt us more than most because we were used to an active life with plenty of exercise. The only saving grace was the food. At this stage there was no shortage and we became rather fat. Later on we were to know the meaning of starvation rations, but at this period we had far more than was good for us. We soon saw that, with a guard on a tower just above our yard and also one inside all night, escape was hopeless for the time being.

Two weary months passed before we were promoted to the top compound where all the other officers were housed. In the meantime we were feeling the stress of living together in such cramped quarters. Geoff Jowett, our Canadian backwoodsman, became more and more mopey. Gerry Daley set himself mathematical problems to solve. Christopher Lea and I had pipe dreams about mad schemes to escape, but the sage old Tag ever counselled patience till we were sent to the top compound. He was right, of course, but it was irksome to us at the time. We were beginning to feel the strain.

I kept wondering whether our efforts on Colossus had been worth it. We had done the job, but we were all in the bag. Had this really been intended all along? I could not believe that this had been anticipated by our headquarters in England. Judging by the fact that our clothes had all had items of escape kit sewn into them, perhaps it had. Maybe there never was going to be a submarine waiting to take us off. Records in the Public Record Office show that there was.

Was it worth it?

Being wise after the event, and half a century later, one is bound to ask whether the effort put into Colossus was worth it. Purely from a military point of view it was of negligible importance. The aqueduct was repaired within a month, during which time local reservoirs kept the water flowing to the three ports. In the summer it might have been different.

There is no doubt, however, that the raid presented a new threat to the whole of Italy. The British had chosen a target in the mountains no less than sixty miles from the coast. A re-examination by the Italians of all important targets was undertaken and arrangements made to guard them as necessary. We had shown that we could breach their homeland and nowhere was it safe to assume that another raid was out of the question. Large numbers of troops were deployed to assist the Carabinieri in their efforts during the remainder of the war.

At home the main aim was psychological. When the news of the raid was published many people were encouraged – we had taken the war into Italy itself. Britain, by itself in the war at this time, had shown it was not only capable of aggressive action, but that it could attack targets a long way inland. By comparison, normal seaborne commandos could only have attacked targets near the coast.

The raid did at least demonstrate that the techniques of parachuting had been sufficiently mastered and a joint operation with the RAF was technically possible. We had vindicated the formation of No 2 Commando. We had done the job and done it successfully.

The choice of an inland target well away from the sea was surprising. Most informed officers, including Admiral Keyes, expected that some of our parties would be captured on the way to the coast. I do not think anybody at home realized that the going would be so difficult or that the Italian population would be so thick on the ground. If it had been like Scotland, most of us would have reached our rendezvous by the sea, but I am afraid only to find that there would be no submarine. One of the Whitleys on a diversionary raid had developed engine trouble and the crew had been forced to bale out near the coast. Unfortunately they chose the same spot which we were trying to reach, although the Captain of the aircraft had no knowledge of our plans. In his innocence he sent back details of where he was baling out in a simple code in the hope that the submarine could also pick up him and his crew. This was more than enough for the submarine to be cancelled, but, as it turned out, this was just as well. The mouth of the Sele River would have been a very hot place for any submarine, if it had gone in that far.

Official records* show that Admiral Keyes tried to get the decision by the Navy to cancel the submarine reversed. It was just as well he was not successful.

* Public Record Office DEFE 2/152 – 3 Combined Headquarters records on Operation Colossus 40/41

* 6 *

PRISONERS OF WAR

At last the great day arrived and we were led up to the top compound. We were held up for about twenty minutes before being let in. We grouped together and sang 'God Save the King'. It sounds extraordinary now so long after the event, but it just shows how tense and worked up we must have been. The gates then opened and we all trooped though, feeling very self-conscious. Having seen nobody except each other for so long, it was really quite astonishing to be once more in contact with the outside world, or so it seemed to us at the time. Soon we were to tire of the company of even the hundred or so officers in our new compound and once again became more and more introspective.

While we had been down in the tiny bottom compound the Italians had been strengthening the wire obstacles. They had erected three barbed-wire fences, each ten feet high, round the complete perimeter of the camp. The fences were well constructed with taut strands of barbed-wire six inches apart, with the bottom one running along at ground level. Each fence was spaced four or five feet from the next, and just outside the outer one lights had been put on the top of twelve-foot poles. These lights were ten yards apart and were kept on all night. In addition, every third pole had a powerful double floodlight pointing each way along the wire. These could be switched on from the nearest sentry boxes, which were dispersed every twenty yards between the first two rows of wire. As the camp formed a rectangle about 300 yards long by 150 yards broad, a guard of forty-five was required to man the sentry boxes alone.

A track for carts ran round the whole camp between the wire fences and the compound walls, which were also ten feet high with broken glass set in the cement along the top. Inside each compound were two Carabinieri who patrolled by day and night. Still not content with what were by now most formidable defences, the Italians had erected two towers thirty or forty feet high in the middle of the camp. By day two sentries could look down on all our activities, and by night they could continue with the aid of a moveable searchlight.

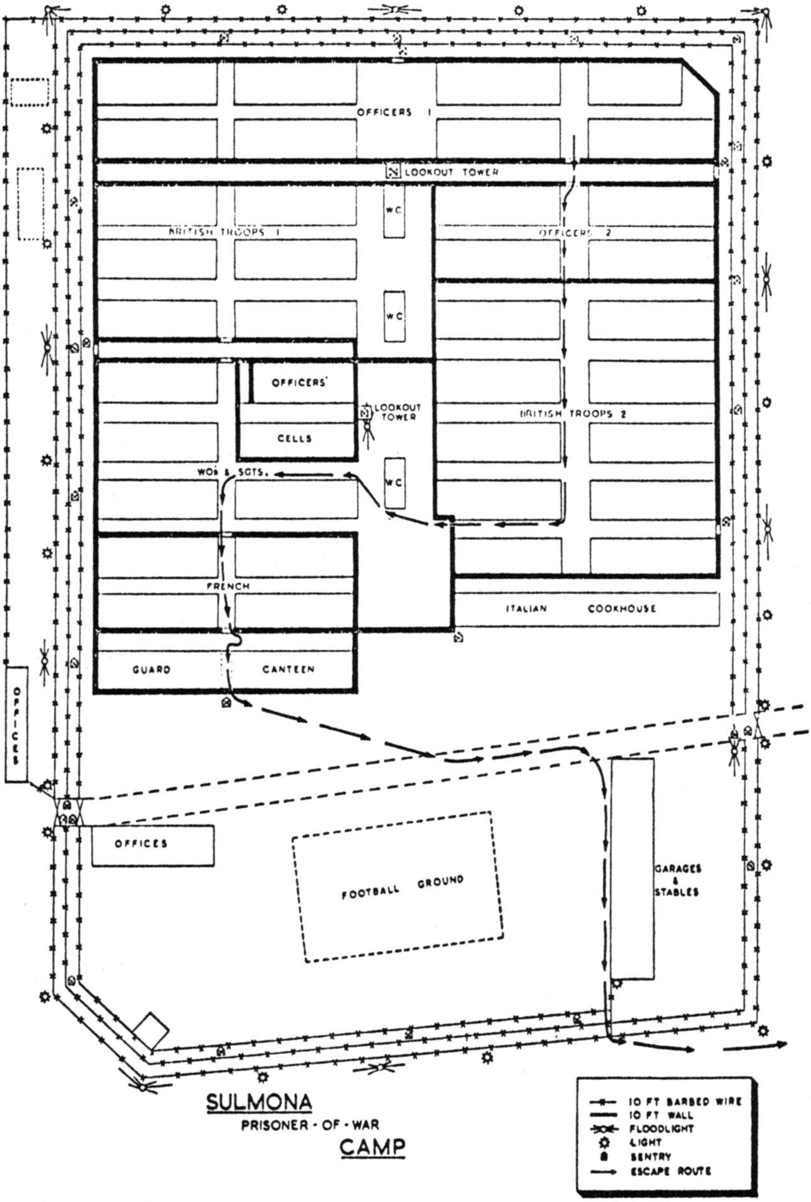

SULMONA
PRISONER - OF - WAR
CAMP

Such was the problem set to every would-be-escaper. The liberal use of wire obstacles, walls and a standing guard of fifty to sixty men on duty at any one time, made the camp an extremely difficult one from which to escape. Most officers said it was impossible except through a tunnel. Nearly everybody agreed that the chances of reaching a neutral country were negligible. We were about six hundred miles from Switzerland through the mountains and no help could be expected from anybody on the way. Italy was in the war and making progress on most fronts – or so said the radio and newspapers. No peasant could be relied on for assistance, although this was to change completely after the Italian armistice two and a half years later. Carabinieri police stations in most villages and towns were the eyes and ears of an efficient system covering the whole country. There was no chance of staying free for long in the countryside.

Our new compound was 150 yards long by 20 yards broad, which felt almost spacious after our previous quarters. Down each long side were four low brick bungalows with tiled roofs, which were to house us for the rest of the time we spent in Sulmona. A wide gravel path ran down the middle, and we were to find out that six round trips to each end and back again would give us a mile's worth of exercise.

Geoff Jowett, George Patterson and I shambled off to our dormitory. Our room held twenty and I was given a bed near the door. In the middle stood a red earthenware stove with the pipe going out through the wall.

By each bed there was a small cupboard and one or two dilapidated chests of drawers were scattered round the room. On some beds officers were lying reading books and one was working away at a table with a pile of heavy-looking volumes in front of him. Our guide turned out to be Lieutenant Bob Ross from Western Australia and he had the bed next to mine. Short and stocky and with a swarthy appearance, he looked more Greek than Australian. He was a wonderful teller of stories and he would ramble on for hours about his past loves and adventures.

Soon after arrival we were summoned to meet the Senior British Officer, who was an Australian Lieutenant-Colonel. Short and grizzly, with close-cropped hair, he squinted at us through glasses with obvious disfavour.

'I want you to realize,' he said in a high pitched twang, 'that I have had very great difficulty getting the Italians to give us the few privileges we have. The Commandant tells me that you are very dangerous prisoners and he hopes that I can control you. I do hope you will cooperate with me and help us to keep our few comforts.'

He was the only Australian I ever met who lacked all charisma. Bob Ross was very apologetic about him when we came back. We must have looked bewildered.

'Senior British Officer, my fucking oath. Son of a Bitch or SOB for short we call him,' explained Bob.

Tony Rowley, another Australian, chimed in,

'SOB giving you his old woman pep talk I suppose?'

'He told us to be good boys,'

'Take no fuckin' notice, cobber. The old man sweated out all his guts in New Guinea before this goddam fuckin' war, and now he has none left.'

Tony Rowley was in typical dress. Crumpled open-neck khaki shirt, khaki shorts and leather sandals, he looked sunburnt and healthy. With a shock of fair hair and a wide open grin, which displayed two or three badly chipped teeth, he accepted you at your face value, 'And no fuckin' about,' as he called it. He had left school at seventeen to go and fight as a mercenary in China against the Japanese. By the time war broke out in 1939, he had already served three years in Chiang Kai Shek's army and had been earning £100 a month. This was a fortune in 1941.

A bell clanged and a cry of 'lunch up' came from outside. We drifted off to the mess room and, arming ourselves with a couple of plates, were doled out our meal at the door to the kitchen. Food was still good and plentiful at this early period in the war and was chiefly limited by what a 2nd Lieutenant could afford to pay. No rations were issued free. Later on, in September, 1941, Italy suddenly introduced very strict rationing which became smaller and smaller as the months went by.

Shortly after arriving in the top compound, all six of us feverishly looked round to find a way out, causing not a little amusement to the rest of the officers. They knew it was impossible, but eventually a tunnel was projected and was soon under way. A piece of cracked concrete served as the opening and this allowed the entrance and cover to be prepared. The big mistake with this attempt was the number of officers employed on it. Some twenty were digging and scattering the soil, and at least another twenty were in positions round about watching for the approach of any of the Carabinieri guard.

The entrance gave on to a fifteen-foot shaft, lined and revetted with firewood to stop the loose sand crumbling and filling in the tunnel. From the initial shaft a tunnel some eighteen inches square went straight under the wire, a good forty yards away. It would then have to continue at least another thirty yards before it would be safe to strike upwards.

Six weeks of hard work went into it with the usual tunnellers' method of scattering earth everywhere in thin streams from pockets. If one saw a collection of officers shambling around, hands in pockets, one knew that a steady stream of sandy earth was coming out of sacks held inside their trousers like hour-glasses running out. But tunnels in this camp were doomed to failure, especially when large numbers were employed on making them. Somehow the news always leaked out and sooner or later the other ranks' compound heard of it. As soon as this happened the Italians seemed to know. There was at least one informer among the other ranks and I don't believe he was ever caught. One day a party of Carabinieri came in and walked straight to the tunnel entrance and dug it up. All our labours in the last six to eight weeks had been in vain.

Ever since this occasion I decided that if ever I should escape it would be solo or, at most, a dual effort. There would then be no chance of anybody getting to hear about it. Many said it was not feasible to go many hundreds of miles through Italy by oneself. I always felt that alone I would only have myself to worry about and, given self-confidence and a lot of luck, there were good chances of success. My later experiences proved to me that I was right. Since then I have talked to several other successful escapers, most of them from Germany, and they have all agreed with me that very few complete parties were ever successful, and nearly all those who got away arrived in a neutral country by themselves.

My first idea on a way out came to me while watching the garbage being wheeled out in barrows and dumped just outside the wire. The snag was that the Italian form of wheelbarrow was small and the garbage was carefully looked over by the guards. But I thought that if a very large sack of vegetable peelings went out every day as a matter of course, then one day when all suspicions had been quietened, I would substitute myself for the vegetable peelings. All went well during the next three weeks. I had to take into my confidence one of the soldiers who was authorized to do the wheeling out, so that he would not be surprised by an extra heavy sack. Two days later, the day before my D-Day, the guards suddenly started searching every sack and even pushing bayonets into every barrowload. My first serious effort to escape had been thwarted. I had a long talk to the chap in whom I had confided. He eventually admitted that he had bragged about it to a pal in his compound. During that long summer and autumn of 1941 some of us were very depressed by the distorted war news put over by Fascist Italy. The Russians withdrew hundreds of miles at a time and the annual circular tour from Egypt to El Agheila, Cyrenaica and back seemed to show precious few rays of sunlight in a cloud-darkened sky.

The prison routine became monotonous. Sleep, breakfast, roll-call, work on a language or do a mile or two up and down, listen to a lecture by some expert on an unusual subject, lunch and so on. Week in, week out. Boredom mixed up with an eternal longing for freedom. Occasional 'black days' when everything seemed futile and a waste of time; occasional rosy ones when an innate optimism strove to show that there must be a silver lining somewhere.

Naturally we kept worrying the Italians to give us more privileges, take us on longer walks, buy us more things from the shops. Anything important we raised officially through the Senior British Officer who had to go and see the Italian Colonello who commanded the camp. For smaller things we nagged at the Italian interpreters, who were mostly quite helpful, but nearly always they returned with the story that it was not possible.

'If only you would all sign an undertaking that you would not try to escape, we could do much more for you. We know that your army says it is your duty to try, but surely you can see it is quite impossible and it would save all this unpleasantness.

'Of course, we know why you want to escape, and we sympathize deeply'.

'Oh really, what is the reason then?'

'Women, beautiful women. We don't understand why you don't all go crazy. We know where to look, if you do get out.'

We heard later that camp standing orders laid down procedures in the event of an escape. All bordellos within ten miles were to be contacted immediately.

I, myself, was not seriously worried by lack of feminine company after the first month or two. Civilization was so far away. It was no good longing for the company of women, there just weren't any. We were not in a position to covet our neighbour's wife, he had not got one with him.

When we came up to the top compound we discovered to our surprise that no attempt had been made to help escapers or to centralize the camp's slender resources of escaper's equipment such as money and maps.

Tag immediately put forward the idea that some sort of escape organization should be set up. He then had to convince everybody that it was a good thing. Using a great deal of tact and gentle persuasion, he eventually won over even the oldest of the camp's inhabitants, many of whom had acquired invaluable adjuncts to escaping such as wire cutters, compasses, maps, money and even civilian clothes. Major S. Clayton DSO, of the Long Range Desert Group, soon became an expert forger of documents. Lucky extracted railway timetables from the Colonello's office whilst acting as a spare interpreter. Information was obtained on what happened on Italian frontiers and a lot of other data. But the first and most difficult task for us all was to get out.

Any officer who thought he had an idea on how to escape had to register his scheme with the committee to prevent two rival parties attempting the same method unbeknown to each other. If approval was given, then sufficient of the camp's resources would be allocated to ensure the maximum chance of success. To preserve secrecy we did not know who was on the committee; only the name of our representative. Naturally Tag was ours and I am sure he was the leading spirit who inspired the whole thing.

The one source of stimulus for me and a few others was the idea of making a successful escape to a neutral country. To some, the only object was to get out of the camp, have a good walk round and taste some freedom from prison routine. To me this was not half enough. I could see little point in getting out if a sound plan did not exist to get to Switzerland. The mere fact that practically everybody in Sulmona said it was impossible to make the six-hundred-mile journey to the Swiss frontier was an added incentive to prove the know-alls wrong.

The summer passed and still we had made no serious attempt to escape. Prison routine was beginning to numb our senses and like the older inhabitants we had half-convinced ourselves that it was impossible.

It was Christopher Lea who broke the spell. One morning, when we were striding up and down the compound, he said:

'You know, Tony, it is high time we made some effort to get out. It is all very well to say it is well nigh impossible, but there must be a way out somewhere.'

'I only wish I could see one.'

'Well what about putting a ladder against the wire in the corner, one on top and then just running across.'

'You have two sentries within a few yards and they would have plenty of time to shoot at you'.

'They might miss.'

'Not at ten yards. No Christopher, we must do better than that. We must have at least a fifty per cent chance of getting out undetected.'

'We must just do something.'

'All right. Let us do it methodically. We must examine every inch of the whole perimeter wire and see if there is anywhere which is less well covered by sentries or where the wire is not continuous.'

'That's right. And having found the weak spot we must then work out a way of getting there from our compound. Come on, let's draw a plan of the outside wire and check it off as we get a chance of looking at it.'

The best opportunity we had of inspecting the outside wire was when we were taken for walks. Four or five weeks elapsed before either one or other of us saw the place we were to use about six weeks later. It was right down at the bottom end of the camp where the ground changed level at a wall. The three rows of wire ended there and then started again at the higher level. The end poles of the top three fences were spaced back from the edge of the wall by about eight inches to allow the poles to be stayed by wires running at an angle. Apart from these stay wires, the ledge was free of obstruction and led to freedom.

We had found a gap in the wire which had seemed so impregnable, but there were many snags. In the first place a sentry box was placed about fifteen yards away on the lower level. Secondly a light shone continuously on the gap from the wall of the stable and kept the whole ledge lit up. Thirdly the gap we had found was at the diametrically opposite end of the camp from where we were. To any but us poor caged birds, the problems would have appeared insurmountable, but we had now been prisoners for nine months and we were willing to take any reasonable risks. It took us a month to work out a plan between the two of us. First I would have a bright idea and then Christopher would have a better one. Each of us spent all day and every day with our minds concentrated on solving the problem. We were beginning to live again.

We first of all decided that, provided the night was dark enough, we could get out along the ledge if the light was put out. This was crucial. A really wet night with no moon behind the clouds would be just what we wanted.

How on earth could we put out that light? We thought of everything. Perhaps we could fuse the whole supply to the camp, but turned this down because it would alert all the guards and the fuse might be repaired before we could get to the right place. We then discovered that the perimeter lights were on a separate circuit from our own.

Our next scheme was to bribe the Italian electrician. We did not like this one. The guards appeared to be singularly incorruptible and we both thought there was a strong change of being double-crossed. Only a few weeks before, one of the officers had tried to bribe a guard who immediately told his officer about it. He was allowed to keep the bribe and was promoted lance-corporal. We found out later that this had become standard practice in all walks of life in Italy with the aim of stamping out corruption.

Our next idea was to wait for a thunderstorm and hope that the lights would go out. They often did. But we could not hang around waiting for thunderstorms.

One morning I had a brainwave whilst sitting on the lavatory – surely a great stimulant to intensive thought the world over. We would carry a ladder to the light and, pretending we were Italian electricians, would climb up the ladder and unscrew the bulb. It all seemed so simple once we had thought of it. The solution had been staring us in the face.

There were difficulties. We had to manufacture a ladder and also Italian uniforms to wear over our escaping clothes. We had to devise a method of transporting ourselves and our ladder over the compound walls to start our walk to the light. The top three sides of the camp had sentries facing the outer walls and only a few paces from it. We could never have dropped over that wall with a twelve-foot ladder and got away with it. The only place where the sentries were away from the outer wall was at the bottom end of the camp, beyond the French compound and between the Italian guardroom and their canteen. A passage went straight through just here, although there was a sentry box outside. He would surely never suspect two electricians apparently coming out of his own guardroom and carrying a ladder?

Towards the end of November, 1941, we heard that Donald Stuart had reached Switzerland to make history with the first successful escape from an Italian prison camp. Gradually the details leaked out. He had pretended he was sick with kidney trouble at Sulmona and had been sent to Chieti hospital only five miles from Pescara on the Adriatic coast. He had some advantages. He was trilingual in French and Italian and looked like a Latin. He went by train from Pescara to Como and crossed the frontier near Chiasso. News of this success encouraged all of us.

We made our ladder by splitting a plank down the middle and used pieces of firewood and bits of chairs for the rungs. Our own excellent NCOs, Sergeants Lawley and Clements, offered to take the bits and pieces of the ladder down to their compound and we let them carry on. They came up to our compound, carried the different parts of the ladder down to their compound over two of the intervening walls and practically under the very eyes of the 'Crows' patrolling in the compounds. They would wait until they were looking the other way, or round one corner of the building, to rush the pieces of wood another fifty yards on their way. As the searchlight's beam from the tower swung round, it would find them and their load motionless in some shadow. Lawley and Clements completed this operation with a hundred per cent success. The ladder was assembled by them in the next few days without any suspicions being raised.

We were now ready. It was 4 December, 1941, and we had been in the bag for nearly ten months. We were both keyed up and excited. Adrenalin was flowing again. Full moon was on the night of 2 December, which meant that by the 7th or 8th the first half of the night would have no moon at all. The year was getting late but unfortunately the weather was still fine. We would make our attempt on the night of 7 December.

Christopher and I disagreed violently on the best method to use once out of the camp. Mine was to walk the fifty odd miles to Pescara and buy a ticket on a train from there. His plan was to hop goods trains all the way up Italy. Mine was certainly the quickest and more spectacular, but Christopher thought it had little chance of success. He did not think that an Englishman with fair hair could go into an Italian railway station, buy a ticket hardly knowing a word of Italian and get away with it. The Escape Committee agreed with Christopher. But I managed to persuade them. I insisted that booking office clerks had a difficult time. All they wanted to hear was 'Third single London' or 'Milan'. They would then push over a ticket automatically. I learnt and relearnt the phrase asking for a ticket to Milan. *'Terzo Milano'* became my sleeping song and my pronunciation was said to be perfect by Lucky.

I told the Committee that I planned to walk to Pescara in three nights. The first night I would go straight up the mountains behind the camp and get over the top. The second night I would drop down on to the main Rome-Pescara road and walk along it about twenty miles each night. I thought I should arrive in Pescara on the third morning and buy my ticket on the 8 am to Milan. From Milan I planned to buy another ticket to Como and from there to get over the Swiss frontier only two miles away at Chiasso.

The Committee could see I had worked out a reasonable plan and they wished me luck. But not one of them thought I would be successful. Once again I had to prove them all wrong.

* 7 *

ESCAPE FROM SULMONA

December the 7th was a lovely day. A glorious feeling of tenseness rose within us. My nerves and brain were working at a speed they had nearly forgotten in the previous dulling months. Maps, money, and a tiny compass were all concealed in oilskin and stuck with sticking plaster well up under my fork.

I pulled on my homemade corduroy trousers and made a bundle of the raincoat and sham Italian uniform. We would put these on at the last moment before going over the wall of the French compound. A battledress jacket covered up my coloured shirt so that in the dark my clothes would pass as reasonable uniform. Christopher was dressed likewise and we both moved off at 8.30 pm after a good meal. We arrived down in the NCOs' compound at 9 pm with about two hours to spare before the moon came up.

Unfortunately two patrolling Carabinieri kept talking to each other in the one place where we had to get over the next wall. They went on talking until 10.30 pm, by which time light from the rising moon, still below the horizon, was beginning to cast shadows in the camp. We decided to go back to our own compound and try again the next night. We both handed over our packets of money and maps to Sergeant Clements to keep for tomorrow. Christopher got over the wall alright and I was just about to follow and was actually hanging by my hands from the top when I heard shouting behind and two Carabinieri came running up. I could not pull myself up and drop over the other side in time, so I let go and came down in the NCOs' compound. I tried to make a run for it, but I had not gone more than a dozen paces before I tripped up and went flat on my face. The two Crows pounced on me from behind. I was led off with the muzzle of a rifle drilling the small of my back, with its owner screaming at me in high-pitched Italian that I would get twenty-eight days on bread and water. I thought I would too. As I was wearing no badges of rank I was mistaken for an other rank. I was in no hurry to advise them differently until after I had been searched.

We arrived at the guardroom and I was then searched fairly well, all seams being felt through, and was then led off to an other ranks' cell. My name soon trickled through to the Italian officers and I was yanked out and taken back to the officers' compound because all the officers' cells were full. I was in real luck. We would have another go on the 8th.

'Fish Eyes', the interpreter, had great pleasure in calling me out at the Roll Call the next morning and telling me that I would have twenty-one days' solitary confinement as soon as there was room.

'Just to make sure you have a happy Christmas,' he said as an afterthought. We called him Fish-Eyes because he had been born with his eyes rather far apart. I was furious with the horrible little man, but outwardly I showed a blank face and went away to discuss with Christopher the plans for the night's work. We decided to go through with the same timings because it would give us an extra hour, with the moon rising an hour later every night.

By this time many officers realized that we were up to something, but very few knew what we proposed to do. Evening came and we had a superb meal with Gerry Daley and Nigel Strutt. They had a Canadian Red Cross parcel, and this produced a sumptuous repast of biscuits, cheese and butter, followed by soused herrings. Not exactly a Lord Mayor's banquet, but it was a feast for us and we were to need every ounce of energy in the days to come. Because we were intending to sidle along an eight-inch wide ledge with a wire fence on one side, we both decided we could not afford to bulge ourselves out with supplies of food. I took only two packets of biscuits and a pound of chocolate. Later on I discovered that thirst and not hunger was to be my principal enemy. On my timetable, it would be five days before I crossed into Switzerland and surely anybody can go without food for five days and feel none the worse for it?

So far so good. We arrived down in the NCOs' compound after a big send-off from Tag and Gerry Daly. Soon we dressed up again in our mock Italian overcoats and hats covering our semi-civilian get up. Sergeant Lawley stood by with a ladder waiting for the moment when the patrolling Carabinieri were at the farthermost point from where we were to cross into the French compound.

We were a bit nervous at this stage. It was like walking round the paddock before riding in a point-to-point. My heart was beating a little faster and nerves were taut while we waited for the signal to move off. We both knew that, if we failed, we would not only get solitary confinement for at least twenty-eight days, but also it would be a minimum of six months before we could think of another way out.

A hushed whisper of 'It's OK' started us moving. We used the ladder to help us over the wall and dropped down into the French Compound. We quickly walked across and put our ladder against the bottom wall, the other side of which was the passage running between the guardroom and canteen. A quick glance over the top to make sure there was no sentry and we both dropped silently over. Unfortunately we both cut our hands quite badly on the broken glass on top of the walls. We lay down in the shadow and bandaged them before moving off again.

Then we stood up and, carrying our ladder together with spare coils of flex held prominently in front of us, we walked straight to the open door which led into the corridor separating the guardroom from the canteen. The doors leading into the canteen and the guardroom were ajar, but, without looking into either, we walked straight through, past the sentry outside who made no effort to challenge us. So far so good. Everything was so normal that it was uncanny. Sentries were in their boxes, perimeter lights outlined the edge of the camp and faint noises of some concert came from one of the compounds. But, unfortunately, the sky was starlit. We had hoped for a cloudy night, but we had taken the decision for better or for worse and now we were on our way. There was certainly no going back and we walked grimly on, wondering what the next few seconds would have in store. We came level with the end of the football field and turned down towards the lamp. I could see the sentry quite clearly outlined against his box and a moment later we were standing underneath the light. Christopher put the ladder against the wall and I climbed up. As I was climbing up the sentry shouted something to us and my heart missed a beat. We had thought this might happen, so I shouted back '*Lampa*' in as confident a voice as I could muster. We counted on the dumbness of the average Italian soldier not to start questioning us but to accept the extraordinary fact that in the middle of the night we were about to change a bulb that was already burning perfectly. I was always very confident on this point but many to whom I have told this story can hardly believe it to be true.

By this time I was at the top of the ladder and soon unscrewed the bulb. I made a pretence of changing them and screwed the same one back, but only half way. Now came the crucial test. We had to move sideways along ten yards of ledge without arousing the sentry's suspicions. We then made our only mistake. We had decided that, on a really dark night, we could carry the ladder out along this ledge and drop it down outside without the sentry seeing anything. We were so obsessed with this plan that we did not make any allowances for the starlit sky and we tried to go through with our original scheme. I climbed half-way down the ladder and side-stepped on to the ledge and signalled to Christopher to come up too. Then came the tricky business we had rehearsed mentally, of Christopher reaching down with one hand, catching hold of the ladder at the point of balance and passing it to me to hold. We started to move slowly along the ledge. Our coats caught in the barbed wire and seconds, which seemed like hours, went by before we could free each other. We had just arrived level with the first row of barbed wire when the sentry came running from his box and started screaming at us. Christopher realized the game was up a fraction of a second before I did, and shouted at me to throw the damn thing away. If it hadn't been for the ladder we could have both dropped down outside by the time this happened. I tossed the ladder away. Down it came across the three rows of wire and set up a twanging noise that must have been heard all over the camp. The sentry must have then realized that it was up to him to stop us and he fired a shot. Something flicked past my cheek and I could feel the sting and blood started to run. By this time I was hanging by my hands to the parapet on the outside of the camp and dropped into the road. The sentry had only managed to get off one round and as this had apparently grazed me, I assumed Christopher was alright and walked straight off. Our plans were to divide immediately on dropping outside the camp and so confuse any pursuers.

I heard later that Christopher had been hit in the thigh by the same shot that had grazed my cheek. The Italians, unknown to us, had issued their sentries with a type of bullet that disintegrated on its way down the barrel and came out in fragments the size of buckshot. One of the fragments had grazed me but most had gone into Christopher's leg. He did not utter a murmer or make any sign to me when we dropped down outside. He knew that I would have stayed with him for at least a few seconds if I had known and he waited till I was out of sight before calling for help. He had in fact been very badly wounded in the groin and nearly died. An artery had been cut and he was very ill from loss of blood. One of the doctors in the camp had insisted he be taken to hospital and it was a month before he recovered. The doctor's name was Steptoe and he was to achieve national recognition after the war as one of the specialists of 'in vitro' fertilization. As I walked rapidly away it dawned on me that I had actually succeeded in getting out. I had twisted my ankle but I now had to prove that I could get to Switzerland. What a thrill it was to be free once more. My plan was to circle the camp round to the left and start climbing the mountain in a diagonal direction. Every light was blazing back at Sulmona and my imagination kept telling me that those flashes of light on the hillside below were coming up after me. After an hour's fast climb and pouring with sweat, I decided I was safe and sat down to rest.

On and up the mountain I went, steering by the Pole Star and the outline of the valley below. The moon was just rising and soon the whole hillside was lit up as clear as daylight. The snow on the hills just above me stood out in startling whiteness and I could see the snowy peaks of the Gran Sasso range thirty miles away to the north. I sat down for another rest just below the snowline. Out came my chocolate for the first time, which I washed down with a lump of snow. My seat felt very cold and I realized that my beautiful homemade corduroy trousers had split all the way up the back seam. I had no cotton to mend it, so I would have to go through Italy with a split up my backside. I also tried without much success to wash the blood off my face with melted snow, in case I had to walk through a village.

I decided to skirt the mountain just below the snow line and to drop down on to the Sulmona-Pescara road just beyond Popoli, which was a tiny village at the head of the gorge leading out of the Sulmona valley towards Pescara. At last I climbed over a spur of the main ridge and could see round the corner down the Pescara valley. Pinewoods grew on any available soil and would have been lovely to walk through with their heavenly smell and glorious views through the trees in more normal times. There was little undergrowth and signs of newly cut trees warned me that woodcutters might be at work. I decided that the best spot might be in one of the scattered clumps of juniper bushes that grew here and there over the whole hillside. Nobody would be likely to tumble on my hiding place as there were so many bushes from which to choose. At last I found a really good-sized bush and crept in underneath. After a little scraping with my hands I had my legs covered with dead foliage and, with my green Italian overcoat over my head, I must have been nearly invisible. I then settled down to a little sleep and did not wake up until about 11 am, feeling rather cold and cramped. The rhythmic tap of the woodcutter's axe and an occasional splintering sound as another pine tree crashed to the ground were the only noises to disturb the peace. I stretched my legs and tried to make myself more comfortable, at the same time looking out from my perch on the hillside to get a wonderful view over the sunlit valley. The snow was only a few hundred feet above me and out of the sun it was bitterly cold. I attempted to eat some chocolate and biscuits but my mouth was so dry that I could not get them down.

At about midday I heard the tinkling bells of a flock of goats getting nearer and nearer as they fed. I hoped that the shepherd did not have a dog with him. I felt safe from anything except a dog. The goats were now grazing all round my bush and I could see an old man coming up the hillside. He had a lined and weatherbeaten face and wore a black coat, a sackcloth cape and dirty black trousers which were patched all over. He came straight for my bush and seemed to look straight at me. My heart stood still, while I rapidly thought out what I would do if I was discovered. I decided to reason with him as best I could and as soon as he had gone away I would get as far away from the spot as possible. At that time in Italy, nobody, not even shepherds or peasants, would help escaped prisoners of war. This had been proven by Dan O'Regan who had got out of Sulmona before we arrived and before all the wire fences went up. He went for a ten-day walk in the hills near Sulmona before being given away by an old woman. Everybody lived in terror of the Questura, which was a type of Italian Gestapo. There was no virtue in helping an obviously defeated enemy, as they thought of us then, especially as such an action might easily cost them their life, or at best a long term of imprisonment. This attitude was to change completely after the Armistice, when it was brought home to all Italians that they had in fact lost the war and the fear of the Questura was removed. They could then see that by helping an escaper they might gain favour with the new order. I was to find this out for myself in under two years' time.

The old man sat down with his back to my bush and only a yard or so away. There was no dog, which was a mercy. I hoped I would not sneeze. I did not dare move my legs which were getting more and more cramped. He stayed there about two hours but then got up and wandered away with his goats down the hillside. I breathed a heartfelt sigh of relief and decided that my luck was in after all. It was a good omen for the rest of my journey.

* 8 *

BY ROAD AND RAIL

Little by little the tapping in the woods petered out and all was silent as dusk fell. There were no houses at that height and all the peasants who worked up there probably lived in one or other of the villages down in the valley. Slowly I climbed to my feet and stretched myself, massaging my stiff muscles back to life. I was looking forward to some exercise to warm myself up, but what I really wanted was a drink from a stream. I started off along the track used by the shepherd when he went downhill. I was now as high as I need be and should be able to drop down on to the main road running through the gorge. The track became well worn and led straight down the mountain, although it might come out rather close to Popoli. A series of deep crevices and ravines with vertical rock faces on either side gave me no choice but to follow the track and hope for the best. After three hours' walking, I crossed a brow and there was Popoli, not a couple of hundred feet below me. I would have to go right through the village to get to the main road on the other side. The time was 9 pm so there should be plenty of people in the streets through which I would have to pass. My main worry was the possibility of checks on the main road as a result of my escape. I decided to risk it because it was a main road and should have lots of people like myself walking along it. This was common practice in wartime Italy when many people chose to walk from one village to another by night. The dangerous time was between about 11 pm and 4.30 am. This period must be avoided but I still had two hours to go before finding a suitable culvert under the road to spend the night.

My track led straight into the village with high walls of houses on either side. It was smelly but the road went on dropping by steps every six feet or so without any doors opening on to it from the houses. I was determined not to appear a stranger and walked on in as carefree a manner as I could muster. Quite suddenly a window banged open high up in a house overhanging my road and a bucket full of shit just missed me. Hell! I must be walking through the town's main sewer. With all my pride lost, I retraced my steps and found another way through to the centre of the town without attracting any attention.

The main road was soon found and was full of people. I walked straight through and nobody took any interest. There were no checks and I was now on the main road which ran through steep-sided ravines to Pescara.

My walk that night was uneventful and on several occasions I passed two or three Italian soldiers on the road without exciting attention. Many a long drink I had from watering troughs spaced out along the road. I could not have enough and used the occasion to wash dried-up streaks of blood from my face. The idea was to get to within 25 kilometres of Pescara that evening. Almost on the 25 kilometre stone and at 11.45 pm, there was a large dry culvert about 6 inches deep in leaves, running under the main road. This was ideal. Footsore and weary, I dragged myself inside and went into the deep sleep of the mentally and physically exhausted.

Numbness and cold woke me up just as it was getting light at 6.30 am. The plan was to stay there all day until nightfall and then walk to within 5 or 6 kilometres of Pescara that evening. It was cold and boring but nobody came near me.

My foot was hurting quite a lot now and, with a steady limp, I trudged along the main road resting every half-hour or so. There were many more houses flanking the road in the coastal plain. The nearer I came to Pescara the more populated it became. I was getting quite worried about finding a resting place near enough to the town. Fortunately the country opened up a little and soon after the 6 kilometre stone I found a ploughed field at least four hundred yards from any house. I lay flat on my back in a furrow in the centre of the field. This would be a most unlikely place to stumble on by accident in the middle of the night and would have to do until daybreak the following morning.

By 4 am I was getting myself ready. A dry scrape with a razor to remove the worst of my beard – nobody is too fussy in Italy – and my Italian overcoat was pushed into a ditch after it had been used to rub most of the mud off my boots and trousers. The mackintosh was a little bedraggled with small triangular rents caused by the thorn bushes in the mountains. By rubbing the material between the palms of my hands I managed to remove most of the bloodstains from the mac and my trousers. The sticking plaster holding my maps and money were unstuck from between my legs. The money was carefully folded into the breast pocket of my coat where I would not have to fumble for it when buying my ticket. A Swastika badge was clipped into my buttonhole and I had a faked German passport in my pocket. This was a product of the imagination of Sandy Clayton and probably bore little relation to the real thing. However, it looked good and had plenty of rubber stamps with German and Italian signatures authorizing nearly everything.

By 5.45 am I was ready and started on the last lap to Pescara which was reached at 7 am. I stopped the first woman I saw and asked her the way to the station in halting Italian, introducing my question by '*Io sono Tedesco*' (I am a German). The station was right at the north end of the town on the other side of the Pescara River. Nobody took the slightest notice of me as I walked through. Like everybody else I carried a little bag. This gave me a *raison d'être*. Nobody walks anywhere or travels long distances without at least a small bag. Mine was actually a British army officer's satchel made of canvas webbing dyed in blue-black ink.

At twenty minutes to eight by the station clock I walked into the main entrance of Pescara Station past two Carabinieri on duty by the door and joined a queue at the ticket office. Nobody took much notice. A five hundred lire note was in the palm of my hand and I was only two paces away from the window. Silently I mouthed to myself my oft-repeated phrase for getting a ticket. I felt as though everybody's eyes were on me as I took my turn and uttered a barely audible '*terzo Milano*' at the same time pushing my five hundred lire note over the counter. Before I knew where I was, a ticket and change were pushed at me and the man behind me in the queue was asking for his destination. The blood rushed back into my cheeks, and with renewed confidence I quickly followed the man in front on to the platform, brandishing my ticket like a passport. The ticket inspector punched the ticket and said *terzo* something or other in my ear. On past two more Carabinieri and I joined a few others also waiting for the train. A bookstall was selling papers and I bought a copy of *Signal* which was a German propaganda illustrated paper published in each language all over Europe. This would act as a further outward visible sign in addition to my fair hair and Swastika badge. I felt I was now the complete German shipyard worker going home on leave from Taranto. The time was now 7.55 am and the train was due in five minutes. My timing could not have been better.

The train came in five minutes late and a corner seat was soon found in which I was going to sit for the next fourteen hours. To my horror two Carabinieri came in to my compartment and sat down one next to me and one opposite. Questions went racing through my head. 'Had I been spotted and were these two following me?' My confidence came back when one of them cleared his throat in true Italian style and spat on the floor, rubbing the spittle in with the toe of his boot. Three other civilians were in the same compartment and they all added to the quota of spitting. I felt I should also spit but I couldn't. Perhaps the Swastika would explain my abnormality.

One horribly over-talkative passenger tried to speak to me and find out who I was to satisfy his curiosity. In halting Italian I told him I was working on German destroyers in Taranto and was on leave to Germany to see my family. Everybody in the compartment took a quite unnatural interest in my doings and I cursed them under my breath for their questioning. However, it was meant well and nobody had any suspicions that I was not who

I said I was. Nearly every siding had German coal trucks in them. Every time the talkative one saw them, he said, '*Tedesco - buono*'. Eventually he got out and the other occupants left me in peace. The main danger was meeting an Italian who could speak German. I had worked out that the better educated would surely be most unlikely to travel third class.

One of the passengers in my carriage leant out of the window at one of the stations and bought a '*cistina*'. This was a cardboard box containing a roll, a leg of chicken, an orange and a bit of cheese. The smell nearly drove me mad with a reawakened hunger. I decided to risk buying one at our next station which was Bologna. Sure enough a trolley was pushed along the train and I bought one for nine lire. I have hardly ever enjoyed a meal so much. This was to be my one and only meal on the whole journey. I could have eaten half a dozen with ease except for the suspicion it might have caused.

My confidence was increasing with every mile and when at last at about 9.45 pm we started to rattle through Milan suburbs, my morale could not have been higher. With a bit of luck I might get the train on to Como straightaway. A sudden doubt crossed my mind that a more thorough check might be in operation at a big terminus like Milan. Provided I moved with the crowd I should be safe. At 10 pm exactly the train pulled in and everybody got out. The ticket collector at the barrier had two Carabinieri standing beside him. I went through sandwiched in amongst a lot of people with no problem. The Carabinieri were probably only looking for people without tickets trying to give them the slip.

Unfortunately the last train to Como had left ten minutes before we arrived. I was in a quandary what to do till 7 am the following morning when the next one was due to leave. An awful reaction set in as a result of the anticlimax to my plans and in a fit of gross over-confidence I decided to spend the night in a Milan hotel. I told myself that if I could get away with it on a fourteen-hour train journey, surely I could do the same in a hotel. I suppose this idiotic decision was partly due to my tired mental and physical state and partly to an overpowering confidence that grips escapers as they get close to freedom.

Be that as it may, I walked down the long flight of steps from the platform level to the main booking hall, went straight up to a porter and asked him for the name of a hotel after explaining I was a German. He immediately gave me a name and a little urchin was button-holed to lead me there. We stumbled across the blacked-out square outside the station and then went down a small street to the right to find the entrance about two hundred yards further on. The name of the hotel was 'Vittoria'.

The receptionist was standing behind his desk. Once more my bad Italian came out asking for a room and some coffee to be sent up. To my horror he answered me in German! He was presumably an Austrian or Tyrolean and that was why I had been sent to this hotel. I mumbled back something in the schoolboy German I had learnt in prison. His only answer was 'You are no German' in German. My pulse beat a little faster but I was determined to have my say and told him '*Ich bin ein Sudetener – Heil Hitler*'. This seemed to satisfy him and he pushed across a card for me to fill in which I did, giving the details from my bogus identity card. He looked at it and shook his head. He had never seen one like that before. I interjected by saying it was only for Sudeteners – of course. He then led me upstairs to a comfortable room with a bath next door. Five minutes later a cup of coffee came up on a tray and as the door closed I wolfed it down. A rough wash in cold water and a scrape with my razor made me feel almost respectable again. I then collapsed on the bed in a state of semi-exhaustion.

In spite of being dog tired, I began to reflect on what the receptionist had said. My brain at last started to work and I began to appreciate what an idiot I had been. The man had most probably realized I was not who I said I was and was even now telephoning Police Headquarters for someone to come round and look me over. I decided to dress and leave the hotel straight away. My clothes flew on like lightening and I went downstairs. The same man was sitting at his desk and not unnaturally he was surprised to see me. I mumbled something about making a mistake in my train timings and put down thirty lire for my bed. He got up slowly from his seat and said quite softly in German 'You are not a Sudetener, you are an Englishman.' I drew myself up as best I could and asked for my change and told him he was not only making a fool of himself, he was also being most impertinent. This took him aback but he still looked very suspicious and asked where I was going. I told him 'Torino' which was opposite in direction from Como and quite likely to have a train in the middle of the night. He slowly pushed the change across, and trying hard not to hurry, I put it in my pocket and walked out of the door. It was a narrow squeak. I am sure he had asked the police to come round. I could feel it in the tone of his voice. With shaking knees I walked straight back to the station and decided to spend the rest of the night in the waiting room. This was big and half-full already with sleeping bodies. It was an ideal place to hide away until morning.

6 am the next morning saw me queuing up at the main booking hall for a ticket to Como and I was cheered up when out it came as easily as before. Back upstairs and into the 3rd Class Buffet for three cups of steaming hot *caffe al latte*. It was synthetic coffee, but it was hot and wet and tasted wonderful. After the coffee the inevitable happened. The public lavatory in Milan station was looked after by an old woman who wanted fifty centismi for her trouble. She indicated an open door and because my appearance was pretty scruffy, she began a loud harangue on the merits of her lavatories. She had two sorts. The squatter hole in the ground type or those with seats.

Unfortunately all her squatters were occupied and therefore I would have to use one with seats. She then proceeded to demonstrate how to use them. They were not to be stood upon. Milan was a very modern station. It even had lavatories '*di nuovo tippo*' as the old woman put it!

I stepped aboard the 7 am electric train for Como and was soon rattling out of Milan towards the frontier. My main worry was that there might be a check on all trains going towards Switzerland, but I was in luck. My spirits were rising with every minute and soon we were passing through countryside which was looking hillier and more alpine. The train stopped at every station and there was no sign of police boarding the train to check papers. At last we pulled into Como Station with the lake just visible over the houses to the north. The ticket collector took the ticket and I walked straight past some more Carabinieri near the entrance. I was now on my last lap but unfortunately I had the whole day to waste before starting towards the frontier at nightfall.

This was my second mistake. I should have remained with the crowds in Milan all day and come out to Como at dusk. As it was, I was so keen to get out of Milan after the hotel incident that I took the first train in the morning. Como and its area were suburban and it was going to be very difficult to find a hiding place for the day. I was soon walking through the streets towards the north and realized I should have to go some way before finding a path off the main road into the country. A little further along I could see my road climbing a small hill, half-way up which there appeared to be a possible turning-off. When about three hundred yards from this turning, I saw two frontier guards coming in the opposite direction dressed in their Alpine uniform. I don't know why it was, but I had a feeling that all was not going to be well before I came up to them. On the other hand it would look even more suspicious if I turned round and went back. How I afterwards cursed that decision! I could easily have turned about when they were still two or three hundred yards away and they would never have been any the wiser.

Unfortunately they stopped me and asked where I was going. After a little blustering, I showed them my papers. Very politely I was told I would have to come along to their HQ which was only a few hundred yards away. This I did and was given a drink of wine whilst I waited. Nobody in the HQ could speak German so I was told they would take me to the frontier post where there was a German speaker. My heart felt suddenly very heavy. I might perhaps give them the slip on the way but my foot hurt quite a lot now and I would not have a chance against two fit Alpinis. By now it was 12 o'clock on a glorious sunny day.

We boarded a trolley-bus which took us down to the frontier post at Chiasso, a village half in Switzerland and half in Italy. I knew the game was up but I thought I would put up one last show. I was ushered into a room occupied by an unattractive little man with outsized horn-rimmed spectacles and wearing a large chauffeur's cap. I gave him a heel click and a '*Heil Hitler*'. It was just faintly possible that his German would be worse than mine. It wasn't!

Almost immediately he sized me up and told me I was English and asked me who I was – in English. I told him my name and, sure enough, he found it on a list given to all frontier posts. I was then searched and nothing was discovered except some money.

The frontier post official was delighted at his capture and became quite affable. 'There will be promotion all round for this,' he said and asked me if I would like anything to eat. I told him I could eat a horse. I also asked him if the two soldiers who had stopped me knew why they had done so. The two men were at a loss to know why, but one said it was my general appearance and above all my dirty boots! Another lesson for the future.

I was put into another room with two guards watching me. A meal was soon brought in from a local restaurant and paid for by the money taken from my pocket. It was delicious but my morale had hit an all-time low. So near and yet so far. This might be my last chance in the war to be so close to freedom.

I have never been so depressed, before or since. My world, which had been getting brighter and brighter, was now inky black. Whilst I sat cursing myself, I dropped off to sleep in fits and starts, hoping the guards would follow suit. Unfortunately they didn't.

Two hours later three plainclothes policemen arrived and took me off by fast car to Police HQ in Milan. Two Carabinieri were detailed to look after me. One of them had a morning paper and he started to bait me. Japan was now in the war, he said, and had just sunk the whole American Navy in Pearl Harbor together with two British battleships. England was in a hopeless position and the war would soon be over. There was then a short pause. '*Duce e forte. Viva Duce*,' they chorused. All this was news to me but I pretended I knew all about it. It was all propaganda and lies. '*Tutte mensogne*,' I told them. 'Look how your papers lied about the Eritrean and Libyan fighting and see where we are now. The British always win the last battle, as your own Garibaldi used to say.' My reaction had surprised them and they stopped trying to tease me.

In the evening I was shown into a cell and told that I would be questioned in the morning. There was a pile of straw in one corner which I spread out and with two blankets round me slept the sleep of the truly weary both in body and spirit. What a day it had been. My life had crumbled all around me but my weary bones at last put me to sleep. All this happened on 13 December, 1941.

* 9 *

SOLITARY CONFINEMENT

My interrogation started next morning and went on more or less continuously for over twenty-four hours. I was sat on a hard seat with a powerful flood-lamp shining in my face. A little, suave man was sitting behind a desk. First he started by pleading and coaxing.

'All I want to know,' he said, 'is the name of the Italian who helped you to get to the frontier.'

They just could not believe that anybody could have reached the frontier without help. The one thing I did not want to happen was any tightening up in the railway regulations, so I told him, 'I can't say.'

This answer became mechanical and I must have repeated myself thousands of times during the questioning. After four hours his relief came in and started off with the brilliant idea that I could be bribed into saying who it was.

'If only you will give me the name of the Italian,' he said, 'you can choose the camp you go to, be it by the sea or up in the mountains or in the south.'

So it went on all morning until midday when I told him, 'I am sick of all this nonsense. I want some lunch.'

'You can have some lunch when you answer my questions like a gentleman should.'

'You know perfectly well that I will not answer your damn silly questions. If you won't give me anything to eat, which I remind you is contrary to the Geneva Convention, then please allow me to use the lavatory.'

'All right and I will look forward to seeing you this afternoon after I have had my own lunch,' he said with a sneer.

After relieving myself, I was put back in the cell for an hour or so and then the whole performance started over again. It was due to go on all afternoon until the evening when one of them lost his temper.

'You filthy Englishman sitting there so smiling. Roma has telephoned to say that any methods can now be used. If necessary you will be shot as a spy, and for wearing the uniform of our Army.'

'That won't help me to answer your questions.'

'Oh, you think yourself funny do you? So, you will now stand up and answer. Do you hear me? *Answer* my questions.'

He ended up in a high-pitched shout and told the soldier behind me to take away my chair and keep the muzzle of his rifle in my back.

All night long the same old questions were put to me. Sometimes he used a quiet voice, pleading to my better judgment and what he called my 'instincts as a gentleman'. More often he was angry and insulting. If I tried to move at all, the rifle in my back gave me a hard jab, and by morning had made it quite tender. It was several weeks before the soreness wore off.

About dawn the following morning I heard a burst of firing and it was announced dramatically that yet another British spy had been shot.

'Now will you tell us? Surely it is not worth dying to save one of your enemies?'

I told them I was bored, tired and not amused. This enraged them and a torrent of invective came out in rapid Italian before the once suave interrogator could be calmed down. Then at last he told the guard to take me away and give me a meal. As I went out of the door, he said with some malice that he would see that I would get very special treatment for the next month or two, just to make sure that I did not try and do the same thing again. He had given up, thank goodness. I quite enjoyed the meal of pasta and a glass of wine which came with it. Next morning I went by car to the station between two burly Carabinieri. We took the 9 am train to Piacenza, a small town in the Po valley about seventy miles from Milan. We climbed out at a little station between Alessandria and Piacenza and had to walk about three miles to Montalbo. This was to be my new home, where I was to undergo solitary confinement for escaping.

Montalbo was an old castle built on top of a little hill overlooking the Po plain and held about eighty officer P.O.Ws. An officer's punishment cell had just been built adjoining one wing of the castle, which was surrounded by a narrow perimeter of barbed wire only a few feet from the walls. Immediately on arrival I was put straight into the cell, accompanied by the usual Italian shouting and screaming whenever things were not quite right.

Life was very uncomfortable, except for the food which was comparatively good and came from the officers' kitchen in the main camp. No books were allowed, nor were writing materials or even pencils. I only had half-an-hour's exercise each day in a kind of bird cage outside the door of my cell. This was about twenty yards long by two yards wide. The most exercise I ever got was to walk to the lavatory in the castle. Three times a day (the maximum allowed) I had a lovely hundred-yard walk.

Whilst eating my lunch on the second day, I discovered under some cabbage a stub of pencil and a note. It told me to write my needs on a piece of lavatory paper the next time I went there and to leave it on top of the cistern. This I did, asking for books. I also told them who I was and where I had been caught. Next time I went to the lavatory I collected a book and hid it under my coat on the way back. The pencil was invaluable and I was soon making up crossword puzzles complete with clues on pieces of lavatory paper.

A few days after I was in the cell it started to snow. When it was not snowing, there was a fog. The walls of the cell were running in water and my top blankets were sopping wet with moisture.

The books lasted till Boxing Day when the guards discovered the trick and stopped me using the castle lavatory. All that was offered as a substitute was an empty tomato tin that leaked on to the floor. As my boots were given to me only once a day for my half-hours exercise, I was forced to give up pacing back and forth in the cell because of muck on the floor. When I complained to the Italian commandant, on one of his visits, he just laughed and went away.

My thirty days were up on 14 January, 1942, but the Italians refused to release me. It was not until 19 January that I was told that I was being taken back to Sulmona and would leave straight away. A captain, a lieutenant and two private soldiers had come up from Sulmona specially to escort the 'very dangerous prisoner'. It was really rather ludicrous, but it gave me some satisfaction to realize how troublesome my escape had been to the Italians.

The guards became quite friendly on the way back. They told me the Sulmona Commandant had been sent to the Russian front as a result of our escape from the camp. I enjoyed that news and laughed. They thought my merriment was in very bad taste. They also told me that Christopher had been wounded but was now all right. As this was the first news that I had heard of it and I could scarcely believe their words, I was delighted to hear that he had recovered.

Evidently the guards thought that I had hopped on to a goods train in the Sulmona valley; they even said that railway guards had seen me doing it!

A car met us at Sulmona station and I was driven back to the camp from which we had escaped six weeks before. It was almost like coming back home and there was a great welcome from all my friends. My account also helped to dispel the bogey that it was impossible for anybody to escape and also have a reasonable chance of getting to a neutral country.

I was so ashamed of my stupidity in the Milan hotel that I never breathed a word about it. I felt I might be branded an idiot who threw away a good chance of success and therefore should not be allowed to try again.

I had not been back in Sulmona more than a few days when the Italians announced that a special camp for dangerous prisoners was being started near Pisa. Seven officers were to go there straightaway, including Commander Brown, RN, and Tag Pritchard. Although neither of them had escaped, they were suspected of having organized them - as they had. I was not included but was told by the interpreters not to worry.

'You will certainly go there as soon as Rome realizes you are back here.' Sure enough, three weeks later, I was on my way.

A captain and a lieutenant acted as escort to take me to Campo 27 and an Italian private soldier came to carry my kit. By this time I had accumulated quite a lot. I took with me two suitcases, an army pack, a roll of blankets and a wooden crate full of books. It was surprising that a mere prisoner was allowed to take so much with him; it was even more surprising that a private soldier was produced to carry the luggage.

We climbed aboard the train for Rome accompanied by my escorts, one of whom had been instructed to keep a loaded revolver in his hand at all times. They repeated over and over again that if I budged an inch off my seat, I would be shot. Having harangued me, my escort would turn to the other passengers and tell them that I was a most dangerous prisoner who had escaped over twenty times before, so they must keep well clear. The passengers then edged closer to have a good look. I became rather tired of this unwanted attention but could do little about it.

We arrived at Rome at 7 pm and had a three-hour wait before catching the train to Pisa. I told the escorts that the Geneva Convention insisted that all prisoners of war must be reasonably fed and suggested that we should go and have dinner in a hotel. They did not buy this one, but after a lot of argument we all trooped into the station restaurant.

We had a good meal of five courses including whitebait, roast chicken and two bottles of a good Chianti. My escort was ever-watchful and tried to eat his meal with one hand while keeping the other on his revolver pointing at me under the table. The waiter saw what was going on and every time he put food on my plate he did it with a big wink.

After many more delays, and changing trains, we climbed down from a train at 6 am at a little station about half a mile from our new camp and about a third of the distance between Pisa and Florence.

My new home was part of an old monastery. From outside it looked like a prison and this impression was reinforced by the massive iron and oak doorway leading into the cloisters. From here another stone staircase led to the monks' cells, each of which now housed two prisoners-of-war.

There were eight British officers including myself and about thirty Greeks. All the British had come from Sulmona and had either made an escape or had been suspected of organizing one. The Greek officers were an odd looking lot. Most had deserted during the war in Albania and were active Italian sympathizers. A few were excellent types, who had been made prisoner after being wounded and warned us about their brother officers.

'If it wasn't for these Greeks,' said Tag, 'we would be out of this camp by now, so easy are the obstacles compared with Sulmona. Every scheme we have thought of so far has had to be turned down because the Greeks would rat on us. The defences are within the camp rather than all round it.'

'Let's go and have some breakfast.'

This consisted of exactly 150 grams of bread to the nearest crumb and a large cup of ersatz coffee.

Lunch consisted of a plate of vegetable soup and any bread left over from breakfast. Supper was much the same except that the soup usually had half an inch of rice in the bottom of the plate. The macaroni ration was saved up for a *bonne bouche* on Sunday. Our canteen allowed us half a litre of vino a day and occasionally we had fruit – but at a price.

At first these starvation rations appeared to make little difference to our health. But gradually over the weeks we became thinner and no longer had any desire to go out for walks under escort in the countryside. Getting up in the morning began to be more and more of an effort. After three months we just wandered listlessly round the garden, praying and hoping for Red Cross parcels. To our delight, these turned up unexpectedly two days later. Solid bully beef and biscuits, scrumptious cheese, packets of raisins, chocolate, tea, milk and even sugar. How we blessed the Red Cross and their parcels. Every mouthful was chewed and savoured to the full. We limited ourselves to one a week although I expect we could have eaten several straight off. We now had a smile on our faces and once more felt hope for the future.

It was towards the end of our second month that we gradually produced a scheme to get us all out. During those eight weeks Lucky had been piecing together the geography on the other side of the wall, by pretending he was a Roman Catholic and asking for confession with one of the monks next door. He was taken round regularly each week and contrived to be taken back a different way each time. This built up a clear idea of the layout. The corridors, off which led our bedroom cells, had once upon a time communicated with the rest of the monastery. We discovered that the wall of an end cell led into a deserted passage on the monks' side. Unfortunately all the cells in this corridor, except for the end one, were occupied by Greek officers. It would be impossible to tunnel through the wall without the whole passage knowing about it.

We had a clue how we might distract the Greeks when they had a party about two weeks later. They invited us to attend as guests. The party started at about 6 pm and went on more or less continuously for thirty-six hours. After about twenty-four hours they were all decidedly merry and nearly hoarse from singing weird Greek songs and shanties; by 6 am next morning they were all sleeping the sleep of the dead drunk. What a party! They were quite offended when we tried to leave at midnight on the first night. At last we crept out at about 2 am when it dawned on us that the party was due to go on all through the next day and night. They all looked terrible for about a week afterwards.

We decided we would save up our wine for the next two months. That should keep the Greeks going for at least twelve hours and should be sufficient. Lieutenant Sullivan, a Naval Swordfish pilot, revealed himself to be an expert forger and produced a series of excellent identity cards. All the usual adjuncts to escaping were sorted out and we all learnt standard phrases. Our equipment was first class and the plan was to take a train to Florence and from there to Milan and the Swiss frontier. We all felt that our chances would be excellent once we were clear of the camp and given an eight- or nine-hour start before we were discovered.

We drew lots who should make the hole in the wall and it fell to Commander Brown and me. The chosen day arrived and we started to ply the Greeks with drink as rapidly as possible, starting after lunch at about 2 pm. We reckoned they would be nicely merry by about 9 pm, when we planned to start work. We thought we would be through the wall and away by 11 pm. Although the wall was only one brick thick, it was no easy matter to make a hole without any noise. We had just pushed the point of a sharp piece of iron through the wall when a light was shone on the hole from the other side and somebody was shouting in Italian and banging on the wall. We had obviously been discovered and so ran back to our rooms and gave the alarm. Our kit, maps, food and clothes were quickly hidden. In a few seconds we had undressed and were in bed. Just as we pulled the sheets up, the Italians arrived, having taken about five minutes to get organized. We all pretended to turn over sleepily in our beds, but this did not impress the Italians, who were livid. They started to search all the rooms and only found incriminating articles on Tag and George Patterson. The next day poor Tag and Pat were both doing twenty-eight days' solitary. If the Italians had been clever and come round to us silently without flashing torches, they would have caught both of us red-handed.

Unfortunately we had chosen the one night in the week when a monk cleaned out the chapel. On this particular night it had been raining and to avoid getting wet he had decided to use the corridor. We were all heartbroken.

The local general came down the next day to see what had happened. He had us all paraded in a small room that just held the nine of us. He screamed at us in rapid Italian ending up with 'I, General Bolo, ordered you not to escape or even try to escape. You are all officers and know what orders are. If you disobey these orders, you will be shot.'

Ending his little speech with a high-pitched shout, he turned about and marched out of the room, followed by the Italian officers from the camp.

There was a slight pause and we all had a good laugh. That is everybody except Tag and Pat. But it kept us cheered up for quite a long time to come.

* 10 *

FLORENCE TO SWITZERLAND

At the end of April we heard a rumour. Rome had decided that our camp was not secure enough for desperate characters like us. A really escape-proof prison was going to be opened up somewhere in the south of Italy. Later on, this camp was destined to be the notorious Number 5, which was located even farther north than our monastery near Pisa.

We were only warned on 7 May that we would leave on the 15th. There was no time to plan a new way out of the camp, so my only chance was to get to a hospital and escape from there. I had been operated on for mastoids behind my left ear when I was a boy, so it was not difficult to pretend extreme pain and deafness. The local doctor said I must see a specialist at once, so next day I was taken to Florence Military Hospital.

The snag of escaping from hospital was the difficulty of taking suitable clothes. I had to travel in what I wore at the time. As a result of my experiences on the Italian railways six months before, I decided that the clothes one wore did not really matter so long as they were not obviously uniform. My mother had just sent me a navy-blue roll-neck pullover, which I always thought might be worn during an escape. I also wore battledress trousers, with the outside pocket removed, and brown shoes. As a hat I had one which had been issued by the Italians. It consisted of one of their own field service hats dyed a dark chocolate-brown colour with a small peak. When the straps going over the top were cut off, it would make quite a presentable peasant's cap as worn all over Northern Italy. My money and maps were stuck in the usual place between my legs.

The train journey to Florence and the cab ride out to the hospital were uneventful, but I tried to remember the way, especially the direction of the station. The hospital was a large building facing the main Florence – Bologna road, and stood about two miles from the centre of the town. I was hustled up to the top storey and was searched quite thoroughly by the Carabinieri who signed for me from my escort. I was then shown into my room which was not unlike that in many English hospitals and contained three beds.

I was in the hospital nearly a month. It was a great change after the monastery. The food was excellent compared with prison fare and the Italian nurses were kindness itself. The specialist came on the second day and said he did not think there was much wrong with my ear, but he understood that life in the prison camp might not be very amusing and told me I could stay as long as I liked. My treatment consisted of two injections of insulin a day and a visit from the specialist once a week. To this day I have no idea why insulin had been specified. I was certainly not diabetic.

Most of the nurses were volunteers for the duration of the war and came from well-to-do Florentine families. The one who had most to do with me was a pretty girl, a little older than me. Her name was Senora Traxler Camerana, and she brought flowers for the room and pre-war English books and magazines for me to read. Her mother was Swiss and her father Italian. I am sure she hated the war and the government in Italy but in no way did she ever say anything against them. She could speak French and German as easily as Italian. Usually we talked in a mixture of French and German so that the Carabinieri outside my door should not hear what was being discussed. Her husband was in the Navy and she had two pretty children whom she brought to the hospital to see me. My German improved considerably during the month and I could speak quite fluently, if a little ungrammatically, at the end. She told me of her home, her love for peace and the English visitors who came to Florence before the war. She described a hundred and one anecdotes about life in wartime Florence – the difficulties with rationing and the black market, a description of a cocktail party or a holiday by the sea. In fact she opened the window to the outside world a little and helped me to become more normal again after life in prison.

'I am sorry,' she said, 'that I cannot help you any more. As you know I have my children and my home to think about.' I was very concerned that she should not be penalized when I escaped. I heard from her after the war that the Carabinieri had searched her house and she was questioned for a long time but not otherwise harmed.

The wing where I was had four rooms all about the same size, two on each side of the corridor. In addition there was a sitting room and a balcony where I was allowed to sit in the morning. This balcony looked on to the main road outside the hospital and gave me a bird's-eye view of life outside. The room next door to me was occupied by a Blackshirt Lieutenant who had been wounded in Russia, and whom I rarely saw. On the other side of the corridor one room was empty and the second occupied by two Yugoslav generals who had been captured when their country was overrun. One had had an operation on his eye and the other on his ear. Both were at least sixty years old. We used to meet on the balcony every morning. They were cheery souls and we got on quite well, talking in German.

FLORENCE MILITARY HOSPITAL

PART OF FOURTH FLOOR.

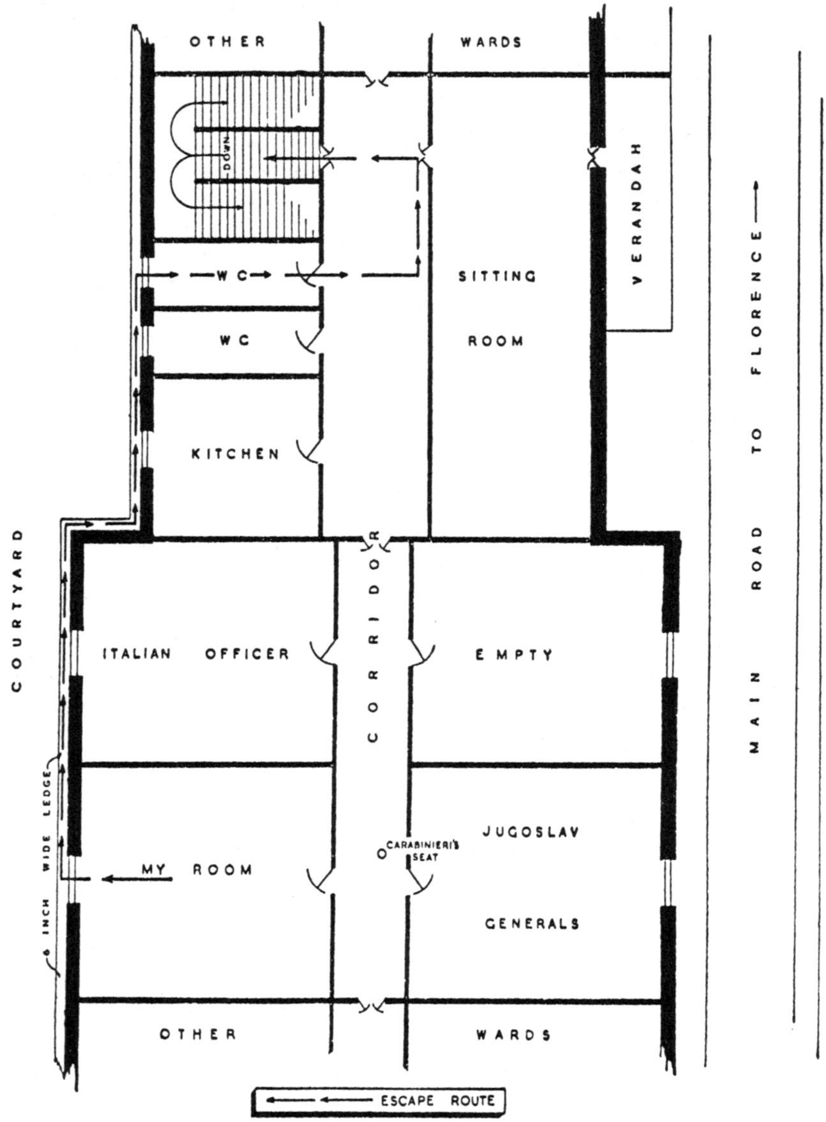

One of them had a letter one day to say that his whole family, wife and three children, had been shot by the Germans because there had been sabotage on the railway near the village where they lived. Poor old soul, he grew ten years older overnight; everything he had been living for had suddenly been cut away from under his feet.

The Carabinieri guard was on watch outside my room continuously and was relieved every eight hours. The door was kept locked. Every time I wanted to go to the lavatory I had to bang on it. The Carabinieri then unlocked it and went with me to the lavatory just down the passage. At first he insisted I kept the door ajar, but this was relaxed after a week or two. When I sat on the verandah he came too. The prospects of getting away did not seem very bright. Luckily the prison camp had not warned the hospital that I had escaped before and was considered 'dangerous'. Six months later in England I heard from Tag that the wretched commandant of the prison camp was sent off to the Russian front for not having warned the hospital.

Outside my window was a seventy-foot drop to the courtyard below and there were no handy drain pipes to slide down. I was too high up to risk using knotted sheets; anyway there were not enough. There was, however, a decorative moulding about four feet below my window which ran round the building. The top of the moulding was slightly sloping outwards and about four to five inches wide. This would have to serve as my way out.

Gradually my plan evolved. I would get out of my window and move along the ledge in spread-eagled fashion, past the Italian officer's bedroom window, round the corner of the building and then in at one of the lavatory windows. I could easily make sure it was open by going to the lavatory about midnight. I would then go through the lavatory door, which I would also leave open and then down the stairs which were in a well of their own and separated by doors from all the landings. The snag was that I could not very well open the door leading down the stairs when I went to the lavatory, but I hoped over a course of days I would be lucky one night and find that it had been left open. The Carabinieri always sat in his chair facing my door and he would be most unlikely to hear me flit in stockinged feet between the already opened lavatory door and the stairway doors. Having reached the ground floor I would jump out through a window into the courtyard and, circling round the building to the right, I could quite easily get on to the main road leading down into Florence.

I had been in the hospital nearly two weeks before my plan had crystallized. About then a Flight Sergeant Cox came into my room for three days with tonsilitis. He was working as a batman in the General's Prison Camp at Fiesole, just outside Florence. He had been with Air Vice Marshal Boyd, when he had landed by mistake in Sicily instead of Malta. He told me how Air Marshal Boyd spent his whole time doing carpentry, how General Gambier-Parry was a very able sketcher and artist and how General Younghusband was a most successful gardener within the limited area which was available. General Carton de Wiart was the only one he could not understand. 'He has only one arm, one eye and a VC, so that must explain a lot.' I agreed. I also remember my father telling me that in the 14 - 18 War he had known Carton de Wiart quite well. In his young days he had been regarded as crazy, clever and very brave.

As soon as Cox had gone back to Fiesole, I started my midnight visits to the lavatory. Ten days went by before the doorway leading down the stairway was left open. This was 13 June, 1942, and St Anthony's Day. This must be a good omen.

I had worked out that I should start from my room at 3 am and be on the road by 4. This would give me two hours to walk into Florence and get the early train to Milan. Back in the Monastery we had planned to take the 6 am train to Milan and this was the one I hoped to catch.

I dressed as silently as possible, putting one shoe in each trouser pocket where they would not be in the way. At 3 am, in my stockinged feet, I swung my legs over into the darkness and found the ledge with my toes. Holding on to the shutter outside the window with one hand, I started to move sideways to the left, flattening myself against the wall as much as possible. I had not gone more than a few steps when an attack of vertigo grabbed me, and I quickly went back, just managing to clutch on to my shutter again. My knees were shaking and teeth chattering with excitement as I climbed back into my bedroom.

Ten minutes went by while I recovered my breath. An occasional grunt came through the door from the Carabinieri or a squeak from his chair as he shifted his seat, but otherwise the night was silent. My imagination told me that I might slip off the ledge or it might crumble under my weight. But I knew I must do it. This was my chance.

Once again I tiptoed to the window and, without looking downwards, levered myself out and slowly slithered my feet down the wall on to the ledge. This time I was not going to get back into the room and, to make sure of it, I swung the outside shutters across the window and I heard a click from the latch on the inside.

I had always meant to do this to keep the Italians guessing how I had got out. On my first try I had forgotten all about it in my tenseness. I had bought some particularly obnoxious and sticky hair oil while I was in the hospital and I had used this to lubricate all the hinges and catches on the shutters and the lavatory door. They were all dead silent.

There was no going back now. I held on to the closed shutter with my right hand and slid as far as I could along the ledge. My left hand could not reach the shutter over the next window but I forced myself on and, inch by inch, moved along the ledge. I wanted to press against the rough wall as tightly as possible, but if I did this it made a scraping noise which might alarm some wakeful patient.

After six feet with nothing to hang on to, I reached the next lot of shutters and, using them as hand-holds, quickly passed under the window. I then came to the worst part of the ledge, where it went round the corner of the building and out of reach of all shutters. I had to leave go with my right hand and move spread-eagled to the corner. Here the finger tips of my left hand were able to follow the wall around and give a little more security. At the same moment the ledge under my left foot suddenly felt loose. I had visions of the whole corner of the building breaking away. All at once my vertigo or giddiness came over me and I felt sweat slowly trickling down the side of my nose. My knees shook, but I held them still by pressing against the wall, while I gingerly transferred my weight to my other foot and felt around with my left toe to see what was loose.

Something was very wobbly right on the corner and looking down I could just see that the cement surface was quite free and, if dislodged, a three-foot length would crash into the courtyard below. The moulding underneath the surface felt strong enough. It made a gritting noise as it wobbled and felt very insecure but I slowly worked my way round the corner and then along a short length of wall to another corner, which was an inside one and much easier. A few more yards and I was under the lavatory window.

I heaved myself up and dropped on to the lavatory floor where I stood for a minute or two to get my breath. I had not enjoyed that traverse along the face of the building in pitch darkness. It might have been child's play to a skilled rock climber but unfortunately this was an activity that I had never tried.

I could just see the Carabinieri round the corner of the half-open lavatory door and could see him looking disconsolately at the ground in front of his chair. I opened the door fully and then quickly moved over to the other side of the corridor. This was out of sight of the guard. I then moved down to a position near the doorway leading down the stairs. Although the door was ajar, I had to open it a little more to allow me to get through and without a murmur and like a flash I passed through and down the stairs without the Carabinieri realizing what had happened. I would have a clear five-hour start till about 8 am when I was called. By that time I hoped to be well on my way to Milan. In case the Carabinieri put his head inside my room during the remainder of the night, I had rolled up a greatcoat to look like me in bed. I was confident that this would pass any casual look.

Creeping down the stairs I arrived at the bottom and dropped into the courtyard through an open window on the ground floor. I crept round the outside of the hospital and then through an allotment to come to the wall bordering the main road. I put on my shoes and pulled out a brown paper parcel from inside my trousers, which I planned to carry instead of a bag to give the necessary *raison d'être*. It was five minutes to four and at four o'clock precisely I swung over the wall and started to walk down the main road to Florence.

The centre of Florence was reached by 5 am and after some directions from an old lady the station was reached twenty minutes later. To my relief I found there really was a 6 am train to Milan, but decided to wander round the station till about ten minutes to six before buying my ticket. By that time there ought to be a good-sized queue and this would give the booking clerk less time to look at me closely.

I had decided to wear no outer insignia to suggest that I was a German. I had no papers with me because it would have been risky to bring them into hospital. Only if challenged would I say I was a German and then only if I had to speak more than a word or two in Italian.

When the time came I pulled out my money and rose to join the queue for tickets. My turn came and I said my usual '*Terzo Milano*' and at the same time pushed over the note. To my horror the official started turning the note over and over, examining it against the light and, after what seemed hours, asked me if I had another. I replied with a shake of the head and a monosyllabic mumbled 'no'. However, with a shrug of the shoulders he pushed the ticket and change towards me. The passengers behind me were getting restive. Panic over. The 500 lire note had been slightly torn when it was pushed up the tubular leg of an iron bedstead back at the monastery. Cold sweat had started on my forehead and the palms of my hands were quite damp as I walked away.

The express from Rome came in ten minutes late and was very full. As soon as it came to a halt the crowd surged forward, myself included, and we fought for places on the steps leading to the carriages. Putting my head down, I got aboard after giving a kick on the shins to a man on my left who had tried to pull me back to get in himself. At last we crammed into the corridor, where I stood in the corner, chin on chest, pretending to doze. I kept my ticket in my hand and whenever the collector passed up and down the train, which happened frequently, he just took the ticket out of my hand, punched it and put it back without apparently waking me up.

A lot of people got out at Bologna and I was glad to find a seat to myself in a compartment. Unfortunately no '*cistina*' lunches were being sold on the stations. Rations in Italy were much shorter now than when I had travelled to Milan six months earlier.

On one occasion when the ticket collector came round he had two railway police behind him and they took a good look at me when punching the ticket. He took the ticket out into the corridor and started examining it closely with his back towards me. After a minute or two he returned it and passed on to the next person. Scare over! I discovered later that they used a special template which fitted the ticket exactly for detecting forgeries. In all my travels on the railway I saw hundreds of Carabinieri, railway policemen and ordinary railway officials. They were always more concerned with the traveller who had no ticket – or one that was forged.

I managed to avoid all conversation by pretending to be asleep in my corner and by 11 am we pulled into Milan Central station. The plan was to hang around the station until about 4.30 pm and then take a train to Varese. This was a small village about thirteen kilometres from Porto Cerisio on the Swiss border and also on the edge of Lake Lugano. If I arrived at Varese by dusk, I could walk to within two kilometres of Porto Cerisio and then strike up the hill towards the frontier.

The waiting room was much emptier this time and I had to kill time by wandering around the station. I had bought my ticket just in case anybody asked what I was doing. This time I took a return to make my travelling to a frontier town more plausible. '*Terzo Varese andate e riturno*', accompanied by a 50 lire note produced my ticket without any questions being asked. I was always a little self-conscious about my dress, but it never appeared to excite any suspicions. Luckily it was fairly cool at the time and the roll neck pullover did not look too out of place.

I had a cup of *caffe al latte* for my lunch and, buying a few papers, took them to the waiting room for a four-hour wait for my train which left at 4.37 pm. I was interested to read in one paper that a German ship had been sunk in the Mediterranean and the survivors had landed at Genoa. This might be a useful story if ever I was stopped. My navy blue sweater would help and I could pretend I was taking a short holiday before going on to Germany.

The journey to Varese by electric train was without incident and I arrived at about 6.15 pm just when it was beginning to get dark. My half ticket was taken without any questions being asked and I went out into the town.

A crossroad on the north side of the town put me on the right road with twelve kilometres to go to Porto Cerisio. By this time it was dark and the sky overcast, but a moon shone behind the clouds for the first half of the night. The road went on for ever. My month in hospital without exercise had not helped and my muscles were very soft. At last the three-kilometre stone to Porto Cerisio was passed and I could see Lake Lugano in the distance with searchlights playing on the water along the line of the frontier. By this time it was 10 pm and I struck up the hillside through a wood. Thorn bushes and undergrowth were so thick that progress was very slow. It was also nearly pitch black. After two hundred yards, I decided to stay where I was until morning when I should be able to see what I was doing. Feeling thirsty, tired and cold, I curled myself up under some dead leaves and went to sleep. The cold woke me up about an hour before dawn and I started to crawl up the hill. After half an hour, I saw I was coming to the top of the ridge. Suddenly, outlined against the morning sky, I saw a sentry box with a tall row of barbed wire behind it. I immediately dropped down to the ground and noted that sentry boxes were spaced about fifty yards apart all along the top of the hill. Just around the corner, and lower down, I could see what looked like a cemetery. This was really too much!

My map did not show the frontier in any great detail but I had never expected to find it so close to the main road or so well guarded. In a minor panic I slithered back down the hill up which I had just crawled and wondered what to do next. I was flabbergasted. I had counted on this piece of frontier being no better guarded than that near Chiasso. Rightly or wrongly, I decided to lie up where I was for the rest of that day and then walk back to Varese and on to Como that night. I would then try to get over a piece of frontier that I knew.

Later on, in Switzerland, I found a large scale map of where I had been. The frontier could not have been there at all and was at least another two kilometres further on. To this day I do not know what I had found. It must have been some kind of military dump which was being extra-well-guarded.

There were about twenty miles to cover to get to Como. I started at dusk feeling very cold and wet after frequent showers during the day. Passing through Varese for the second time about 9 pm, I was soon trudging on my way towards Como. My brown Italian shoes were working up beautiful blisters which did not help progress. If I had had a more accurate map of the frontier I would have gone across country but it was too risky. I might easily bump into a frontier guard like I had at Chiasso six months before.

I do not know what possessed me, but I went on walking after midnight. At about 1 am, while passing through the little village of Ogliati, I was challenged. My spirits fell as I went up to the man who turned out to be a Maresciallo of Bersaglieri —the equivalent of an RSM. He asked me for my papers. I went into a long explanation of who I was and brought out my newspaper to prove it, but all I could get out of him was that I would have to go in '*dentro*' (inside) for the night. The last card I had to play was to knock him on the head, seize his bicycle and make a run for it, but before this I tried my last piece of bluff. I told him that if the German Consular authorities in Como did not see me by 8 am the next morning, there would be trouble for anyone who held me. I spoke out with much gusto and repeated this several times. With much head shaking and more muttering of '*dentro*', he said I could go on this time, but it was most irregular and I must not do it again. I thanked my lucky stars that my Italian was much more fluent than it had been six months before.

My luck had held out but that scare brought me to my senses. I did not make such a stupid mistake again. I walked on through the village and a little further on found a hiding place in a wood for the rest of the night. Creeping in under some thick bushes, I curled up and went to sleep, mentally and physically exhausted, but thankful that I was still a free man.

I woke up at about 11 am to the sound of woodcutting and children playing about a hundred and fifty yards away in my wood. Children and dogs were my worst enemies that day but luckily none came near enough to find me. The day was dry and when dusk came I started out on what I hoped would be my last lap. The country was getting hilly and the road climbed slowly upwards in a series of gentle curves. A few men passed me going the other way, including two or three soldiers. They had no eyes for me and I certainly had none for them. At about 11 pm I came to a road junction and turned left towards the lights, thinking it would lead me to Como through which I should have to pass before reaching the frontier area at Chiasso. But I had made a mistake. My road had by-passed Como and I was on my way to Chiasso. I suppose I should have recognized it but it looked very different by night.

I walked on down the hill to Chiasso and did not realize my mistake until suddenly I saw the frontier barrier right across the road and not two hundred yards away. I nearly had a fit on the spot. Trying not to appear hurried, I retraced my steps and found a culvert under the road in which to sleep until about 4.30 am. My culvert could not have been more than a few hundred yards from the frontier but it was a case of safety first at this stage.

At last it was 4.30 am and, making sure that there was nobody looking, I started back down the road towards Como. In ten minutes I found a turning off and was soon following a small footpath which led up the hillside in the right general direction. It would be too early for any woodcutters going to work and also probably too early for a changeover of guards on the frontier. This would be more likely to happen after 6 am, so I left the track at that time and continued to climb straight up the hill. I was now at about 2000 feet above the valley. I could see Chiasso quite plainly with its long goods sidings and the frontier wire running at right-angles up the hills on each side.

I thrust my way up the mountainside until I came to a belt of pine trees, followed by hazel plantations and every sort of mountain shrub. At last I thought I was high enough and started to move cautiously along the hillside in the direction where I knew the frontier had to be. I had not been going more than half an hour when, just across a little valley and not more than four hundred yards away, I saw a sentry box amongst the trees. Crawling a little closer, I could see a few more sentry boxes and the wire beyond. I found a comfortable little hollow, surrounded by gorgeous ripe bilberries and full of dead leaves in which I could sleep and also from which I could watch the frontier.

Sentries changed every even hour and appeared to be about two hundred yards apart. I carefully noted the route I would have to take that evening to bring me exactly between two sentries. None of them wandered out of their sentry boxes by day, so they were most unlikely to do so by night. A light rain started about 10 pm and I started my crawl through the undergrowth and across the open patch at the bottom of the valley. The rain pattering on the leaves made all the difference as it blanketed any noise I made. I could just hear one singing away to himself in his box, little suspecting that a British officer was at that very moment within a hundred yards of his post.

By 11 pm I had reached the path used by the sentries and beyond I could see the frontier wire. It was a fairly formidable obstacle made of diamond mesh wire and about twelve feet high. Poles in the form of an inverted V suspended the wire from its apex. All along the top, bells were hung which would start clanging if the fence was touched. The problem was how to get over, through or under. No branches overhung the wire and, as I had no pliers, my only alternative was to try and burrow a way underneath. I could have risked the bells and climbed over the top, but it might have gone wrong and was not worth it if I could find another way.

The foot of the fence was pegged every six inches with eighteen-inch wooden stakes. Luckily the soil was mostly leaf mould and the stakes came up easily without shaking the fence. I had soon freed about a three-foot length, pausing between each stake to listen for any footsteps.

All was quiet. The sentry on my left was still crooning away to himself about his '*Mama mia*', and I could hear nothing from the one on my right. The rain came down a little harder now and a damp moist smell came up from the disturbed earth that reminded me of an English wood in autumn after a dry summer. But it was no time for nostalgia. I slowly scraped away, using one of the stakes to loosen the earth, which I then removed with cupped hands.

After ten minutes there was quite a respectable hole and I tried to squeeze through. I became stuck with one arm and one shoulder in Switzerland and the rest of me in Italy.

Several things happened at once. The bell above gave a small tinkle, a branch crashed down nearby, the sentry stopped singing and the noise of shunting wagons in Chiasso suddenly became very loud because of a change of direction in the wind. I prayed that the sentries would stay where they were whilst I slowly pushed myself back into Italy. The hole would have to be bigger.

After a few very long seconds, I was clear and crawled back over the track and lay in a bush for a few minutes. If a sentry had heard anything he would surely come down to see what was going on.

My luck was in. Five minutes went by in complete silence except for the rain on the leaves and the noise of the shunting. I crawled back across the track and worked away for ten minutes before the hole was big enough. My hands reached through to Switzerland, this time much farther. I grasped a tree root and slowly pulled myself through without shaking the fence. I was free at last!

* 11 *

SWITZERLAND, JUNE, 1942

I was now in Switzerland! My hunger, tiredness and sore feet were all forgotten in my elation and satisfaction. Walking erect and no longer afraid of making a noise, I went a few hundred yards away from the line of the frontier before turning down the hill towards Chiasso. I then got stuck in the most enormous patch of thorn bushes. I scrambled free but decided to sleep the rest of the night on the hillside. In the morning I could see where I was going.

I woke up at about 4 am to see the eastern sky just beginning to lighten. Overhead the clouds had gone. By 5 am I was threading my way down a path to Chiasso. The atmosphere was altogether different, the people just stirring at the backs of their houses looked clean and hospitable. The occasional Swiss sign reassured me that the almost unbelievable had come true. I had actually arrived in a neutral country.

I sat down on a bench in Chiasso in a state of euphoria. Should I present myself to a Swiss policeman, explain who I was and ask to be taken to the British Embassy in Berne, or should I try and get there under my own steam? After all, I had succeeded in travelling by train through wartime Italy with few problems. Surely the same could be done in peaceful Switzerland? My first task was to change my money and this was done in the bureau de change in the station. I received twenty-five Swiss francs in exchange for about four hundred lire. So far so good. I next bought a ticket, speaking German this time, and rather to my surprise out came my third class ticket to Berne. It was almost too good to be true and could not last. It didn't!

I had an hour to spare before the train went and was just walking out of the station when a Swiss policeman politely asked me who I was. The game was up and so I told him in German that I was a British officer escaped from Italy. I was just going out to have a shave before taking the 7.15 train to Berne. This took his breath away and all he could mutter was, 'It is most irregular'. I agreed with him and said I did not suppose it happened every day, but then I was lucky and would he mind telling me the way to the nearest barber?

By this time he had come to his senses and told me in Italian that he did not believe a word that I had said and that I was probably a German spy.

Anyway, I would have to come down to the frontier post for interrogation by his boss. Once again I was searched and questioned, this time in English. All the officials were most polite and, after I had told them that I had not washed, eaten or slept for three days, immediately sent out for some breakfast and a barber.

A huge bowl of coffee soon slipped down, accompanied by several crisp warm rolls spread with delicious butter and jam. My morale was picking up with every mouthful and, after a wash and a shave, I felt like a new man. Everything was wonderful, the countryside clean, and everywhere I could see happy smiling people who looked so different from their neighbours across the frontier. I wore rose-tinted spectacles all that day.

The Swiss police had been told over the telephone to take me to Berne and hand me over to their military headquarters. We reached a large stone building in the middle of Berne about 7 pm. A courteous young Swiss officer interviewed me and said I could stay in a hotel for the night provided I promised not to try and communicate with my Embassy. I readily agreed and walked round to the hotel by way of his flat, where he lent me some of his own clothes. He thought I might be embarrassed in my battledress trousers and now dirty roll-neck pullover in a large Berne hotel. This was kind of him and most thoughtful. I was shown my room by the hotel manager, who became most effusive as soon as he knew who I was. In the luxury of a steaming hot bath, I lay back and forgot all my worries.

The next day I was questioned and soon satisfied them that my story was bona fide. The following two weeks in Switzerland were almost like a fairy tale. Cocktail parties, dinners, dances, sailing and swimming. I had my first real holiday of the war and I did not let the grass grow under my feet. The feeling of freedom was so pleasant.

I wrote a postcard to Tag from Aunt Agatha and also sent a parcel of goodies. From memory it went like this -

'Dear Tag, I have only just received your address and hope you and your friends are not too uncomfortable. You will like to know that I have just come out of a nursing home where I had to spend a month. I am now very healthy and recuperating fast. I do so hope you can join me here, but I suppose we shall have to wait for the end of this horrid war. Keep your chin up. I am also sending a parcel.

Your loving Aunt Agatha'

I heard after the war that the card came through quite quickly and cheered everybody up. How I wish they could have been with me.

The British Embassy in Berne was very helpful. Colonel Cartwright, an escaper from the 14-18 war, was the Military Attaché. He told me that I now had to be very careful until I arrived on British soil. He would send me down to Marseilles and from there I should be able to get to Gibraltar.

I then moved down to Geneva to start on the next lap. This time I did not have to work out how to travel or what dress to wear or the money I would need. It was all done for me.

A grey suit was chosen for its continental style and cut. It had wide trousers, padded shoulders and patch pockets, A dark blue beret and an attaché case completed my outfit for my new disguise as a Czechoslovak refugee.

Two RAF sergeant pilots now joined me. They had walked all the way to Switzerland from northern France. All three of us were to travel together down to Marseilles. We stayed in an unobtrusive hotel in Geneva for nearly a week waiting to go. In the meantime I went for long walks round the city every day, bathed in a swimming bath and went out for sails on the lake. In the evening my still insatiable hunger got the better of me and I would go to one of the open-air lakeside restaurants. Meals at restaurants were rationed and no more than three meal coupons could be expended at any one restaurant for a single meal. As I had a whole month's coupons to last a week I was able to have hors d'oeuvres and fish in one restaurant and then move on and have the rest of the meal at another one, I was still about thirty pounds underweight and my appetite always appeared to demand more.

Our moment came at last and about an hour before dawn a car picked us up and drove to a little churchyard on the boundary between Switzerland and Vichy France. A guide led us to a crossing place and after wishing us 'Good Luck' we crossed a small stream to meet our next guide called Simon. We all walked to his house where Madame produced the biggest and best omelette I had ever tasted.

After breakfast we cleaned up and were taken by another guide to catch the train to Marseilles. Henri arrived at 9 am and he led us by a carefully chosen route to his house. We had another excellent meal with Henri and passed the rest of the day in his house. He had many tales to tell of the difficulties and dangers of a patriot in France. German gestapo men in plain clothes were everywhere and nobody knew who was friend or foe.

With tickets already in our hands we walked a few hundred yards to the station and went straight into the buffet to wait the arrival of the train. Plain-clothes men were wandering around the platform and occasionally checked papers. For some reason, they never came into the buffet.

The train rumbled in and Georges, our new guide, called us on to the platform and we ran for the end of a coach to climb aboard. We sat in opposite corners of the same compartment pretending not to recognize each other. We spoke not a word all that night on our way down the Rhône Valley to Marseilles, which we reached next morning at 7 am.

Marseilles was meant to have about 30,000 police of one sort or another, but it was such a large town that any crook might well have hidden away in it for years without discovery, which was in fact well known to every wanted man in France. Georges led the way down the main street from the station, past the hotel where the German-Italian Commission was housed and into a little café which had opened early for the sale of coffee and rolls. They were delicious. Jean, our next guide, came in a few minutes later. We thanked Georges profusely and were led off for quite a distance through the streets.

No praise can be too high for these guides from the French Resistance. They asked for no reward and they looked embarrassed when thanked. They wanted to contribute something towards the day when France would be liberated. Each had his sector to work and did not know where the next guide went.

We walked through a very poor quarter and up the winding stairs of a dirty apartment house. This was not our final goal and we collected our next guide, a young girl of about twenty, who took us to a modern block of flats overlooking the old harbour. A gendarme happened to be standing outside the door to the block, but without faltering we went straight in and up the lift to Madame Renée Nouveau's flat, a luxurious apartment through which many an escaper had passed during this part of the war.

We were on the fifth floor with a lovely view over the Old Harbour. A large bay window opened out on to a typical fishing scene with every sort of fishy aromas, drying nets, and baskets full of newly caught fish. Renée was dressed in her Red Cross uniform which no doubt allowed her to move around unmolested by police. She drew us all over to the centre of the room and asked us all to put on carpet slippers which she provided.

'Try and keep clear of the windows,' she said. 'We do not want any official visitors knocking on the door to see who you are. You must all wear slippers so that the flat below does not realize we have so many guests. We still have some old English magazines and books and we hope you will all be comfortable.'

This was the famous 'Pat' escape line which had become a resting place for large numbers of escapers like me, before moving on over the Pyrenees to Spain. I thanked Renée from the bottom of my heart for taking us all in. She could not have been kinder or more hospitable during the ten days we spent there from 2-12 July, 1942.

Her husband, Louis, was up north on a job for the Resistance and Renée was standing in for him in his absence. She wanted to know more about me and where I had been. She was fascinated to hear about Colossus. I then gave her a thumbnail sketch of life in Italian prisoner-of-war camps.

'I am afraid the Italians are very good at holding on to their prisoners,' I told her. 'I believe I am only the second person to get away since they entered the war nearly two years ago.' We were talking in her large library with thousands of books in shelves which went from floor to ceiling.

She got up and found a book in the middle of one shelf and turned over some pages. She wrote in pencil in the margin my name, unit, where captured and my home address. I was actually the 123rd ex-prisoner to pass through her hands. I was overcome. I could not thank her too much for the enormous risks being run by both of them. We would all try and make our stay with her as inconspicuous as possible.

Six months later Louis was caught and put in Buchenwald Concentration Camp for the rest of the war. He had only been arrested on suspicion or otherwise he would have been executed. Luckily Renée heard of her husband's arrest in time to go underground, and she remained undetected for two years until her hideaway in the Haute Savoie was overrun by the US 7th Army. Before fleeing she had stripped her flat of everything from books to carpets and from ornaments to heavy oak chests of drawers. All her friends took what they could and promised to keep it for her until the day they were liberated.

When the day came and Renée returned, her friends brought everything back and she told me she did not lose even a tiny ornament or any of her books. I revisited her flat in 1945 when my plane taking me to the Middle East broke down at Istres. This gave me an extra twenty-four hours and I took a chance to hitch a lift into Marseilles and found the flat I had known so well in 1942. With trepidation I knocked on the door, and to my enormous surprise and relief saw both Louis and Renée together in their flat, which looked exactly as I had remembered it in 1942. I soon heard their news and once again we looked up my entry in their book. They both told me I was the first of those whom they had helped during the war who had revisited them. Right royally did they welcome me once more and once more all I could do was to thank them again and again.

Squadron Leader Whitney Straight had arrived at the flat a few days before we arrived. He had been shot down in northern France about a year before and had walked all the way to the Pyrenees, with the help of the French Resistance. Unfortunately he was caught by Vichy gendarmes and put in a prison camp in the Alpes Maritimes. With others he escaped from this camp and as soon as he got out was escorted like us to Marseilles.

At last the day came for our departure. We were told that the passes over the Pyrenees were too dangerous to be used at this time and we were going out by a special method only used in the past for Polish refugees. We went by train in two parties to a station quite close to the sea and about fifty miles west of Marseilles. We walked to a small wood which we reached at dusk and were joined by two more parties of RAF evaders, to make a total of eight British plus half-a-dozen French guides.

We were all in the highest of spirits and talked with excitement about what we would do when we arrived home. Were we going to leave by submarine or how on earth could we possibly get away by any form of surface ship? We soon found out.

At 11 pm we moved off in single file. The night was dark with no moon. After a mile or so we reached the shore and went along it to end up about half-way along a ten-mile beach of white sand. The time was midnight and we had another hour to wait until 1 am on 13 July. At 1 am precisely we saw two faint blue flashes come out of the darkness in the bay and were answered by a signal from one of our guides. So far so good, but nothing happened. At 1.30 we flashed and again at 2 am. Our guides were getting really worried. We would have to move back from where we were by 3 am at the very latest because we were now quite a big party. This would only allow an hour and a half to find somewhere to spend the next day. I remember telling Whitney Straight that it was bound to be all right because 13 was my lucky number and today was 13 July.

'Well, I hope you are right,' he said. ' I am not too happy myself.'

The words had hardly left his lips when a blue flash came from the sea not more than a few hundred yards out. A rowing boat was coming ashore with padded rowlocks. A midshipman in naval uniform was in the stern and a couple of husky ABs were at the oars. The offshore wind and current had been very strong and they had taken much longer than expected.

We piled aboard and pulled off after saying goodbye with many Au Revoirs to our brave guides. Two of us lent a hand at the oars and in ten minutes we sighted the outline of a small ship against the night sky. A scaling net over the side had us all aboard and we were soon munching bread and jam washed down with large mugs of steaming hot Navy cocoa.

The Captain of the ship came in to speak to us and see who we were. He told us it was so nice to pick up Englishmen. All his previous trips had been to collect Polish refugees. We asked him how on earth he managed to sail so close to an enemy shore with so small a ship. A twinkle came into his eye as he said, 'You see, we look just like a peaceable fishing trawler.' 'And by the way,' he said, as an afterthought, 'if any planes come out and have a look at us in the morning, I want you all below decks. All my crew have the right clothes to keep up our pretence. I don't want any plane to become suspicious at the numbers we are carrying.' He bade us a cheery good night and we turned into some spare bunks. Thank God that it had turned out so well. We slept soundly that night.

Morning came with a bright blue sky and I was on deck to see what sort of ship she was. Outwardly she looked a dirty brown trawler flying the Portuguese flag, with bits of rope strewn everywhere and nothing at all shipshape. Some of the crew were working in old reefers and the Captain was on the bridge in a garb not much better.

On close inspection, the little trawler became more interesting. The big steam winch was a 3.7 inch gun. Another gun was fixed aft under the engine-room hatch. There were machine guns under wraps which could be put quickly into action. We were something like the 14-18 War Q ships, but on a much smaller scale.

We still had to pick up the Poles. No less than eighty came aboard from an open boat captained by a gallant Polish sea captain. His guise was so good that he sailed right into small ports on the Southern French coast to take aboard a new load to ferry out to our trawler. It had become almost like a bus service and was never suspected because of the tiny size of his craft.

We were now on our way to Gibraltar. With thirty-six hours sailing yet to do, our Captain announced that tonight would be 'Painting Night'. It was the thirteenth complete coat of paint that he had given his little ship in four months. By morning we had to be a nice grey HM trawler in all its glory with White Ensign flying, guns oiled, decks scrubbed and ropes neatly coiled everywhere. We were all dished out with a pot of grey paint and a brush. We painted all night until, by 4 am, the transformation was complete and our little ship had had its face lifted again.

The authorities in Gibraltar were astonished to find a party of escapers mixed up with the Poles because nobody had warned them we were coming. Everybody was very helpful and somehow we were all squeezed on to a troop-ship which was sailing for Britain the next morning.

We dropped anchor off Gourock in the Clyde after ten days of zig-zagging in convoy across the Atlantic. A Movements Officer came aboard and I was singled out to land first and get to London as quickly as possible.

The sight of some WVS doling out tea on a platform brought me to my senses. They were doing things for others. I realized what I owed to all my friends still in prison in Italy and to the dozens of brave Frenchmen and their wonderful organization. If it had not been for them I would still be languishing behind barbed wire with all its mental anguish and petty horrors.

As I fell asleep I thanked God for my good fortune and prayed that others besides myself would have some of my luck. Much later, after the war, I heard that only two officers had made successful escapes from Italy before the Italian armistice over a year later. It made me feel quite humble that I was one of them.

* 12 *

TARANTO TO TERMOLI

After ten days' leave I was on my way to Bulford to serve as Signal Officer to Brigadier Eric Down, who commanded the newly formed 2nd Parachute Brigade. Eric Down was a superb infantry officer and had taken over command of 2 Commando (or 11th SAS) in the spring of 1941 when we were all in Italy. He did not agree at all with small party operations and set about the task of creating a light infantry battalion which went to war by parachute. This was to become 1st Parachute Battalion. He set the standards and was ruthless in applying them. Affectionately known as 'Dracula', the fantastic achievements of 1st Parachute Brigade in its many battles in North Africa were largely due to the groundwork put in by Eric Down in 1941/42. He could see more clearly than most what the essentials for success really were in airborne operations.

I was now a Captain and it was wonderful to be able to do a useful job again. I hoped some of my enthusiasm rubbed off on to my soldiers as we trained hard in the next six months for the battles to come. My senior sergeant was a Sergeant Goodman and he told me that he had never worked so hard in his life and that applied to everybody. 'We can tackle anything now,' he said.

We had time off on very occasional weekends when many of us went up to wartime London to see a show and stay a noisy night in an hotel. Sounds of AA gunfire and sights of weaving searchlights did not worry us. German bombs were few and far between, but we tried to leave London before dark to get back to Bulford.

On one Sunday afternoon on 14 February, 1943, I had nothing to do. Two of us had heard there was a fun party going on in the Grosvenor House Hotel. It was too. I was sat at a table where there was a spare seat. Next to me was a quite delightful brunette with laughing eyes and a welcoming smile. She danced beautifully – which I didn't, but we had great fun all that afternoon until the time came to leave before dark.

I discovered later that a group of 'matrons' from all over London wanted to cheer us all up by organizing parties for their daughters and their friends for officers on leave. One of these 'matrons' was to be my future mother-in-law.

After three months and a few more weekends, some of which started off from her parents' home in Hampstead, we became engaged on 10 April. This was the day before we sailed for North Africa. Naturally I now had to put my mother in the picture. I was able to tell her by phone that I had just been promoted Major, that I was going to North Africa tomorrow – and I was now engaged. Naturally she was full of congratulations but dearly wanted to meet my future wife. Evie made the long journey down to the Cotswolds by train and bus while I was away abroad. I heard later from my mother how delighted she was with my choice.

We sailed for North Africa on 11 April, 1943, with the task of preparing for the invasion of Sicily. In this operation 2nd Parachute Brigade was ordered to capture Augusta by airborne attack, but the assault forces advanced so quickly in the early stages that the drop was cancelled. We all felt let down when we returned to our hot and dusty camp in the olive groves near Sousse.

Two days later, on 13 July, we enviously watched the aircraft and gliders streaming overhead carrying 1st Parachute Brigade to their jump into Sicily. Primasole Bridge was successfully captured in spite of inaccurate dropping on the part of the American aircrews.

The American commanders were deeply ashamed of the performance of their pilots. With characteristic thoroughness they instituted a period of intensive navigational training. By D-Day the following year nothing but praise could be heard for the pilots who flew their unarmed and slow transport aircraft at a mere 1000 feet to a pinpoint dropping zone over enemy territory.

On 6 September the whole 1st Airborne Division was given forty-eight hours notice to embark at Bizerta to sail to southern Italy. We were to be taken as deck cargo on five cruisers and a minelayer of the Royal Navy and one cruiser of the US Navy.

On the evening of 8 September we sailed from Bizerta with a bare minimum of transport. Jeeps and trailers were slung in odd places all over the ships and were even lashed to the tops of gun turrets. Next morning we heard of Italy's unconditional surrender and saw for ourselves the majority of Italy's battle fleet sailing past us on the way to Malta to give themselves up. Somehow that sight gave me a lot of satisfaction. In the evening we disembarked at Taranto and by midnight had taken over intact the whole port and its important naval installations.

For the next three weeks 1st Airborne Division were the only allied soldiers in the 'heel' of Italy. Taranto had to be held at all costs. With the limited numbers of troops at our disposal all that could be attempted was a series of aggressive patrol actions on as wide a front as possible. These were singularly successful. 1st Airlanding Brigade was not withdrawn until they had reached Foggia, 120 miles from Taranto. By this time 78th Infantry Division had landed and took over from 1st Airborne Division who were brought back into reserve.

At the beginning of October our thoughts returned to the prisoners of war. What had happened to the 30,000 British when Italy had capitulated? Allied HQ in Algiers had apparently advised the War Office to tell all camps that prisoners should remain where they were and not try to come south to the Allied Armies. This quite disgraceful blunder was to sentence many officers and soldiers to many more months behind barbed wire, when some of them might have had a good chance of going free. As an ex-prisoner of war I probably felt more strongly than most. It was said to be administratively much more 'convenient' to deal with whole camps rather than have 30,000 officers and men wandering about all over Italy. It made me spit with rage at the incompetence of some brother officer. To this day, I have no idea who he was.

Unfortunately many camps obeyed these orders to the letter. At Chieti, for example, the Senior British Officer posted officer guards to prevent the remainder getting out. Only a few managed to escape the vigilance of their brother officers. The Germans arrived after a few days and removed the whole camp to Germany.

Intelligence reports were coming through that, in spite of War Office orders, large numbers of officers and other ranks were wandering about Italy. The Germans had not bothered to take over the soldiers' camps straightaway and in many cases the prisoners had become tired of waiting and had taken to the road. A few of the officer prison camps were occupied immediately by the Germans, such as the notorious No 5 where Tag was located. The inmates were given no chance to escape. A few more officer camps had completely disregarded the orders and all were on their way, either going north to Switzerland or south towards our own lines.

The authorities now realized what a fiasco the stay-put policy had been and felt they must help the ex-prisoners get back somehow. One problem was how to contact them. The decision was taken to send in a number of small parties whose job it was to round up the maximum numbers and bring them down to a designated beach on the coast where they could be picked up.

By the beginning of October several 'round-up teams' had been landed along the Adriatic coast from Ortona to Rimini. One had even been dropped by parachute a few miles inland from Pescara. An HQ to control the operations, together with craft to be used for retrieving the prisoners, had been set up at Termoli.

The snag was that there were no communications with the round-up parties. There was no way of telling Termoli how many prisoners had been collected or whether the selected beach was suitable, let alone last-minute alterations or breakdowns. 1st Airborne Division, now under command of Major-General Eric Down, was asked to provide the necessary communications.

I was then sent for by the General and told to see what could be done to improve the situation. 'One last point, Tony,' said General Down with a smile, 'I want you to understand absolutely clearly that you will not set foot behind the German lines.'

Two days later I arrived in Termoli together with some of my best operators and a complete base radio station. I planned to attach two operators and their sets to any future collecting teams that were sent in by sea. We were given for this purpose some suitcase radio sets which were normally only issued to agents.

Termoli was a small natural port just north of the 'spur' on the Italian boot. The village was built all round the harbour on the side of a hill. Houses tumbled over each other in typical ramshackle style. Narrow little alleys and streets burrowed their way between tiny ill-lit shops and houses, in which the fishermen lived.

The HQ had a house on the sea front. I was shown into the Colonel's office by a swarthy looking ruffian who mumbled in a strange language and wore a mixture of American and British clothing. Colonel Tony Simmonds was sitting at a rough wooden table covered with Italian maps, with a cigarette hanging out of the corner of his mouth. A bandage went right round his head and under his chin, leaving a small shock of sandy hair sticking out at the top. He told me he had not been wounded – he had some sort of dermatitis.

'Oh, I was expecting you,' he said. 'You have joined an unconventional army. The gangster who showed you in is a Jugoslav agent and we have another one as our officers' mess cook. Our fleet consists of two Italian E boats complete with Italian naval crews, an LCI [Landing Craft Infantry] manned by the RNVR and four Italian fishing boats equipped with ancient diesel engines. What have you brought with you?'

I told him and said we could operate as soon as we had set up our base station and had learnt to use our new sets.

Nearly every night during the next month I went up the coast in one or other of our strange craft. On one occasion we took the LCI up to a beach fifty miles north of Termoli expecting to take off three hundred prisoners. When we arrived only twenty-three were there. Not twenty minutes before we arrived, over 250 panicked when a burst of German Schmeisser fire had been heard. One of the ex-prisoners of war had shouted, 'It is a trap'. In spite of frenzied efforts by the officer in charge of the team, nearly all had streamed back to the farms and villages from where they had been collected.

On one night I had trouble with the commander of an Italian E boat. We were twenty minutes early and standing off the beach with engines stopped. We could see through binoculars a convoy of German lorries moving south along the main road. He gave the order to start up the engines and return to port. I told him in my best Italian that unless he cancelled his orders he would die and pulled out my Colt.45 automatic. He quickly changed his mind! Exactly on time I sent off my sergeant in a rubber dinghy to pick up six prisoners. I thought it best to stay on board because the dinghy could only bring back two at a time. I did not want any last-minute change of mind by the E boat.

One night when I did not go out an E boat failed to return. We heard later that it had been engaged by a light AA gun on the shore and one of the torpedoes on board had exploded, blowing everything to pieces. Two of my soldiers who had gone out that night were in the dinghy when it happened. They had a sticky time avoiding capture for the next few days. They managed to return through our lines to tell their tale two weeks after they had set out.

One day an Italian agent came in with a message from one of the parties that had been dropped over a month previously. A radio set and operators were desperately needed to pass back information about prisoners coming back through the lines. I selected Sergeant P. Phillips and Signalman D. Stewart. They were both small in height and Phillips could have passed for an Italian anywhere, besides being a very expert and experienced radio operator. They had worked together for a long time and were a good team.

Two nights later I rowed the two ashore just north of Pescara and wished them good luck. One was carrying the set and the other a heavy accumulator. Their first task was to find the party who had asked for them. After a few days searching near the map reference I had given them, they gave up trying. Sergeant Phillips then decided to establish an escape team of his own. First of all they had to organize a regular flow of prisoners, then to reconnoitre a route through the German lines and finally to collect parties of prisoners and lead them back to our own lines.

Every day Sergeant Phillips came up on the air with a brief message saying what was happening and what he proposed to do. I asked him how he was keeping his battery charged up. Back he came in a masterpiece of understatement describing how he had set up his set in an attic over a German Brigade HQ. At night he was getting his battery charged up on a German engine which was kept running all night.

Almost every night for over a month Phillips and Stewart personally conducted a party of twenty to thirty ex-prisoners through the lines and then went back for more. The Germans had wind of their activities and on three occasions they had to change their location and route. They only managed to clear out of one village by vaulting over some walls at the back of a farmhouse when the radio set and battery had to be dumped in a pig-sty. The Germans blew up the whole of that small village and shot all the men who were left.

Routes through the lines became more and more difficult to find till at last they decided to return themselves. They had brought through over four hundred prisoners and were by far the most successful of all the teams. This was all the more remarkable because the Canadians were having a full-scale battle to capture Ortona over the same ground that Sergeant Phillips brought back whole platoons of ex-prisoners every night.

Well did they deserve the personal congratulations of General Sir Oliver Leese who commanded the Eighth Army at the time, and the Distinguished Conduct Medals for both of them which came through three months later.

At the beginning of December we received word that the Division was returning home before Christmas and I was ordered to hand over all our activities at Termoli to other troops.

1st Airborne Division was to take part in the cross-channel invasion after all. We were delighted that we were coming back to participate in what was obviously going to be the climax of the war.

1 "In places this watercourse surfaced and then became a bridge, including one crossing the Tragino Torrent" (p.11). The bridge in 1989, with the author in the foreground. Signs of repair are clearly visible.

2 The author in N. Africa, 1943 (p.82)

3 Sulmona Camp (see diagram p.33). Photograph taken in 1989 showing the spot where the author (on right) crossed the wire.

* 13 *

ARNHEM PLANS — SEPTEMBER 1944

I woke up cramped, thirsty and hungry. Was it yesterday that I had escaped from Italy, only to find myself today hiding in a tiny wall cupboard in Holland? My memory took me back two years with breathtaking clarity. Once more the horrors of life in a prison camp were hanging over me unless I could find a way out.

★ ★ ★

When 1st Airborne Division had returned to England nine months before, it had been given Lincolnshire as a base area. Nearly every village and town had its quota of troops wearing red berets. Large country houses, barns and stables were all requisitioned to house us. Soon the whole county was strewn with unit direction signs, all bearing the Pegasus symbol of Airborne Forces.

At first the good Lincolnshire people were a little apprehensive. Were these troops a lot of undisciplined roughnecks who would make their lives intolerable? Would it be safe to walk through the streets at night?

These doubts were soon laid at rest when they saw a standard of discipline and smartness which they had never seen before in that part of the country. The villagers' feelings turned into admiration. After only a few weeks they began to take a possessive pride in their local Airborne Unit. Arnhem Sunday is still celebrated throughout Lincolnshire by parades of Old Comrades. A few more go every year to Arnhem on an annual pilgrimage to join Dutch people at ceremonies on Arnhem Bridge (now renamed John Frost Bridge) and the cemetery.

But first things first. Evie and I were married on 29 January, 1944, in Hampstead Parish Church. Evie looked delicious in her white wedding dress and bridesmaids were found from our sisters. For a honeymoon we had six very short days at a delightful old pub with a reputation for good food at Winsford on Exmoor. Coming down from cloud nine was quite a shock when I went back to Lincolnshire and she to her job in the Admiralty.

We were all part of the British Airborne Corps headed by the legendary General 'Boy' Browning, who had been in charge of Airborne Forces for nearly three years. He had set high standards of dress and discipline, and was responsible for our Red Berets and Pegasus signs. Unfortunately he had never commanded Airborne formations in action and this was to have its significance later on.

We had to be ready for operations by the end of April barely four months hence. There was no time to lose and we entered on a period of extremely intensive training, culminating in divisional exercises in Yorkshire and in the Cotswolds. By the beginning of May every man was convinced that he belonged to the best unit and best division in the British Army.

Our new commander, Major-General Roy Urquhart, had taken over from General Eric Down, who once again had been denied taking the Division into action. Most unfortunately, Eric Down had never commanded in action. I heard in 1989 from Brigadier Austin Eagger* that Montgomery himself had decided that 1st Airborne Division must be commanded by someone with a good track record in action. Roy Urquhart was just such a man. Eric Down was sent off to India to start up the Indian Airborne Division. The only other really experienced airborne Commander was Major-General 'Windy' Gale, then in command of 6th Airborne Division.

Roy Urquhart was well liked by everybody, although he had never commanded airborne troops before. A large man with an imposing figure, he was overweight to parachute but everywhere he went he radiated self-confidence. He himself planned to land by glider with about half his HQ. The other half would go by parachute.

The Division consisted of two Parachute Brigades, one Airlanding Brigade (gliders) and one attached Polish Parachute Brigade. 1st Parachute Brigade consisted of veterans from the North Africa and Sicily campaigns. It was still commanded by Brigadier Gerald Lathbury and must have been one of the most efficient and battleworthy brigades in the British Army. 4th Parachute Brigade, under Brigadier Shan Hackett, had been formed from British units in the Middle East and India. Although not so experienced and battle-hardened as 1st Parachute Brigade, it had an *esprit de corps* all of its own. 1st Airlanding Brigade, under Brigadier Pip Hicks, was made up of ordinary infantry battalions who were carried to battle in gliders. The three airlanding battalions were both efficient and experienced as a result of operations and in the glider assault into Sicily. In addition there was the usual complement of gunners, sappers, signals and service troops. All these were on a much-reduced scale when compared with a normal division, due to weight restrictions.

I was second-in-command of the Divisional Signals and we had to make do with small radio sets of much reduced power compared with those used

* Personal letter to author from Austin Eagger.

in a normal division. Soon after our return from Italy, I put forward a proposal in writing asking that this policy be reviewed. Although airborne divisions were lightly equipped, their brigades might be as far apart as we were in Italy. I realized, of course, that this would mean an increase in the number of gliders allocated to signals because heavy radio sets, as issued in normal divisions, could only be carried in jeeps. This idea horrified the staff who quickly laid down that the Airborne Division would never be employed on a wide front. 'Landings would invariably take place on or near the objective and within a small perimeter, perhaps as much as three miles in diameter.'

This was sensible. Every past airborne operation had shown that landings must take place either on the objective or within a mile or so of it. This had been demonstrated in North Africa and Sicily. It was shortly to be confirmed by 6 Airborne Division's landings in Normandy. This opinion was also reinforced by American experience. General James Gavin was in command of 82nd Airborne Division and had established a reputation as a highly respected and successful commander. In his book he states 'It is in general better to take landing losses and land on the objective than to have to fight after landing in order to reach the objective.'* I was delighted that our own staff was now crystal clear on our limitations. We would soldier on with our small radios, and would have to produce a higher standard of training to make up for some of their deficiencies. Unfortunately this could not possibly make up for sheer lack of power.

D-Day came on 6 June and with it the eternal question from the soldiers, 'When is the Division going to be used, Sir?' We read of great doings in France and felt sure we should be there too. We had worked the men up to a pitch of training that only action against the enemy would satisfy.

We soon had our answer. We had to prepare to land on the hills to the south of Caen in Normandy and help capture this important feature in conjunction with 7th Armoured Division. We loaded up our transports and gliders, but on 13 June the operation was cancelled. Altogether sixteen operations were planned for 1st Airborne Division in the fourteen weeks between D-Day and Arnhem, but of these only four came to the ears of the troops. Four times the aircraft were loaded up and four times unloaded again within a few hours.

After Caen it was Falaise, then south of Paris, but all were cancelled. Tournai seemed a safe bet because it was on the road to Brussels. The British Army was getting very strung out in its rapid advance. But it too was quickly by-passed by the Guards Armoured Division and so became yet another plan to be discarded.

* Chester Wilmot, *The Struggle for Europe*, p.499. Quote from James M. Gavin, *Airborne Warfare*, p.81.

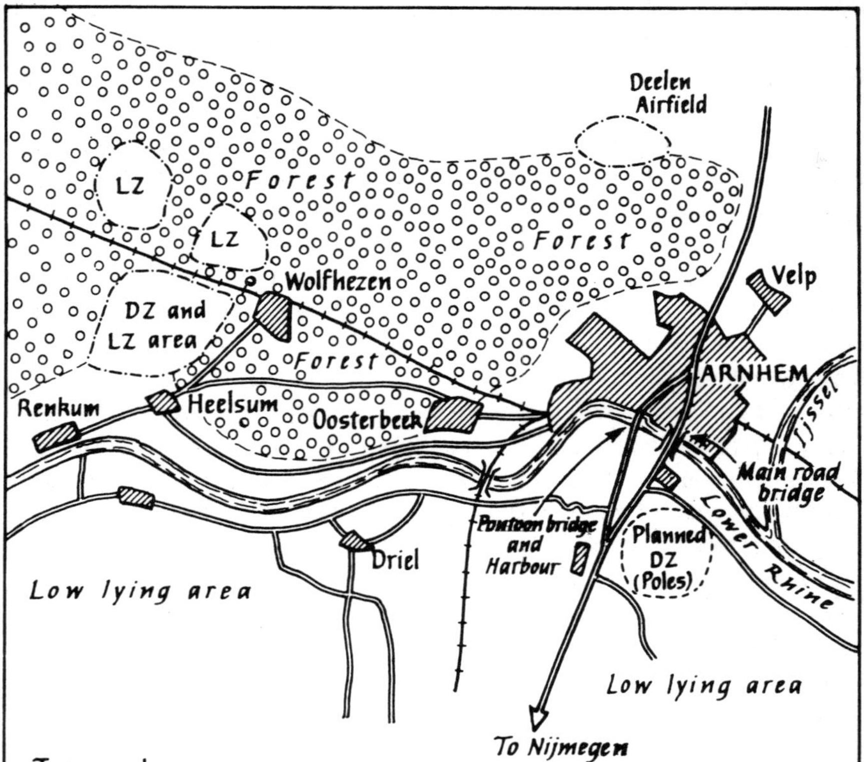

Topography
Area north of the Rhine up to 200 ft above sea level. Forests growing on sandy loam. Very large, ideal DZs carved out of forest

Area south of the Rhine low lying and flat. Wet in winter. Fields divided by drainage ditches

Arnhem: DZ areas and topography

The men's efficiency had reached a peak on D-Day, but as each operation was put off their spirits went down lower and lower. There was nothing wrong with them that properly planned action could not cure, but our standard excuses were wearing a bit thin after the fourth time.

'The main value of an airborne division,' said a visiting Brigadier from the War Office, 'is as a strategic threat to the enemy's lines of communications, which is lost as soon as the Division is landed.' Arguments of this nature did not appeal to the men, however true they might have been. We all had a difficult time keeping up our own enthusiasm as well as that of the troops.

On 12 September yet another airborne operation was planned, this time to take place in Holland between Eindhoven and Arnhem. No less than three Airborne Divisions were going to be used, together with our own Airborne Corps HQ. Once again we loaded our aircraft and gliders, a task which had by now become a well-known drill and did not take long. The same old procedure of briefing the men took place and all the time we expected a cancellation to come through.

I only heard details of the whole operation 36 hours before we took off on 17 September. The task of 'Market Garden' was to seize a sixty-mile-long corridor spanning eight major water obstacles including the Meuse, the Waal and the Lower Rhine at Arnhem. If this could be done, Field-Marshal Montgomery would be able to sweep forward into Holland and thence towards the north side of the vital Ruhr, thus turning the flank of the Siegfried Line, which ended at Aachen. Once across the Rhine the open plains of Germany lay ahead, unlike the broken and difficult country in front of the Americans on our right. But, unbeknown to us, there had been major arguments going on between Monty and Eisenhower. Monty wanted one major single thrust based on the British Twenty-First Army Group and the adjoining American Twelfth Army Group, commanded by General Bradley. If necessary, he offered to serve under General Bradley to allow this to happen. He believed that this was the only way to end the war before winter set in and make the best use of the limited supplies which were available.

Eisenhower did not agree. He favoured the broad front which allowed the maximum freedom of action to move forward by all the Armies. Undoubtedly General Patton's advance, in command of the Third US Army, had caught the imagination of the American public.* Any idea of restraining Patton to help Monty was unacceptable from a political point of view,

* Cornelius Ryan. *A Bridge too Far*, p.61. Report of discussions with Eisenhower. 'The American people would never stand for it and public opinion wins wars.' Montgomery disagreed. 'Victories win wars. Give people victory and they won't care who won it.' Also supported by General James Gavin. 'If Montgomery had been allotted the extra Corps he had wanted, he would have succeeded in breaking through to the North German Plain.' Obituary, *Times*, 27 Feb, 1990.

although the sheer military logic of a single massive thrust in the north was probably the quickest way to end the war before Christmas. Although all available transport aircraft were allotted to our Corps for the duration of Market Garden, there was a severe shortage of supplies within the British Second Army under General Dempsey. Most of these supplies for all the armies came over the beaches and then on by truck for 400 miles. The Channel ports had been bypassed and were still held by the Germans. Only XXX Corps under General Horrocks had sufficient supplies to support the advance towards Arnhem. As General de Guingand, Monty's Chief of Staff, said later, 'Montgomery was correct in his prognosis; no individual group was strong enough on its own to force its way across the Rhine that year. Yet, having predicted what would happen, Montgomery attempted to defy his own logic in the most ambitious Allied operation of the war – the airborne assault on Arnhem.'*

The detailed planning had been done by 1st British Airborne Corps under General Boy Browning at Moor Park near London. There were many difficulties to overcome.

In the first place and by far the most important, there were only sufficient aircraft to lift about half the force. As has already been mentioned, lessons from all previous airborne operations had emphasized that formations must be landed complete and as near to the objective as possible. Operation Market Garden split everything into two parts and landed the whole Division seven miles to the west of the bridge with a forest and a town in between. This was a risk only justified in face of negligible enemy opposition or if the relieving ground forces could cover the sixty miles from Eindhoven to Arnhem in under sixty hours.** Both these suppositions proved to be wrong and it took General Horrocks and his XXX Corps seven days to reach the Lower Rhine.

The task given to 1st Airborne Division was to seize the bridge over the Lower Rhine at Arnhem. Corps HQ had planned the operation in conjunction with the US Allied Airborne Army HQ nearby. A major flight plan was produced to arrange the flying in of hundreds of aircraft and gliders required by the three airborne divisions. Some 1544 planes and 478 gliders were to take off from twenty-six airfields on 17 September. It would take one and a half hours for the whole airfleet to become airborne and formed up for the flight.† There was no moon in the middle of September and this had made

* Sir Francis de Guingand, *From Brass Hat to Bowler Hat*, p. 15.

** Cornelius Ryan, *A Bridge too Far*, p. 79 and p. 126. Report of briefing by General Horrocks before the Market Garden attack. 'He expected to pass 20,000 vehicles over the road to Arnhem in 60 hours.'

† Lewis Brereton, *Brereton Diaries*, p. 345.

a daylight drop essential. The coordination of this plan with over 1200 fighter sorties and the air sea rescue service ruled out any prospect of two lifts on one day.

RAF air photographic experts reported that Arnhem was heavily defended by flak and that to fly closer than five miles to the town would invite up to two-thirds casualties in the slow-flying transports and gliders. They also said that the low-lying open farmland just south of the Bridge would be too 'difficult' for parachute troops and the smaller fields surrounded by drainage ditches would result in many accidents to gliders. Both these recommendations proved to be wrong. There were few active flak guns and the ground south of the Bridge would have been eminently suitable for landing gliders, although there would have been more crashes. The Air Forces enjoyed air supremacy at the time and could have taken out many of the active flak positions. As I was to see for myself during the battle, the Germans had put in numerous dummy flak positions. This was belatedly acknowledged in the official RAF report made after the operation.*

There was no doubt that the RAF was dead set on using DZs to the west. They appeared to be mesmerized by their excellence from an airman's point of view. Every possible snag was put in the way of using DZs to the south of the Bridge. There were good reasons for their choice. The DZ areas to the west were very large and ideal for massed landings. Suitable flight plans could be arranged for the aircraft to keep well clear of supposed flak. As I was to hear after the war, one of the principal air photograph interpreters was left in no doubt where the Army *had* to land.** General Roy Urquhart was also given no option. He reckoned the RAF's job was to get the Division to the landing area and he could not interfere with it. He left his staff to work out with the RAF the details.†

There were only two senior officers available with sufficient airborne

* Public Records Office. W0205/870. Report on British Airborne Effort in Operation Market by A. V. M. Scarlett-Streatfeild commanding 38 Group RAF (1 Jan, 1945).

** Discussion by author with a pre-war and post-war gliding acquaintance at Dunstable Downs in 1960. During the war he was Squadron Leader Lawrence Wright and an expert air photo interpreter on the air staff. It was not difficult to paint a horrific picture near the bridge. He told me he had pointed out to the Air Staff that some of the flak positions looked like dummies. This was not passed on. Lawrence Wright died in 1985.

† Letter to author from General Urquhart in October, 1988, and confirmed by Col. Charles Mackenzie, his GSO 1. There was no contact with General Gale. Ryan quotes Gavin in *A Bridge Too Far*, page 106. All Divisional commanders were asked to describe their future plans for Market Garden at Browning's Corps HQ at Moor Park on 13 September. 'Gavin was so astonished when he heard of Urquhart's choice of landing sites that he said to his operations chief, Lt. Col. J. Norton "My God, he can't mean it." Norton was equally appalled. "He does, but I wouldn't care to try it." He was surprised that Browning did not question Urquhart's plan. Still Gavin said nothing, "for I assumed the British with their extensive combat experience knew exactly what they were doing'."

experience who could have challenged this decision. One was General 'Windy' Gale, then commanding 6th Airborne Division. The other was General Eric Down. Windy Gale was the more diplomatic, whilst Eric Down would have been explosive. Both would have considered the DZ choice and the divided drop for the whole Division as disastrous.

General Windy Gale had apparently been called in to Moor Park during the planning stage for Arnhem to give advice.* His opinion was that 'If these DZs have to be used, a minimum force of a parachute brigade *must* be landed south of the Bridge in a *coup de main* role'. General Browning must also have asked Gale not to pass on these opinions to Urquhart.

In the event, the Corps plan for the fly-in was virtually set in concrete and orders issued to use the dropping and landing zones to the west of Wolfhezen. As a result there arose yet another difficulty. As the Division had only enough aircraft to arrive in two waves (or in three if the Polish Parachute Brigade was included) a significant part of the first day's drop had to stay in the dropping zone area to protect it for use twenty-four hours later. This weakened the striking force still further and moreover spread the Division over a large area of enemy-held country. If the enemy were to attack before the whole Division could be landed and concentrated around the objective, there would be a grave danger of being defeated in detail. Again the plan relied on negligible enemy opposition in the Arnhem area and yet again was found to be wrong. 9th and 10th Panzer Divisions were refitting in the Arnhem-Hertogenbosch area. This information had filtered through to General Dempsey and Second Army by 10 September.** High-grade decrypt had identified both divisions by 15 September, although Second Army's summ-

* Discussion by author with Major G. Norton, curator of Airborne Museum 1968-88, and confirmed later by letter. General Gale visited the museum in 1970/71 and said he had been called in by General Browning to Moor Park during the planning stage for Arnhem. When asked for his opinion, he said that 'The whole Division would have to be landed on or close to the bridge to be certain of success, or at the very least, a *coup de main* drop of a parachute brigade to hold the bridge until the main force arrived'. 'Without such a drop, the chances of success were slim,' he thought. He was also particularly critical of the drop on two days. This reinforced the need for the parachute brigade drop adjacent to the bridge. When Browning asked him what he would do if he had to accept the plan, General Gale said 'he would resign'. I believe Browning must have asked Gale not to contact Urquhart with these opinions. Letter to author from General Urquhart confirms that these major issues were never raised with the RAF. The reason this anecdote has not been published before was that:

1. General Gale wanted the Airborne Museum to have a record of what took place.
2. He had no wish for any comment he had made during the short planning phase to be used as a criticism of Roy Urquhart, with whom he deeply sympathized and who he believed had been given a raw deal (Roy Urquhart died on 13 December, 1988, aged 87).
3. General Gale asked that publicity for this should be withheld until after the main participants were dead.

** *British Intelligence in the Second World War*, Vol III, Part II by Professor F. H. Hinsley and others, p.383

ary on 13 September tended to downgrade this threat. On 16 September it was upgraded again that 'German armour was present in the Arnhem area'. A report had also been received from Dutch Resistance on 14 September that 9th SS Panzer Division had been located in the Arnhem-Apeldoorn area and had been equipped with new tanks from Cleves.* Field-Marshal Model was also reported to be at Oosterbeek about two miles from Arnhem and between the DZs and the Bridge. The GS02 Intelligence at Airborne Corps was a Major Brian Urquhart, (no relation to General Roy Urquhart).** He had also received similar information from Dutch Resistance through Second Army and Dutch liaison officers at Corps HQ on 12 September. He became very concerned that 1st Airborne Division would be written off by German armour. General Browning would not listen to his warnings. Brian Urquhart even asked the chief doctor, Brigadier Austin Eagger, to plead his case with General Browning,*** who told Eagger, 'Urquhart may well be right but the responsibility is *mine* not his if we can shorten the war and save hundreds of lives.' Brian Urquhart was working himself up into a state of considerable anxiety, so he requested a low-level air reconnaissance of the Arnhem area which took place on 12 September.† This confirmed the presence of German armour†† but it did not impress the Corps Commander,††† who sent him off 'sick'.

Some of this information penetrated down to us. There were said to be considerable numbers of low-grade troops in the Arnhem area, but infor mation on the 'presence of a Panzer division was weak or that the division was not fit for action'.†††† The German Army had apparently taken such a thrashing in its retreat across France and Belgium that there were no fighting formations left. We must get there before the whole thing packed up.

* Ibid, p.385

** Personal letter to author from Sir Brian Urquhart. See also his book *A Life in Peace and War*, p.73

*** Personal letter to author from Brigadier A. Eagger.

† Ibid, p. 384

†† Ibid, p.387. The German armour available to Model and used against 1st Airborne Division was a battle group formed from 9th Panzer Division with one company of Panther tanks, an armoured infantry regiment, an artillery battalion, two assault gun batteries and its reconnaissance battalion.

††† The US Official History reveals that a complete operational plan for Market Garden was captured from one of the gliders of the US Airborne Divisions which landed short. It was probably available to Model before giving out his orders. Other accounts suggest that it had not reached him or was considered to be a plant. (As he could see for himself what was happening, the author doubts if this affected the first day's operation in the Arnhem area. Undoubtedly it helped for D + 1 and subsequently. Fortunately the D + 1 drop was delayed by fog in the UK. In the meantime the German Air force had concentrated its total effort of 190 planes airborne and in ambush. As they landed to refuel, the Allied airborne Armada was running in to drop.)

†††† Ibid, p.384

Unfortunately General Boy Browning was going through a bad patch. On 3 September Browning had complained to his boss, U.S. General Brereton, commanding the Allied Airborne Army, that on one of the previous cancelled airborne operations insufficient time had been given to distribute maps of the area so that proper briefings could be given. Brereton must have formed a low opinion of Browning and this was the last straw. Brereton's answer was to direct Major-General Matt Ridgway, commanding the American 18 Airborne Corps, to be prepared to take over Browning's command.* Later that day Browning wrote to Brereton tendering his resignation as deputy commander of First Allied Airborne Army. The next day peace was restored and Browning withdrew his resignation. Later still, on 12 September, Brereton was to have another major disagreement with Browning,** who maintained that Montgomery himself had said he wanted 101st US Airborne Division to land spread out along an axis 30 miles long with seven separate objectives and DZs. (I very much doubt if such an instruction was ever issued. Montgomery would never have told a subordinate commander how to do his job. It was more likely that Browning may have suggested that 101 would land in this manner and Montgomery would have then agreed.) Brereton decided to go over to Belgium with General Taylor (commanding 101st Airborne) to see whether this plan could be changed. They saw General Dempsey who immediately understood the problem and agreed to a more concentrated drop. Brereton's comment was that 'General Dempsey seems to have a better appreciation of the employment of airborne forces than other British ground commanders.' Browning was then told of the change.

All this did not make for a happy relationship or one which would acknowledge any obstacle in the path of Market Garden, however real it might be.

There was no doubt that if Browning had bitten the bullet and cancelled 1 Airborne Division's part of Market Garden, he would have been sacked by Brereton. Browning even decided at two weeks' notice to take his Corps HQ to Holland with the aim of 'better controlling the three Divisions', leaving his Rear HQ and base radio stations back at Moor Park.† Tactically this

* *Brereton Diaries*, p.337

** Ibid, p.341, 342

† Personal letter to author from Maj-Gen. R. Moberley. The so-called Corps HQ was in reality only a static administrative HQ to look after the two Divisions in the field. It was never designed to be an operational HQ. Quite naturally, Boy Browning relished the idea of commanding in the field. The rapid advance in France persuaded him that the German Army was smashed. He became obsessed with the idea of flying in with his 'Corps HQ' apparently to the exclusion of all other factors. Brigadier Moberley was given two weeks to arrange scratch radio teams. His advice that this could have been better done by XXX Corps was rejected.

was ridiculous and unnecessary. The airborne divisions would probably be withdrawn as soon as ground forces relieved them. They would have been better served by links to XXX Corps. Unfortunately the thirty-eight gliders needed by Corps HQ* could have provided additional and invaluable support to assist 1 Airborne Division on the first day. As a *coup de théâtre* it might have been dramatic; as a means of waging war against the background of an acute shortage of aircraft, it was absurd.

Another result of spreading the Division over such a large area was the inadequacy of the radio sets with which we were equipped. They were designed to communicate up to three miles and all our previous exercises and operations had been planned and had worked on this basis. At Arnhem the sets would have to work seven or eight miles to the bridge through a forest and built-up area and no less than fifteen miles to Corps HQ at Nijmegen. I only heard of the plan late on 15 September and immediately contacted my commanding officer, Lieutenant-Colonel Tom Stevenson. I told him that we were unlikely to have proper communications until the Division was concentrated around the bridge. I felt so strongly about it that I asked to see the General or at least the GSO1, Charles Mackenzie. I was told that it was too late to worry them. He told me firmly to do no such thing. He was probably right.

In the event my prediction that communications would not work or be most unreliable until the Division was concentrated proved to be accurate. Even if the radios had worked when the Division was widely spaced apart, it would have made a negligible difference to the outcome. Some unfair comment made in the heat of the moment was resented by my excellent soldiers.** The cause of failure was strategic or tactical, and nothing to do with signals.

So much for the plan and the problems. We were all in a state of euphoria. We were now going into action. We had to demonstrate just how good we knew we really were. The whole plan would have gone brilliantly if there had been little or negligible resistance from the enemy. Unfortunately this was not to be. Risks were taken in the Arnhem operation with eyes wide open. The prize was great if success came our way. If the German opposition had been as insignificant as had been expected, the whole plan would have been completely successful. The commanders concerned would have been congratulated on their nerve and their timing.

* Public Records Office. WO 205/870. Report on British Airborne Effort in Operation Market by A. V. M. Scarlett-Streatfeild commanding 38 Group RAF (1 Jan, 45)

** Lewis Golden, *Echoes from Arnhem*, p.139 et seq. Unlike many 'instant' stories from *Arnhem*, mostly based on erroneous repetition of quotes from R. Urquhart's book *Arnhem*, this is a well researched account of the tactics, the problems, and recorded messages from War Diaries. In spite of their low power, the radios worked, albeit with difficulty, unless destroyed by enemy action.

* 14 *

ARNHEM — THE ACTION

Sunday, 17 September, 1944 dawned fine. To our great surprise we had not yet received any cancellation. A lorry arrived at our country house billet with our parachutes. An hour later more lorries arrived and we climbed aboard to drive to an airfield near Grantham. Everything seemed so unreal. Never before had we got as far as this on any of our previous abortive operations.

All down one side of the airfield were about fifty C47s (Dakotas), lined up in staggered rows. We drove to our allotted aircraft and rechecked the loading which had been done on the previous day. Everything was all right and our American crews came over and helped us. They were a grand lot and mutual respect for each other had grown up in the preceding months. We could not have been served better. But for them there would not have been any large-scale airborne operations.

The word came to put on parachutes and get into the aircraft. A few minutes later we were roaring down the runway at thirty-second intervals. The planes flew in a wide circle, low over the villages we knew so well, allowing the rest to take off and join our air armada. Now we were in tight formation, all fifty of us, flying south-east over the sunlit fen country. I rose up and moved forward to get a better view through the door to the pilot's cockpit. I could see that my aircraft was the leader of our V formation and that half a mile ahead were another fifty Dakotas, flying steadily on, all bunched together. Behind us was a similar lot, making 150 in all, carrying 1st Parachute Brigade complete, together with the parachuting part of the Divisional Signals and the Reconnaissance Squadron. The next day the same aircraft would bring the 4th Parachute Brigade and, the day after, the Polish Parachute Brigade, if they were required.

The glider element was taking off simultaneously from eleven airfields in Gloucestershire and Oxfordshire, carrying two-thirds of the Airlanding Brigade, the remainder of Divisional Headquarters plus its Signals and the Reconnaissance Squadron in 345 gliders. The towing aircraft were all found from No 38 and No 46 Groups RAF. They too would return for a second lift of another 300 gliders on the following day.

The flight plan phased in all the aircraft into one continuous stream. What a magnificent sight it must have been! From the air we could see the streets of the villages we passed over thronged with people looking upwards. Occasionally I could see a handkerchief waving a farewell. About midday we crossed the coastline and flew out across the North Sea. For once this was like a millpond with scarcely a ripple to disturb its brown-looking water.

The men in my plane were nearly all asleep by now as is the custom of the British private soldier. He had few worries; he placed supreme confidence in his officers. Little did he care that he was taking part in the largest airborne operation ever launched; all that mattered was that he did his own job to the best of his ability. Therein lay his strength as a fighting soldier in adversity. I was proud to have them in my company. They were to need all their qualities in the days to come.

Twenty-five minutes after leaving the Suffolk coastline there was a bustling amongst the crew in the cockpit up forward. I could see they were strapping on steel helmets. The Dutch coast was in sight and a few minutes later we flew in low over the island of Schonwen just south of Rotterdam. A moment later I saw several fighters with United States markings come up level with us for a second or two and then fly away out of sight. At least 1200 fighters were on patrol to protect us during our flight. The Luftwaffe missed a golden opportunity on that Sunday.

A little later on when we crossed the Dutch coast proper we were surprised to see some Horsa gliders already landed in the fields below us. We heard later that about ten percent had broken their tow ropes and had come down short of their landing zones.

The Dutch farms, surrounded by green fields and ringed by dykes, looked peaceful enough from above. There was no sign of any enemy. As in England we could see Dutch people looking upwards and an occasional handkerchief could be seen waving. I heard afterwards from a Dutch patriot who watched us from below that it was the most thrilling spectacle of his whole life and was not surpassed even by the day of his final liberation by the Canadians some eight months later.

There were now only twenty minutes left to the time we were due to drop at 2 pm. So far we had not suffered a scratch. No enemy fighters had come near, nor had any flak guns seen fit to fire in our direction. It was almost too good to be true and I was just congratulating myself when a noise like a sledgehammer beating the outside of our fuselage woke everybody up. This even included my batman/driver, Lance-Corporal Nick Turner, who could be relied upon to sleep like a log in an aeroplane. Through our open doorway we could see a light flak gun shooting straight at us. Little yellow tongues of flame spat in our direction and a few seconds later some more hammer blows could be heard. There appeared to be no casualties, so perhaps the shells were hitting the plane where it did not matter. This was confirmed when I saw about a foot of a wingtip suddenly disappear from the aircraft flying just opposite the open doorway only twenty or thirty feet away. We had just time to see six RAF fighters dive down on the flak gun, all cannons blazing with the German guncrew belting for their slit trenches.

Another twenty minutes dragged by as we droned on. At last I was given the word from the pilot and out came my automatic order:

'Stand up, hook up and check equipment.'

The whole planeload leaped into activity. Parachutes were adjusted, static lines hooked on to the wire running down the side of the fuselage and the straps on the steel helmets given another tweak. Some looked a little pale, but most tried to appear unconcerned as I passed down the fuselage checking that each man was properly hooked up. For many it was their first operational jump and, after the incident with the flak gun, they were all most anxious to get the jump over and be on the ground once again. After hooking myself up, I took up position at the open door with the rest of the men as close as they could get behind me. I could hear the engines change their note as the pilot throttled back to jumping speed. A large river flashed by underneath and the red light came on. That must be the Rhine and we were nearly there. Now I could see some parachutes lying at the end of a field. An enormous T had been laid out on the ground by the pathfinder company. 'Green Light.' I was out of the door and a moment later was gently swinging beneath my parachute.

All around me were parachutists as all fifty aircraft ejected their loads. For those privileged to be there, it was a most inspiring sight and one which I will never forget.

I touched down in some heather and rolled over backwards, banging my head on a steel container in the process. For a few seconds I could not think what I was doing, but by now the next group of fifty aircraft were roaring overhead. As if by magic another thousand parachutes came out of their bodies and floated earthwards on top of us.

I had soon gathered my planeload and we moved off to a prearranged rendezvous for Divisional HQ. An occasional rifle shot could be heard, but apart from this the whole landing operation could have taken place on Salisbury Plain. There was hardly any wind and the sun streamed down on a large open heath covered in heather. Pine forests were growing each side of the Dropping Zone exuding rather attractive smells when compared with the sour odours of the planes in which we had been travelling. We were now safely on the ground and much more in our element.

We arrived at the side of the heath amongst a clutter of crashed gliders.

In one corner we met up with the rest of my men who had come by glider and a little further on I could see the General and Colonel Charles Mackenzie, the GSO1. I reported all present and we were soon at work setting up the nucleus of a Divisional HQ based on the two or three jeeps, which had already arrived, after being extracted from the tails of the gliders. Communications were soon working to 1st Parachute Brigade who were ready to move off within an hour of landing.

One essential part of the assault plan was for Major Freddy Gough and his heavily armed jeeps in the Reconnaissance Squadron to move off the Landing Zone as soon as possible and capture the bridge by *coup de main* hopefully before the arrival of 1 Para Bde.* No less than twenty-eight jeeps out of the thirty-one which started were ready to move off at 3.40 pm. Communications had been laid on for the Reconnaissance Squadron to come under 1 Parachute Brigade whose task was also to capture the bridge. Unlike the Orne bridges in Normandy, captured by 6th Airborne Division, when gliders were landed adjacent to the objective, Freddy Gough was some 7 - 8 miles away, with forests, suburbs and the main streets of the town in between. Soon after Freddy had given the order to move off, he was engaged by Germans in the area of the railway crossing on the edge of the DZ at Wolfheze. In the middle of this action he received a message that the General wanted to see him personally on a matter of urgency. Freddy handed over to his second-in-command and went off on a wild goose chase with two of his jeeps to find the General. By now the General was moving up the road towards Arnhem in an attempt to reach 1st Parachute Brigade HQ, but instead found Brigadier Gerald Lathbury at the headquarters of 3rd Battalion. They all came under machine-gun and mortar fire, which destroyed the General's radio and wounded his operator. Gerald Lathbury's radio was working well and later on they heard the good news that 2nd Battalion had captured the bridge.**

In the meantime Freddy Gough had failed to contact the General, but by skilful navigation through the suburbs and streets, shooting up many groups of Germans on the way, actually arrived at the Bridge with his two jeeps each mounting two Vickers K Guns.† These were to prove invaluable later on. The rest of the Squadron had been held up in the woods leading into the town by fierce opposition and were unable to get to the bridge.

Back at Divisional HQ reports began to come in that 1st Parachute Brigade was meeting with considerable opposition on their way to the bridge. Three roughly parallel roads were being used for the advance, one for each battal-

* Lewis Golden, *Echoes from Arnhem*, p. 142

** Gerald Lathbury's diary p 65/66 published by Airborne Museum at Oosterbeek

† J. D. Frost, *A Drop Too Many*, p. 223.

lion. The southern one near the Rhine was the only one found to be moderately clear of the enemy. Along this route Lieutenant-Colonel John Frost and 2nd Parachute Battalion pushed as fast as they could. By 8 pm that evening he had established Battalion HQ and one company at the north end of the bridge. A little later a second company arrived and a large part of Brigade HQ, the signals section and some sappers.

The Division was now in three bits. Brigade HQ minus the Brigadier, together with most of one battalion was on the bridge, while the remainder of the Brigade were about two miles away on the edge of the town. The rest of the Division, including Divisional HQ, was back near the dropping zone. This was a military nightmare, which would lead to disaster if the Germans attacked in strength. Luckily they attacked piecemeal, although precious little was to be saved out of the mess.

Back at Divisional HQ on the first afternoon I was worried. Our communications back to base at Moor Park were weak and erratic with constant interference from a strong German station. We had no communication direct to Corps HQ, although messages could be sent via Moor Park. We had lost touch with 1st Parachute Brigade HQ when they were only about five miles away, in spite of every effort to improve the position and height of aerial of our Divisional HQ sets. My Colonel asked me to move forward as early as possible next morning and see what the trouble was. He also ordered a change of frequency for our main Divisional Command radio set. This change would not be known to 1st Parachute Brigade unless they were informed and he asked me to do this and clear up the trouble. We had no idea how far they had reached.

Soon after first light on the 18th there was still no improvement and I set off with my batman, Lance-Corporal Nick Turner, who was an excellent man to have around in a tricky situation. In peacetime he had been a valet-chauffeur and nothing worried him. His dry sense of humour was a great asset. By keeping our eyes open we were able to avoid trouble and scouted round many pockets of Germans who were keeping up an irregular sniping action on the Brigade's routes of advance.

We soon discovered that the road nearest to the Rhine was relatively free of Germans and were able to make good progress. There were two circular dummy flak gunpits on the Arnhem side of Oosterbeek, with horizontal telegraph poles held up in the middle by a short piece buried in the ground. The Germans must have put in a lot of these all round the Arnhem Bridge. I remember thinking that I hoped our air photo interpreters were not taken in. Might this explain why we were landed so far away from the objective?

We soon arrived at HQ 1st Parachute Battalion under Lieutenant-Colonel David Dobie. The Battalion had just reached the outskirts of Arnhem proper, adjacent to the St Elizabeth Hospital, and was preparing to attack, with the aim of reaching the Bridge through two miles of enemy-held streets. David Dobie had received his orders by radio from Brigade HQ on the Bridge, where Johnnie Frost was now acting as Brigade Commander.

The Battalion was under a certain amount of fire from mortars and snipers. A crash on the wall behind me and just above my head showed that a sniper had fortunately overestimated the range. The enemy had very quickly appreciated our real purpose and was resisting with surprising energy. Little did we realize that Field-Marshal Model, who commanded the German Army Group B, had his tactical HQ at Oosterbeek. This was only a mile away from where we were and he had witnessed the drop on the previous day. He had immediately ordered armoured reinforcements from 9th SS Panzer Division to stop our movement through the town.

Nobody of course knew this at the time and preparation for the attack went through with confidence. I managed to speak to the Brigade Major, Major Tony Hibbert, at Brigade HQ on the bridge and tell him of the change of frequency, although I was to hear after we arrived back that he could not remember me telling him. He had a lot on his plate. I told him I hoped to come through with 1 Parachute Battalion and would see him then. Like everybody else, I completely failed to appreciate the strength of the opposition we were up against. With hindsight, I should have returned to Divisional HQ at this stage.

From the start the going was tough. I found myself encouraging some of the slower men in the Battalion who were cluttering up Battalion HQ. One of the companies which had the job of clearing the river banks along the Rhine was running into difficulties. I could not do anything else except to go forward with Lance-Corporal Turner to find out what was going on. The Company Commander, who had been leading his men with great dash and energy, had just been killed. To take over seemed to be the only thing to do. The main aim of the Division was to seize and hold the Bridge. If I could help by taking over a company temporarily, this might help the Division to carry out its primary role.

Street fighting is always a pretty bloody business and this was no exception.

About four hundred yards farther along our side of the river, just level with the pontoon bridge, the bank was broken by a thirty-foot-wide channel leading to a tiny harbour in the middle of the town. A group of houses stood just short of the channel and I gave orders to capture and hold them whilst the rest of the Battalion caught up with us on our left.

While we were advancing under cover of the river bank, we were under a certain amount of small-arms fire and at one point three Germans threw some stick grenades at us. These did no damage and they soon stopped when we threw back some of our own. By the time we reached our objective, only twenty men were left out of the whole Company. I could see that we had left the rest of the Battalion far to the rear and our position would be quite untenable for any length of time. A check-up on our ammunition showed we only had about a hundred rounds between us. The time was about 4 pm and I gave orders to take up defensive positions in the houses overlooking the harbour. We distributed ourselves between three houses which gave us a commanding view all round. Our big difficulty was that we had no way of telling Battalion HQ where we were or how successful our attack had been. I thought the enemy would attack our position by first light the following day, by which time we would have to be relieved.

A German account of this advance is revealing. 'Spindler's men, occupying the house and gardens bordering the high ground to the left overlooking the low road, grenaded and fired at anything that moved. Fire still continued from the front. Assailed from three sides, the attack collapsed in a withering concentration of weapons of all calibres. There was nowhere for the hapless paratroopers to turn, except to try and gain admittance to occupied houses on their left. Shelter had therefore to be fought for. Advance elements of 1 Para had reached the Old Harbour, barely 1400 metres from the bridge ... Behind, the column was in a shambles. Decimated desperate groups began now to flee or exfiltrate back to the start line. Most of the officers and non-commissioned officers were already dead or wounded. This was the nearest they would ever get to Frost, but 2 Para, totally preoccupied with their own battle on the bridge did not hear a thing.'* The hyperbole of this account may have overdramatized the action but we were in an awkward situation.

We kept up a sniping action to keep the Germans from getting too close. By nightfall nearly all our ammunition had gone. Judged by the sound of firing, the main body of the battalion was still fighting in the area of the St Elizabeth Hospital over 400 yards further back. I decided that we were in a hopeless position and that our best course was to get back to the Battalion by night, even if we had to swim the Rhine to avoid the German-held streets behind us. The time was about 10 pm. To give the best chance to everybody the remains of the company were split into three groups, Lance-Corporal Turner and three other men coming with me. It would have been impossible to get twenty men back through the streets without being discovered. A Lieutenant and a Sergeant, whose names I do not know to this day, commanded the other two parties. We all agreed it was the only sensible solution. I moved with my small team to a house near the water as a jumping-off point and broke in through a ground-floor window. We were just looking out of the window on the other side of the house when I heard somebody, obvi-

* Kershaw, *It Never Snows in September*, p. 169.

ously a German, trying to get in at the front door. I thought it most unlikely that we had been seen. We all dived into a lavatory on the ground floor and locked the door on the inside.

Eventually the German broke in through the door. To our dismay a section of about ten soldiers followed him in and on upstairs. From the sounds of tile-removing and furniture-shifting the house was being converted into a strongpoint in the German defensive position.

We sat in turns on that lavatory seat for the following three nights and three days until 21 September. During this time we could hear the almost incessant firing at the bridge just up river, together with the sounds of more distant fighting from the rest of the Division about three miles away. By night the sky was red with flames from burning houses. Occasionally everything was lit up by a brilliant white light from a star shell or very pistol. We were in an extraordinary position. A German machine-gun position in the roof made a hell of a noise when it opened up and two more had been dug into the pavement just outside the ground-floor windows. When these fired it was comparatively quiet, but still very noisy. We would need a lot of luck to get away with this one!

I could stand it no longer and told the group we would make an attempt to get out on the fourth night. Quite often during those three days Germans would come and try the door. On finding it engaged they politely went away and tried elsewhere. But by the time darkness fell on the fourth night the sound of firing had died down and most of the Germans in the area had pulled out, although the post in our roof could be heard letting off a burst or two very occasionally. The plan was to swim the river and, because of the current and our different swimming speeds, we would rendezvous together on the far side at the blown railway bridge only a mile downstream.

We all took off our boots and heavier clothing and tied them inside our smocks. These could be floated across the river without holding back our swimming. Our plan was to open the front door as quietly as possible and, using the shadows, walk down to the river not twenty yards away. The light from the burning buildings in the bridge area was still annoying but not half as bad as it had been on previous nights. One of the men I had with me had quite a bad attack of jitters. He kept saying, 'We shall be cut to ribbons, Sir, when we poke our noses outside that door.' He ceased to be frightened when we started off. The long spell in the lavatory had allowed his imagination to run riot. He was a veteran of the North African campaign and had received a Military Medal while serving with 2nd Parachute Battalion.

We were all hungry. I had eaten one concentrated ration on the evening of the 17th, but none of us had had anything since, except some apples we found in the cellar of the house in which we were hiding. We would creep down in the middle of the night and lay in supplies for the day.

About 1 am on 22 September we crept out of the lavatory and opened the front door an inch or two. The machine-gun posts outside were no longer manned, although the equipment was still in position. The crews must be sleeping nearby. Waiting for another period of continuous firing, which I thought would blanket the noise we would make, we quickly dodged from shadow to shadow and down to the river bank. A second or two later we were all swimming without making too much noise. Occasionally a burst of firing would shatter the stillness of the night. The reflections of burning buildings in the water made me feel that we could not help being seen. As we came out into the current, I was rapidly swept downstream and lost touch with the rest of the men. The Rhine at this point was about four hundred yards across and, due to the distance, I swam as slowly as possible to avoid getting overtired or out of breath. At last the chimneys of a brick factory loomed above me and I was clambering up the slippery bank. I had hoped that the Second Army might have reached that bank by now. If it hadn't it would mean they were three days behind schedule. However, I was not going to take any risks and moved as though the enemy was still in possession. There was no sign of any of the others.

Having untied my bundle and put on my clothes which were surprisingly dry, I started to move slowly down the river bank to the railway bridge where I had planned to meet the rest of the men. The time was now 2.30 am and we only had three hours left before dawn. Slowly I walked or crawled along the river bank, straining my eyes and ears for any signs of the enemy. A burning haystack to one side showed that the low-lying area we were in was still active. Now and again I could hear more firing coming from my front. After about an hour and a half I began to see the outlines of the railway bridge about four hundred yards away. Once in a while a starshell lit it up as if it was day.

I was getting quite close to the bridge when I had to leave the river bank to skirt round a dyke which flowed into the Rhine. I was just getting over a wide ditch when I heard a shrill whistle about thirty yards away. Dawn was still one hour away. I suddenly realized what had happened. The Germans were manning the railway embankment leading to the bridge and were 'standing to' an hour before dawn, as is the custom in the British Army in case of an attack at dawn.

Hell! I was now in the German front line with only a few yards to go and had arrived in time for 'stand to'. I ran forward quickly to get clear before the sentries woke up properly and fell into a slit trench in the dark on top of a German just beginning to stand up. He let out a scream and one of his pals came over from his trench about two yards away. He found me struggling with a rather sleepy German in a wet trench about four feet long and four feet deep.

The rest of the men all crossed safely but unfortunately all were caught. And so was I.

'The best laid plans of mice and men ...'

* 15 *

A DUTCH CUPBOARD

The game was up and I was a prisoner again. Once more I went through the indignity of being searched, but on this occasion at least I had no weapons to surrender. My sten gun and pistol had been dropped in the water while swimming across the Rhine.

No longer was I a free man and the anticlimax made me remember my hunger. Every bone and muscle in my body ached for rest. Wearily, so wearily, I was marched down the road to Company HQ, watched by sleepy-eyed Germans from slit trenches dug into the verge.

We stopped at a farmhouse and I was shown into a room, after pushing aside a blackout blanket which had been nailed over the doorway. Inside, a hot aroma of unwashed bodies, the acrid stench of stale tobacco smoke and garlic sausage combined to stifle my nostrils. A hurricane lamp turned low gave the only light. In the gloom my smarting eyes could now see gently-heaving bodies wrapped up in greatcoats lying all over the floor, with mounds of equipment taking up every vacant space. The only sounds were wheezes and snores except for the faint noise of a conversation in German coming from the next-door room.

One of my escort of three pushed by and, after mumbling what I took to be swear words, woke up one of the prostrate bodies. He turned out to be an NCO and was soon kicking the other bodies to life. A piece of paper passed hands and I was off again out of the house with three new soldiers to Battalion HQ about a mile away.

This time everything was much more orderly. A German sentry examined the piece of paper carried by my escort and I was led down some steps into a cellar whose roof had been chocked up with large baulks of timber. A clean-shaven middle-aged German subaltern sat at a table with a lamp on one corner. He motioned me to sit down and said in broken English;

'I must to you questions ask. You will answer.'

'Oh.'

'Your name please?'

I told him.

'What day you jumped?'

'I can't say.'

'How many more are you?'

'I can't say.'

His eyes bulged a little behind his glasses and an angry flush spread up to his neck.

'OK, You no speak. We will see.'

He ended with some instructions in German. I was led outside under escort and put in the back of an open Volkswagen car which drove off quickly towards Arnhem.

We crossed the Rhine over the bridge which had cost so many lives. I could see many marks of the bloody fighting which had taken place as we threaded our way in and out of shellholes and burnt-out German tanks. Smoke was still coming from the ruins of the buildings on the north side of the river. Second Battalion must have had a hell of a fight. I remember wondering how long they had managed to hold the position before being overrun. This was the morning of 22 September. I was to hear later that day that the bridge had finally been captured only 24 hours before.

We sped through deserted streets to the outskirts of the town and stopped outside a newly built church which had sentries posted all round it. I was told to get out and wait inside. The church was full of newly captured prisoners of war standing in little groups everywhere. In one corner I could see a few officers, none of whom I knew. I learnt from them that the Division was now fighting inside a small perimeter round Oosterbeek. In another corner I saw Lance-Corporal Turner and the three others who had shared the lavatory with me. They too had been captured that morning in various places not far from where I had been taken.

We all looked pretty scruffy in that church. I had a five days' growth of beard and many more were like me. All of us had the slightly haggard and drawn look of soldiers who have been without sleep and seen their best friends die. Some were rummaging in their pockets or haversacks for any crumbs left over from the once despised forty-eight-hour concentrated ration which we all carried. Many were lying down full length on the pews fast asleep, snoring away with mouths slightly open and heads twisted at any angle.

As the morning drew on, the air in the church became warmer. Many of us laid down where we were on the hard tiles and went fast asleep. I followed suit.

The Germans gave us nothing to eat and by midday we were all getting very hungry and thirsty. Some of the soldiers asked me if I could get the Germans to do something about it.

I managed to get hold of an officer outside who could speak a little English. I told him in a mixture of languages that we expected to be given food within an hour. Otherwise, I told him, I would make sure his name was remembered after the war when the time came to deal with war criminals who disobeyed the Geneva Convention.

He became quite angry and spluttered in German, 'You can all think yourselves lucky to be alive and you will get food when it pleases us. Anyhow, what do you know about Geneva Conventions?'

'You would be surprised,' I replied in German, 'but food we must have and it is your responsibility to provide it.'

'Let me tell you, Herr Major, I have just received orders to march you all to a prison near here run by the SS. I am sure they will feed you,' he added sarcastically.

With a glint in his eye, he turned on his heel. Five minutes later we were on the march with guards on all sides. For two miles we went through the suburbs and saw very few civilians. There were one or two who were brave enough to wave and smile as we went by. But mostly the Dutch kept away and could not be seen.

At last we reached a house on the outskirts of Arnhem in the suburb of Velp. This was used as a temporary prisoner-of-war 'cage' and was guarded by an understrength company of fifty-five men. It was a typical large detached suburban house, about twenty yards back from the road and with exactly similar ones on either side. A row of low bushes surrounded the house itself just below the large windows. Two large monkey puzzle trees stood on the front lawn.

Inside were about 500 all ranks from the Division, whose spirits were high in spite of being prisoners. I met Freddie Gough, Tony Hibbert and many others. I learnt all their news and told them mine. The Germans fed us on tins of lard and coarse brown bread. We were not fussy and I wolfed my share down. I had not had a square meal since leaving England, my last one being breakfast on the 17th, and today was the 22nd. What months it all seemed, and yet it was only five days.

Tony Hibbert told me that the bridge had been captured by the Germans soon after dawn on the 21st, when nearly all the original defenders were killed or wounded and all ammunition had gone. Colonel Johnnie Frost had himself been wounded and for the last twenty-four hours Freddie Gough had been in command. For three days and nights this gallant force had held out against overwhelming odds, including tanks, which came up and gradually knocked down or set on fire every house being used for the defence. Some of these tanks had been stalked on foot and blown up with grenades. Fighting patrols had gone out every night to drive the Germans out of houses which overlooked the bridge. Deeds of heroism were done which are matchless in the history of the British Army, but received little publicity at the time because nobody returned to tell the tale. The Division had been ordered to hold the bridge for forty-eight hours until the arrival of the Second Army. It had been held for seventy-two hours by 600 men, but unfortunately to no avail.

By now we all realized what a failure the whole operation had been. We still hoped that the Division could hold on where it was and provide Second Army with a bridgehead through which the advance could continue. Many were our speculations on what was happening to the rest of our units still fighting, but our hearts were heavy.

Some officers were already saying that they would leave trying to escape till they arrived at the prison camp. 'It would all be laid on there.' This sort of talk was reminiscent of my experiences in Italy. I told everybody I saw that their one and only chance of getting away would be before they left Holland. The farther they went back along the evacuation channels, the more difficult would escape become. I think they believed me, but most of them could not see any possible way out with any hope of success. When I started looking over the whole house and garden, there were many smiles cast in my direction. It was not possible to get away, they said; they had already been over the place with a fine toothcomb. The trouble was that most of them were numbed by the anticlimax of being prisoners. They did not realize that, small though the chances of getting away were at the moment, they were better now than at any future date.

I reasoned that the cage would only be temporary and would last as long as the Division did. From all accounts this would not be long, so one solution would be to hide up in the house itself till the Germans left and then get out. Again it was just possible that the Second Army would continue their advance through the Division's bridgehead and then the whole area would be liberated.

I could not see any way to escape from the house that gave a better than fifty-fifty chance of success, so I looked everywhere for a hiding place which would hold me for two or three days. The only possible place was a wall cupboard in one of the ground-floor rooms which had a flush-fitting concealed door. The whole door was covered with the same sort of wallpaper as the rest of the room and did not stand out. The cupboard was about four feet across, twelve inches deep and about seven feet high. Its interior was divided horizontally by adjustable shelves. I left the top one in place and stacked the rest on the floor. I found I could stand inside in tolerable comfort. Fastening the door was a problem. The cupboard was fitted with the normal type of mortice lock let into the thickness of the door, with a keyhole on the outside complete with a key. By unscrewing the lock and turning it back to front, the keyhole came on the inside of the door and I was able to lock myself in. A piece of wallpaper torn off another part of the room and pasted over the outside keyhole helped to conceal the cupboard's presence.

The next job was to lay in a stock of water and food. All I had was my water bottle and I found an old two-pound jam jar which I also filled up. A one-pound tin of lard and half a small loaf of bread about the size of my fist completed all the provisioning I could do. Some of the officers very kindly offered to give me their water bottles, but I refused. They would need them for their own escape, which I reminded them they must try to make or be a prisoner for the rest of the war.

Little did I think that I would be confined to my cramped little cupboard for thirteen days and nights before getting out. I thought that the limit of my endurance would be reached after three or four days.

The Germans came round on the evening of the 2nd to take all names. I thought I had better give my cupboard try, so I stood in it whilst the names were being taken to avoid leaving a record of my capture. The room was being emptied as the names were taken and I had to start hiding properly. I stood first on one leg then on the other. There was no room to sit down because the cupboard was too shallow. I managed to sleep all right, although occasionally my knees would suddenly give way and would drop forward against the door with a hammer-like noise.

The day after I locked myself in the cupboard the Germans turned the now empty room into an interrogation centre. A chair was placed with its back to my cupboard with a table in front and more chairs on the far side for the use of prisoners. Every officer and man going through that cage was first interrogated in my room. This not only relieved my boredom, it was also fascinating. We had always been told that if ever we were made prisoner, the only information we should give would be our number, rank and name. The Germans knew this, of course, but tried every guile to get more information. The usual trick was to pretend that they were filling out a card for the Red Cross. They would ask a series of innocuous questions until the prisoner was at ease, when a question of military importance would be tossed in. I was surprised that very few officers or men gave only their number, rank and name. Almost everybody gave a little additional harmless information such as the address of their parents or their wives, whether they were regulars or had come from the TA.

The questioning went on for several days, four or five I think. By night the room was used as sleeping quarters for the guard. I had no chance to get out. As I had lasted so far, I thought I could manage another twenty-four hours. My luck must come to my rescue. It had always done so in the past.

Little by little I eked out my rations of water and bread. Four mouthfuls of water every four or five hours and just a bite or two of bread. The water was the chief shortage. After nine or ten days I could not eat any more bread because my mouth was so parched. For the benefit of the curious, I was able to direct my urine into one corner of the cupboard where there was a gap around some pipes going down to the cellar. I appeared to pee rather more liquid than the small amount I drank. I did not understand that. I must check up when I got out. I did not feel the need to do anything more solid during the whole time because there was nothing at all in my tummy. My system started to function again quite normally as soon as I started to eat. My only legacy was a series of nasty boils followed by styes which went on for about a year afterwards.

On the eleventh day I had a fright in the afternoon. The room outside was now a guardroom and, although only one man was left inside, I could hear him getting up and walking towards my cupboard. He stood right outside and started tapping on the door. He then got out a sharp knife – it could have been a bayonet – and started levering the door open. On the inside I was holding on to the key in the lock and pulling the door towards me. I could hear him grunting. I thought I smelt his bad breath. Just when he might have been successful, I heard the main door into the room being opened and the German on the other side gave up. I heard a few words and then both of them sat down on the floor. One of them had a wife in East Prussia and the other one was unmarried. As far as I could understand, they both talked about the women with whom they had slept – or hoped to sleep.

I woke up in the early morning of the thirteenth day of my voluntary confinement. It was 5 October, 1944. My water was nearly at an end and the cramp in my muscles hurt acutely most of the time. Patience and caution were now finished. I would have to make an attempt to escape that evening.

The room outside was still full of Germans, but, provided no new prisoners came in, there would be a good chance of the whole guard leaving the room empty for half an hour or so at sunset. On the previous evening they had all cleared out of the room and hung over the garden wall adjoining the main road outside my window to watch the passers-by in the twilight. I suppose it is a world-wide habit to come out of houses on a warm evening for a breather before going back inside for the night.

I slowly shifted my weight from one leg to the other, and leaned alternately on my right shoulder and then on my left. By now, shifting my position had become almost automatic. No longer did it require any thought or even consciousness. My mouth was as dry as a bone but I had already had both my dawn and midday mouthfuls. My evening one was not due for another two hours. Tonight I would take three mouthfuls of water. What bliss!

Darkness should come about 7.30 or 8 pm and I hoped the room would clear by about 7 pm. My plan was to hide up in the bushes near the house for an hour until it was really dark. I would then slip away round the back through the garden and the orchard beyond.

The minutes slowly crept by while I waited for the sounds of Germans leaving the room outside. Occasionally one of them would go out or come in. I could hear two of them snoring. At about 6 o'clock I pulled on my boots and my smock and gathered together all my equipment. Dressing noiselessly in that cupboard was a work of art. It was three-quarters of an hour before I was ready. I had heard two of them stumble out of the room, but I was fairly certain there were one or two more. Sure enough, by their grunts and the bumping of boots being pulled on, I heard two more get up and go out talking about a *fraulein*.

The time had come. Cautiously I unlocked my door and opened it an inch or two to have a quick look round. Damn. Not six feet away was a solitary German soldier sleeping with his hands crossed over his tummy and his mouth wide open. As I had to walk across the floor and open the big windows, I decided to give him another half-hour.

Luckily a few soldiers came into the house with a couple of girls, all talking at the top of their voices. I heard them go upstairs and enter the room directly over my head. There was soon a merry party going on with songs, a gramophone and an occasional girlish giggle or scream. I was in luck. They were certainly not expecting any more prisoners tonight. If the noise increased as the wine flowed, I should have no worries about covering up squeaks as I opened the window.

The noise upstairs woke up my sleeping soldier after about twenty minutes. Glory be, he got up and walked out. This was my chance and, taking a couple of mouthfuls of water, I gently pushed my door open. This time the room was empty. Closing the cupboard door after me, I walked over to the window and could see the guards lining the garden fence on the main road about twenty yards away. I had to get the window open and then wait for a lorry or tank to go by before slipping out into the shurbs growing under the sill. The Germans would be most unlikely to look back towards the house when anything interesting was passing by.

I was in luck and no sooner had I opened the window when a large truck went clattering along the main road. This was my cue. Quickly I was out of the window and into the shrubbery. My luck held good on the thirteenth day in that Dutch cupboard.

Quickly I crawled into the bushes where it was thickest at the corner of the house and concealed myself under some dead leaves. A squadron of tanks then rumbled by on the main road and kept the attention of my guards. I could see about eight or ten of them idly leaning against the garden wall a few yards away. After the tanks had passed I could hear them chatting about the war and their sweethearts at home. From the window above came occasional strains of music which drowned any noise I would make and was sweet to my ears. Even better, the semi-delighted, semi-frightened squeals from the not-too-particular girls.

* 16 *

DUTCH COURAGE

Oh so gradually it became dark. One by one the Germans left the fence and went back inside the house. Forty-five minutes later it was black enough to get going. Dodging round the corner of the house, I crept round to the back and over a fence into an adjoining garden. The bottom part was all vegetables and soon I was munching a beetroot, after roughly cleaning one off on my trousers. The juicy sweetness of the raw beetroot tasted all right, although I do not suppose it did my stomach much good. From the garden I climbed over another fence into an orchard and was soon feasting on some excellent apples. I would not have bothered about the beetroot if I had known about the orchard. I could feel renewed strength and hope coming back as I stretched my arms and legs. My legs were incredibly weak but I was now full of confidence. My brain was again functioning more or less normally. It was 6 October and my last proper meal was nineteen days ago at breakfast before we took off. I was very very hungry.

My plan was to contact a friendly Dutch family who might give me some civilian clothes. Once I had these, I thought, I should not find it too difficult to move about and find a way back to our lines. There was no reason why I should not try the houses nearby. If the Germans did suspect that the cupboard had housed an escaper, which was unlikely, then they would never guess that he had gone into hiding within a few hundred yards of where he had been held in prison. The more I moved around with a fourteen-day beard on my chin, the more likely I was to be discovered.

Stuffing a few apples into my pockets, I moved down to the bottom of the orchard where it joined on to some more gardens at the back of a row of houses. I could see no reason why I should not tap on the first door I came to, telling them who I was and asking for shelter.

I tiptoed past a coal-shed and knocked gently on the door of a house with its ground-floor windows still lit up, but screened with black-out curtains. Someone came at last and I heard a voice asking who was there in Dutch. In halting German, I stammered out, 'I am a British parachutist. Please give me food and shelter.'

'Go away quickly,' he replied in equally bad German. 'My house is full. We have no food. Very dangerous to have you here.'

The whole conversation took place through the locked door. He did not wait for me to answer and I heard him stomping off to another room.

I walked away feeling rather depressed, as I had fondly imagined that most of the Dutch were pro-British or at least anti-Nazi. Although at this stage of the war the majority were wholeheartedly in favour of getting rid of the Germans, there was a minority who neither liked us nor did they welcome the trouble we had brought to the area. What little contact they had had with the Germans had been on a satisfactory basis; what they did not want was to have their way of life upset. I was to hear later that some of this minority were active German sympathizers and I was lucky that I did not bump into any of them that night.

Fortunately England has never been invaded and then occupied. I am personally convinced that in similar circumstances the British people would certainly be no better and, more than likely, the proportion of active sympathizers with the enemy might have been a great deal higher. Skilful propaganda can soon persuade many people that wrong is right.

There were relatively few who were prepared to take the risk of harbouring a British soldier. They knew the consequences too well if they were caught. They would be shot and their families put in concentration camps. All their property would be sold or burnt down as a warning to the neighbourhood. This increased my respect for those Dutch men and women whom I met later, who were prepared to take any risk which would help to win the war. They made me feel quite humble in their company. Naturally I thanked them but how can one thank someone properly who might be shot the next day for giving you assistance?

Disconsolately I walked back a few paces and decided to rest in a small shed and think out what to do next. I would cross the road and try a house on the other side. Round the back I might find a more friendly family.

A German army truck swept by full of troops and as soon as it was out of sight I walked quickly across the road and took a path between two houses. Once more I tapped on a door but to no avail. The time was now about 11 pm and all were in bed.

I tried three more houses and still got no reply. Rather to my surprise there were saucers full of scraps left outside each back door. I was so hungry that I went from door to door wolfing the scraps which tasted excellent. After quite a reasonable if scrappy meal, I decided to lie up in one of the sheds at the back and wait there till morning. I chose the one which had the biggest plate of scraps – they surely must be charitable people – and soon nestled down in an old potting shed full of seed trays and broken furniture. I slept well and woke at dawn to watch for any sign of the inhabitants so that

I could make myself known to them as early as possible. Gradually I heard the house wake up; the alarm clock go off, sleepy yawns come from an open window and I saw a man stretching and looking up at the morning sky. Half an hour went by and the back door opened. I could look straight into the kitchen where a girl of about twenty was cooking on a wood stove. The man then came downstairs to sweep out the kitchen and clean his shoes. He next shaved, put on his jacket and came towards my hiding place to fetch some firewood.

As he came through the door I said 'Good morning' in German. To give him his due, he did not appear to be in the least taken aback. Speaking German in whispers, I told him my story and asked him if he could help. He understood me quite easily but was a bit doubtful. He would do his best but there were a lot of children nearby who might stumble on me whilst playing and give me away. He certainly could not hide me in his house, but he would try and find a place where I could go that night. His wife would produce some food. I was overjoyed and thanked him with a terrific handshake. He turned away with a wink to me and beckoned to his wife to come over.

At first she would not budge, but after some hesitation she came over, looking rather cross. She suddenly saw me standing well back from the door and she let out a scream, clutching her husband for protection and looking thoroughly frightened. I do not suppose I was a very edifying sight, with my ginger beard, filthy camouflage airborne smock and bedraggled battledress trousers. This was the first time, and I hope the last, that a woman has screamed with terror when she saw me. Gradually she calmed down and was most sympathetic. Back she went to prepare a meal, although she still had rather a scared look in her eyes.

In the meantime I had a look round the hut to find a possible hiding place in case any children came near or the Germans made a search. There were some horizontal wooden beams under the roof with a few planks across them to hold up some bales of straw. At first sight this looked the best hiding place, but its big disadvantage was that it was also easily the most obvious. Anybody coming into that hut would immediately be attracted by the pile of straw up in the roof. I therefore decided to hide under a pile of loosely stacked seed boxes and apple trays that littered the floor. By arranging these in the manner of a tunnel, I crawled in underneath and pulled some old sacks over the top. Even if somebody had peered through the clutter of trays, he would only see a pile of sacks at the bottom.

Hiding, always hiding! But I could not afford to walk about in daylight, unwashed, unshaven and dressed as I was. Before I had time to make myself really comfortable, the good lady of the house brought out an enormous plate of boiled potatoes over which she had poured a savoury gravy. It smelt like a banquet for kings. I had soon swallowed this down together with about a pint of ersatz coffee. This made me feel as though I had not slept for weeks.

I woke up to the clink and thud of heavy military boots tramping in the yard outside and the sound of shouting German voices. They were accusing the Dutch family of sheltering a British officer. In halting German, I heard my host flatly denying these accusations. The back door banged open and I could hear someone going upstairs, emptying the drawers on to the floor and opening all the cupboards. I was worried, but principally for my kind Dutch family. I pulled the sacks even closer over my hiding place and waited for the Germans to visit the shed.

I heard them crashing downstairs, out into the yard and straight towards my shed. I could hear someone breathing heavily as he paused just inside the doorway to allow his eyes to get used to the gloom. I also heard exclamations from my good Dutch host swearing that there was absolutely nothing in the shed. As I had suspected, the first place he looked at was the straw up in the rafters. Muttering oaths, the German climbed up a ladder and pulled away at the straw bales which came crashing down on the seed trays under which I was hiding. As soon as he had satisfied himself that there was nobody there, he did not bother to look anywhere else. They went on to look over the house next door. I suspect that my attempts to get help earlier on the night before, or idle chatter in front of children, may have given the Germans the clue that I was hiding in the area. Once again my luck was in.

About 4 o'clock the Dutchman came back looking like death. His voice shook with agitation and he told me I would have to leave straightaway. I thanked him from the bottom of my heart for what he had done so far, but I thought it might be dangerous for him if I walked away from his house dressed as I was. I would wait until it was dark. Could he find someone who could take me in?

The poor man was in a complete dither and nearly incapable of coherent thought. I told him I would soon be on my way but I would like some idea of where to try next.

Evening came and he returned with an aluminium canteen full of sandwiches and a water bottle full of milk. He was obviously longing for my departure, but felt guilty at turning me away and very generously gave me all the food he could spare. When it was quite dark he led me outside and pointed out the railway line for me to follow for about a mile. 'You will see a large white farm in open country on the left-hand side. I think the owners will shelter you for a short time.' Thanking him profusely for his kindness, I was soon on my way, walking down the cinder path alongside the track. It was pitch dark and my host told me that there were no German patrols on the railway.

I soon recognized the farmhouse and found the back door on which I tapp-

4 'I was first on two of the days but overall I came seventh" (p.145). World Gliding Championships, Leszno, Poland, June, 1958.

5 The author in 1944 when second-in-command of 1st Airborne Divisional Signals.

ed an urgent Victory V tap. The door opened a crack and in a whisper I told the farmer who I was. He replied that German patrols were all round his house. He certainly could not help me and to my amazement slammed the door in my face.

I walked away and half a mile further on I tried another house, only to get the same treatment. By 11.30 pm I had walked two or three miles and tried two more houses with no success. I was very tired and disheartened. I wondered what on earth I should do if I was unable to find shelter before daybreak.

Just then a church clock chimed eleven. What about the vicar? The church was across some fields surrounded by trees. A large rectangular building was next to the church. This might be the vicarage. A light shone under the door on which I tapped. After a lot of scurrying of feet on the far side, the door opened. A young priest dressed in a long black cassock was standing holding a hurricane lamp in one hand, and behind him were about a dozen men, women and children. Who could this be, knocking so gently and after curfew hours?

I quickly told him my story. He too could only speak German and he told me that although I could not stay in the house he might be able to help me. This was a Roman Catholic School which had been partly requisitioned to house German troops serving a newly sited flak gun in the trees nearby. The remainder of the house was full of evacuees from Arnhem and was a most unsuitable choice for a hiding place. My luck was in again. If I had tapped at the wrong door it would have been opened by a German and not the priest.

I was the centre of attraction, surrounded by a dozen evacuees of all ages, with a couple of young priests hovering in the background. Someone brought a large cup of milk which was lovely. There then followed a long debate in Dutch about where I should go. One of the priests then told me that he was sending for the school's private policeman who lived a few hundred yards away.

Twenty minutes later a real old character walked in. He looked more like a gamekeeper than a policeman. He was dressed in a black corduroy jacket and breeches with black leather leggings and boots. His hat was a green 'pork pie' and his face was thin and lined but he looked lively and had a twinkle of amusement in his eyes. Although he could only speak Dutch, he was obviously enjoying himself immensely. I imagine his life must have been rather dull up till now. Secretly he may have longed to take a more active part in the war. This was his chance to show that he was a true patriot.

He led me out of the school doorway and down an avenue of trees to his cottage at the end of the road. The time was about midnight and his wife was waiting up for his return. A genial, fat old soul, she produced some bread and jam which I tucked away with no difficulty. A shaded lamp stood on a shelf on one side of the room, in the middle of which was a heavy pine table with a scrubbed top. Shining copper cooking pots hung over the stove, while round the walls there were all sorts of bric-à-brac on shelves and brackets.

The old lady, in nightgown and curling papers, kept smiling, while her husband tried to tell me his life history in Dutch. I nodded and shook my head as he spoke but without much comprehension as I sat munching the bread, which was washed down with locally made 'tea' made from dried apple and blackberry leaves. He could see for himself how filthy I was, with unwashed hands, torn trousers, and a fourteen-day growth of beard on my face. I must have looked dreadful. After some sign language I was able to wash and gave myself a shave, using my host's old cut-throat razor. He next led me upstairs to the attic and took away all my uniform. He would get me some civilian clothes in the morning. One end of the attic had been converted into a bedroom and I was soon fast asleep between clean white sheets. What fantastic luxury!

The sun was streaming into the room in the morning when I woke up. Outside my window I could see an apple tree laden down with enormous red apples. My watch told me it was twelve o'clock, so I must have slept continuously for about twelve hours. I lay back luxuriously in bed and wondered what would happen next. I did not feel inclined to do anything. Until now I had not realized quite how weak I was. Nervous energy and excitement had kept me going, but now inner exhaustion had caught up. All I wanted to do was to lie back and breathe in fresh air and thank God that I was not a prisoner.

The familiar whine of a shell passing overhead, followed by an explosion a field or two away, brought me to my senses. War was being fought nearby. I must now do something about getting back across the lines. I climbed out of bed and tottered stiffly across to the window. Everything looked so peaceful. A mirror over the washstand gave me a shock. I could hardly believe I was looking at myself. A hollow-eyed, emaciated face gazed back at me and was almost corpselike in appearance. I could stand it no longer so went back to the window to look out across the beautiful green fields over which I had trudged the night before. The shell I had heard go over had landed among some cows and I could see a farmer hurrying out to see what damage had been done. Milk was so short in this dairyland of all Europe that only small children had a ration. The Germans had taken the majority of the dairy herds away to Germany, so the loss of one cow was felt by the whole community.

There was a gentle knock on the door and in came the old man with a large soup plate piled high with savoury macaroni and mashed potatoes. A separate plate had a large slice of apple pie. I blessed them both and soon tucked it all away. He told me in a sign language what he had been doing and also that he had not told the children that I was staying with him. He thought they would be bound to give the show away. I agreed and thanked him once again.

I asked him about the war and if he knew how far the Allies had reached. He only had the vaguest ideas and this appeared to be quite common amongst Dutch civilians. No papers were published and their only source of news was their local radio station, the BBC and rumour. The latter produced some wonderful tales which included anything from additional bridgeheads across the Rhine to airborne landings near the Zuyder Zee. It was very clear that I would have to get up and find out for myself what was going on. Could he get me some clothes and the loan of a bicycle? He thought he could tomorrow but for today I would have to stay where I was. I was in no position to do anything else, dressed only in my underclothes.

I started thinking about Evie. Poor girl, she was expecting our first child in January. She would probably be worried sick by hearing no news. I was to hear later that she had managed to arrange a short meeting with my Colonel in London.

'Do you know when Tony was last seen?'

'I am sorry to say that he was last seen going into a house in Arnhem, which was then attacked and set on fire by the Germans.'

'Well, I suppose he might have escaped at the back?'

'I don't think he did. But it is just possible that he is a prisoner of war, though you should not count on it.'

Next day I felt hot and feverish with my chest wheezing like a steam engine. I had clearly got bronchitis which must have been one result of nearly three weeks without food or exercise. For four days I felt very ill and could not eat at all. The poor old couple looked very worried. At last on the fifth day the fever left me and I began to feel much better, although my legs were weaker than ever. I decided I must get in touch with the Resistance movement and ask for some help to get back across the Rhine. Kind as the old people were I would have to move on.

With some reluctance my host agreed to go and find someone who could help. Everybody in Holland thought they knew who was in the Resistance and who was not. Very few really knew. I think the old man was rather proud of his 'Tommy'. When his best friends called at the house, he would lead them up to my room to show me off like a prize pig. When I reached safety I registered his name as someone who had given me help. After the war he received a certificate, well printed on vellum, to say how grateful the Allies were for his patriotism. When I revisited Arnhem, three years after the war, to thank him again, he had it hanging in an honoured place in his living room.

On the afternoon of the sixth day he came in to say he had arranged for me to go somewhere where I would be less likely to be discovered. His one idea was to hide me. My one idea was to get away and back to England.

I quickly dressed and went downstairs in the fading light to meet another man who had a spare bicycle. I was to follow him at about a hundred yards' distance to a new address. I took leave of the old pair and thanked them from the bottom of my heart for all the kindness they had shown me.

As we cycled slowly along the streets, it felt quite odd to be once more on the road. I was dressed in an old dingy pair of black trousers, a blue shirt and a battered hat to give me local atmosphere. My only concern was that Germans had an awkward habit of suddenly setting up a checkpoint to round up able-bodied men for work on field defences. They were building quite extensive works along the line of the Ijssel River, which joined the Rhine just upstream from Arnhem. We saw a lot of Germans walking or marching about, but none of them took any notice. In due course we arrived at the door of a suburban semi-detached villa in the side streets of Velp. Inside I was met by my new host and hostess, Mr and Mrs Huisman and their two children aged eight and five. What an incredible family! They were already sheltering two refugees. One was a Dutchman who had escaped from a concentration camp and who had to lie low. The other was a Polish-German Jew whose antecedents made him a marked man.

My host was the local headmaster from the primary school. A more jovial, God-fearing and brave man I have never met. His wife was equally wonderful. In a tiny two-bedroomed house they squeezed seven people and cooked for them, using many gifts of food from friends. She even managed to keep the house looking extremely clean. Potatoes were the big filler-up at meals. We refugees used to peel them and wash up. Huge soup bowls full of mashed potatoes with a little meat gravy were helped down with bread covered with a smearing of butter and sugar sprinkled on top.

There was no electricity. It had been cut off the day after we had landed. All the cooking had to be done on a small wood stove in the dining room. We also helped by chopping up wood at the back of the house. Only one of us could do this at a time because there were German sympathizers living in the house behind. At this stage of the war many of these people kept their heads down. The end was in sight and they did not want to become marked men or women.

The Huismans were a religious family. A grace was said before all meals, while we dutifully stood with bowed heads behind each chair, our steaming potatoes doled out in front of us. After the evening meal our host read a chapter from the Bible in Dutch. On Sundays, hymns were sung to Mr Huisman's accompaniment on a harmonium he had in the living room. Many of the Dutch families I met followed similar routines.

They were all members of the Dutch Reform Church which I believe to be strictly Calvinistic in its outlook and preachings.

A hideout had been dug under the floor of the front room. It was entered through a hatch formed from floorboards which would be difficult to notice except during a thorough inspection. At first we all slept in it, but I found it so dank and stuffy that I slept on the floor of the living room just above.

Pete was my real contact with the outside world. I believe he was a proper member of the Resistance, although this was a question which was never asked. He had light red hair and an open smiling face. He did not mind what he did and no job would be too much trouble. He came in on the evening of the first day, with my host on one arm and on the other a big basket full of eggs, butter and potatoes for the household. He told me that Tony Hibbert had got away. This was great news. Apparently he was using a telephone which communicated direct to Nijmegen, fifteen miles inside the British lines. I heard later that the line worked over the Power Company's overhead cables and was never discovered by the Germans.

Planning for our escape across the Rhine was divided into three parts. First, as many British troops as possible who were known to be living in the area would be located and contacted. Then they would have to be concentrated in the woods near the river at the right time and without the Germans realizing what was going on. Then the whole party would have to move down to the river bank and be taken across by boats which would also have to be laid on.

In the meantime everybody was asked to lie low and not excite too much attention because it would take at least fourteen days to organize the whole escape. More than a hundred and twenty British officers and men were scattered over as many square miles all round Arnhem. The majority had evaded capture and had been living during the previous weeks in the woods or thanks to the hospitality of our good Dutch friends. The Resistance had accepted the task of concentrating all of us together. In the meantime Tony Hibbert and Digby Tatham Warter would make detailed reconnaissances in the Ede area to find a suitable concentration point near the river and a route down to it between the German positions. I sent word to them asking if they wanted any assistance. The reply came back saying that the fewer in the area the better so it would be preferable if I stayed where I was for the time being. All I had to do was to sit, wait and wonder how the plan was getting on. Very boring!

Pete also told me that Tony Hibbert had managed to escape by jumping off the truck which was taking them to permanent prison camps in Germany. The guards lost their heads and turned their Schmeissers (similar to sten guns) on to the rest of the lorry, killing two and wounding three more. Tony had jumped off in the middle of a Dutch town and had soon shaken off the two Germans who followed him.

At that moment a refugee Dutchman came running in to say that a German patrol was approaching, so we had better get down into our hideout in case they came in. Quickly we clambered down. One of the children shut the trap door on top and smoothed over the carpet. All we could hear was our own heavy breathing and an occasional footstep in the room above. The atmosphere was tense and we wondered whether we would be discovered.

Twenty minutes later someone came over to our trap and gave the signal to open up. The patrol had passed and we could all have supper. Mrs Huisman had the frying pan out and was soon mixing the batter for pancakes. This was a rare delicacy in 1944 Holland, the children all becoming wildly excited with anticipation for the meal to come. The *pannacuchen* were lovely, the first rich food I had tasted in Holland. Soon the whole house was full of the deep aroma of frying batter. I shall never forget that glorious smell. A continuous diet of potatoes and bread, sufficient though they may be, gradually produces an inner craving for something richer and more full of flavour. The *pannacuchen* were just what was wanted.

I was getting so much out of touch with news of the outside world that I asked if anybody had a radio that still worked. The Germans had cut the power off to all parts of the town except in the street where their own Headquarters was located. My host took me round to a house near the German HQ, where a radio was tuned in to the BBC. It was wonderful to hear the calm voice of the announcer giving out the news. There were a lot of Germans coming and going to their HQ, of course, but they took no notice. I often went round in the evening to keep up to date. On one evening I met a local Baroness who was also listening to the radio together with her pretty teenage daughter. Later on I discovered her name to be Baroness Ella van Heemstra and her daughter was to become the film star Audrey Hepburn.

'You look so thin,' the Baroness said. 'Do you like champagne? I have a few bottles left in my cellar.' She spoke in English and my face lit up with astonishment.

'My word, I do,' I replied. 'But surely you should keep it for the day you are liberated?'

'Not at all. You look as though you could do with some right now. I will send a bottle round to the Huismans.' I thanked her and was delighted to get a bottle of the best Krug champagne the next day. She was even more gratified when I sent a note of thanks which showed that I was aware that Krug was among the best of all champagnes.

The following night was to be the last night we would be staying with the Huismans. Quite a party developed, also helped by bottles of Arak gin brought in by some friends. We all became exceedingly merry, with the

Dutch singing patriotic songs in quick succession at the tops of their voices. Thoughts of war and Germans disappeared into the background. Here at least was a little piece of Holland trying to forget its worries and anxieties.

* 17 *

RHINE CROSSING

We none of us heard it at first. Someone had been knocking on the door and had ended up with an almighty bang. This took away our smiles and the singing like magic. Was this the *Moffen*? We all looked at each other in alarm. *Moffen* was the Dutch equivalent of our 'Hun'. Who was it who was knocking so urgently?

My host spoke through the door to the person outside and, on identification, opened the door. It turned out that we had woken him up in his house about a hundred yards away. He was worried that the Germans billeted with him would also wake up. This brought our party to an abrupt stop. We all had to be up early in the morning.

By dawn we were all dressed and ready to start on the next lap. We thanked the Huisman family for their fantastic hospitality in a house within walking distance of large numbers of *Moffen*. Quite soon a Red Cross lorry, painted white with red crosses on the sides, drew up outside. It was powered by charcoal gas and already had six civilians seated in the back. They showed no surprise as we climbed in and lay on the floor under some sacks in case a German checkpoint should ask for passes.

We bumped and swayed through the streets of Arnhem and on down the main road to Ede. From my place on the floor I could see the second floors of houses as they sped by. This was soon replaced by the sky and trees overhanging the road. I began to feel an elation that I had not had for weeks. We were really on the move again but surely not yet out of the wood. I had a feeling of overwhelming gratitude for the good Dutch people who had sheltered us and were now getting us on our way. For their part they may have welcomed the opportunity to do something for their country, but I was especially grateful for all that they had done.

Through a crack in the side of the lorry I could see burnt-out German trucks which had been caught out by RAF Typhoons with their rockets. Every German in the area had one eye on the sky and the other on the road. Every military car or lorry had an air warning sentry sitting on the front mudguard looking backwards and upwards. Even then the RAF occasionally surprised German convoys on the road before the sentries could shout warnings. Awful bloody havoc and ruin would then result.

We were now moving along the road between Arnhem and Ede. The forest was nearly continuous on either side except for an occasional white-fronted house set back in the trees. The lorry suddenly stopped without warning and the passenger sitting next to the driver jumped out and beckoned us to follow. There was nobody in sight. We were quickly led down a narrow path leading into the forest, with the noise of the Red Cross lorry getting fainter as it drove on towards Ede.

After twenty minutes we came out into a small clearing with a tiny woodman's hut in the middle surrounded by about thirty British soldiers dressed in a mixture of uniforms. They were all busying themselves in small groups. Some were sorting out equipment, while others were boiling up hot water. Many more were exchanging tales of what they had been doing. Another twenty men were crammed inside the hut. As I opened the door a high old stench of stale tobacco smoke and unwashed bodies hit me.

Tony Hibbert suddenly saw me and let out a cheer which was taken up all round. I suppose the others must have thought that our party were all Dutch. My old battered felt hat, black corduroy jacket, blue shirt and patched black trousers gave me a nicely local look. The others with me were not much different.

The news was good. There were plans for us all to move down to the river that night. Assault boats had been laid on to get us across and a Bofors gun would fire bursts over the chosen point at midnight. With any luck there should be a total of about 120 men, including a variety of fighting troops, medical personnel, RAF and American pilots and about ten young Dutchmen who wanted to join the Free Dutch Forces.* We had to carry out a difficult night move through the enemy lines and it was essential that there should be as much order and control as possible.

My shoes were a disaster. I had left my boots with my policeman rescuer at Velp and the shoes he had given me in exchange were horribly uncomfortable with pointed toes and paper-thin soles. Luckily Pat Glover, the quartermaster, was in charge of the hut and he quickly fixed me up with a pair of boots he had scrounged off a dead soldier. Pat had foreseen our requirements and had been collecting weapons, boots and smocks from British dead for the last few days. He also gave me a smock to cover my coat and a sten gun. A number of us were given small groups of men to look after, so that if we did bump into the enemy, we could at least give some account of ourselves.

Our hut was one of two collection points, the other being much nearer to the river crossing. We were still ten miles from the river, whilst the other

* *Brigadier Lathbury's Diary*. p 77 Published by Airborne Museum Oosterbeek.

one was only about three miles away. The first task was to concentrate everybody at the nearer one. We would move there by lorry at nightfall. From there we would be guided down to the crossing point. Digby Tatham Warter had carried out a brilliant reconnaissance the night before. He had managed to find a route that led down to the river and was between German troop positions.

By four o'clock we were ready and the whole area scavenged for incriminating evidence. The Dutch were laying on the lorries. We had to be hidden in the undergrowth fifty yards from the edge of the main road by ten minutes to six. Slowly the minutes dragged by. Everything was fine except for the large size of our ragtail group. However quiet each one might try to be, 120 men moving through the woods at night would sound like an army.

I was half asleep when a low whistle woke me. We moved up to the roadside and at 6 sharp three old covered lorries rattled down the road drawing up in front of us with a squeal of brakes. The fifty of us piled in quickly and lay on the floor, while the Dutch drivers covered us with sacks. We were meant to look like lorries full of potatoes which the Dutch were busy harvesting at the time. If a German checkpoint should stop us, which we were told would be most unlikely, the Dutch would try and bluff it out. If that failed we would have to jump out and overpower the post. I remember thinking that this would mean the end of our escape.

We were soon bumping on our way. After twenty minutes we passed through Ede, which also housed the HQ of the Division manning the sector of the river where we were due to cross. The night was closing in as we zig-zagged through two checkpoints. The Germans waved us through without stopping. Perhaps they thought we really were potato lorries; or maybe we were the rations going up to the regiments on the river line.

After another twenty minutes the lorries drew up at the side of the road and we all jumped out. It was now nearly dark as we filed down a narrow footpath. We stumbled over tree trunks and brambles which led to an open area after about ten minutes. Brigadier Gerald Lathbury and Digby were there and dozens of others. The whole party was now 120 strong.

Everybody was cheerful, although we all knew that the most difficult part of the operation was still ahead. We would wait till the moon rose at 9 pm before we started. This would give us four hours to cover the three miles to the crossing point near the village of Renkum, which we were due to reach at 1 am. To cover our move through the German lines, our artillery was to carry out harassing fire on German positions on the flanks and to our rear.* The operation to get us across the river was being organized

* *Brigadier Lathbury's Diary*, p. 77. Published by Airborne Museum, Ooosterbeek.

by 101 American Airborne Division, whose sector it was, but making use of storm boats operated by 43rd Infantry Division sappers. The telephone line from Ede to the British Corps in Nijmegen must have been working overtime to lay all this on.

At 9 pm we started on our way through the forest. Where possible we went in pairs to reduce the length of the column, but sometimes the path was so narrow that we had to go in single file. All we asked each man to do was to keep in sight of the one in front and to be as quiet as possible. The Dutch provided guides for the first two miles or so. As this was the densest and darkest part of the forest, their help was invaluable.

Sometimes the trees closed in over us like a tunnel. The moonlight was completely shut off except for an occasional shaft of light which came through the branches. The only noise in the forest arose from wild animals; rabbits and an occasional deer could be heard running off as the sound of our approach broadcast a warning. The first time we heard a deer, everybody stopped and listened. We thought we had bumped a German patrol.

By 11 pm we had reached the edge of the forest. Our route then crossed a tarmac road and about a mile of open fields before we reached the edge of the river. We wrung the hands of our brave Dutch guides. This was as far as they were taking us.

Our boots made a horrid clatter as we crossed the road but our visibility was immensely improved by the moon shining through clouds and also some light from a few burning buildings in Renkum. We were now passing through the German forward defences and our success would depend on how skilfully we managed to avoid their posts which were spaced about half a mile apart. We knew that German patrols occasionally moved along the river bank connecting up their positions and we might have to fight for it with our motley army.

We could hear our own artillery doing their stuff. Ear-splitting explosions nearby, followed by the tearing noise of the shells, cut into the still night air. That sounded good. I hoped it would be effective.

A four-foot drainage ditch ran along our route. We were able to use it as cover. We bent ourselves double and half-crawled, half-walked along its length. After an hour we had covered about half a mile and were about level with the German positions. We had a small patrol out front covering our advance. Frequent halts were made whilst the patrol had a good look and listen for any opposition. Half a mile further on we could see the line of the river. The time was midnight and right on cue a burst of Bofors tracer came over and showed us that we were heading exactly right. We had one hour left to get to the crossing point.

More careful crawling, using the best cover we could find, either from hedges or drainage ditches, brought us to a track, where we could see the

Germans had dug slit-trenches in the bank. Digby passed word that the Germans had had a standing patrol in this area the night before, so we should be as quiet and alert as possible. After a quarter of an hour in which we all crawled up as close as possible, there appeared to be no Germans in the position. We quickly crossed the track and jumped down the bank on the far side. The river was now only two or three hundred yards away as we followed the line of a main drainage ditch down to its bank.

Nothing stirred on the river save the gurgle of flowing water and a subdued swish from a nearby weir. A few marsh birds occasionally let out their plaintive cries. This was the no-man's-land between the Germans and the Allies.

We could now see the other side through a layer of swirling mist that clung to the surface of the river. No sign of life or movement could be seen anywhere. I heard some of the men beginning to talk quite loudly and I hissed at them to stop. At the same time a Captain Wainwright, in charge of our own leading patrol, came back to see Gerald Lathbury*. He had seen a number of lights flashing from German positions at no great distance. He thought that we had been located and we might be attacked. We should be ready for anything.

We moved on along the bank to be nearer our crossing point. Several things then happened at once. German automatic fire sounded as though it was only fifty yards away; our Bofors opened up with another long stream of tracer and our leading patrol also returned the fire. We all went flat on our tummies with the shattering noise still ringing in our ears. I wormed my way forward to see what was going on. Luckily nobody had been hit. We could hear sounds of a German reconnaissance patrol withdrawing hurriedly back across the fields. They must have been scared stiff when they realized how many we were, although I doubt if our minor tactics would have coped if a proper battle had taken place.

We reached the chosen point and gave the prearranged light signal. Five, ten, fifteen minutes went by and nothing happened, except for the occasional weird, tearing screech overhead of our own artillery doing their stuff. My imagination conjured up a hundred and one things that might have gone wrong, but at last the rhythmical splash of paddles could be heard. A moment later three or four assault boats nosed upstream towards us through the mist. The swift current in the middle of the river had carried them downstream as they came across. A cheerful confident American voice was hailing us in the darkness from the assault boats being paddled by 43rd Division sappers.

Three trips were needed to get us all across. I was in the last lot and we

* Brigadier Lathbury's Diary P. 78.

helped carry the boats to a farm near the river. This was my fourth Rhine crossing in six weeks. I had flown over it, I had swum it, I had been driven over as a prisoner and now I was carried across in a boat. I preferred the last method, although I did not regret the first.

Everybody was now laughing and talking about what they would do when we arrived back in England. In a carefree manner we piled aboard some waiting transport which was not really adequate for our large party. Tony Hibbert and I jumped on to a jeep which already had five others in it plus the driver. Tony decided to sit on the bonnet in front. Off we drove at a brisk twenty miles an hour without lights and went straight into the back of a lorry in front. Tony bore the full force of the crash on his legs, which were broken in two places. It was incredibly bad luck and we all felt very sorry for him. It was many months before he was able to leave hospital and sad to relate he was subsequently invalided from the Army.

At 3 am on 23 October we arrived at XXX Corps Casualty Clearing Station established in a school near Nijmegen and there we spent the rest of the night. Next day we were thoroughly questioned. I was able to pinpoint the German Divisional HQ in Arnhem and also pass on the names of all those good Dutchmen who had helped me in the previous two and a half weeks.

After another night in the CCS we were driven twenty miles to an airfield where six American C 47s waited to fly us back to England.

At 2 pm we landed at the same Lincolnshire airfield from which I had taken off some six weeks previously. Near the control tower I could see a few cars waiting and I spotted one from my unit.

'Sergeant-Major sent me, Sir.'

'Did you know I was coming?'

'Well, not exactly, Sir. We heard that a party had got back across the Rhine. The Sergeant-Major said you was a dead snip to be with it. I think he had a bet, you see, Sir.'

★ ★ ★

The first thing I did was to ring up Evie and tell her I was back. She was not at all surprised, although she had been worried sick after her meeting with Tom Stevenson. Perhaps the worst hell and greatest heroism of Arnhem was not that of the men who fought there, but of the women who waited for news. In my case, this had been spun out for six weeks.

Two nights ago she had woken up in the middle of the night when I had crossed the Rhine and she knew then that I was safe. 'Was I wounded?' she asked.

'Not a scratch, darling, only about twenty-five pounds underweight.'

The known or suspected opposition which included tanks and the 'remnants' of a panzer division located in forests and built-up areas to the west of Arnhem made sure that the operation would be a failure. The divided drop made certain of it. We were fortunate to hold the bridge as long as we did.

Being wise after the event, 1st Parachute Brigade complete might have managed to get through to the bridge, if 9th Panzer Division had not been galvanized into speedy action by Field-Marshal Model watching from his HQ at Oosterbeek. This reinforcement should have allowed the bridge to be held until the arrival of XXX Corps. Unfortunately the rest of the Division would still have been cut off in the woods to the west of the town. Disaster would not have been far away.

The whole Division should have been dropped south of the bridge and regardless of flight casualties from supposed flak. Only in this way could some compensation be made for a divided drop. Undoubtedly a number of aircraft and gliders would have been shot down and perhaps as many as 10% of gliders would have overrun their fields and become stuck in ditches. The open fields did not provide much cover except along the dykes or in the embankments and life would not have been comfortable for the first few hours on the first day. But our objective would have been held and we would have been astride the line of advance of XXX Corps. Our casualties, including air casualties and during air resupply, would have been a fraction of what took place.

Better still, if Eisenhower had backed the major single thrust we might have won the war before Christmas and perhaps saved half a million allied casualties. There is little doubt, however, that Ike would not have been elected President a few years later.

★ ★ ★

'Since the war, von Rundstedt and other German generals who can speak with authority (Student, Westphal, Blumentritt and Speidel) have all declared that a concentrated thrust from Belgium in September must have succeeded. These generals are all agreed that if even fifteen divisions had driven on after the capture of Brussels and Liège, the Wehrmacht would have been powerless to stop them overrunning the Lower Rhineland and seizing the Ruhr before Christmas, 1944.'* Montgomery was once again shown to be right and Eisenhower wrong from a military and strategic point

* Chester Wilmot, *The Struggle for Europe*, p 539

of view. If Eisenhower could not tackle it for political reasons, then Montgomery was wrong to launch the operation with inadequate forces.

★ ★ ★

The powers that be then decided that I should become a staff officer after a six-month course at Camberley. Our first child was born on 13 January, 1945 — keeping up my tradition of a lucky 13.

* 18 *

TWO MONTHS TO LIVE

The great man droned on almost out of hearing. The scene was a corner room in the Westminster Hospital with a slight tang of disinfectant coming up from the chromium-plated glass-trayed trolleys being wheeled around by efficient-looking nurses. 'Yes,' he said, 'it will have to come ...,' and then his words were lost to me as he turned away towards four or five white-coated doctors looking on. I could see they were most interested in what he had to say. Perhaps they would incorporate his comments when their time came to discuss a patient.

1955 was my last year at the Staff College and, during a break just before Easter, I had the lump in my neck removed in Aldershot. Just before I returned home, the surgeon came back off his own leave to speak to me. I thought this a little strange, but he said, 'Oh, by the way, the pathologists disagree about that lump in your neck, and I would like you to go up to Millbank and see our expert there. I have arranged an appointment for tomorrow.'

This seemed swift work, although, looking back, I suppose he did not want me to have much time to think and had already arranged an appointment as soon as he had heard the pathologist's verdict. I learnt later that the Aldershot pathologist thought I had cancer and so did the one at Millbank, where I went the next day.

The specialist at Millbank was charming, but, after examining me, said that he too had fixed up an appointment that same afternoon to see Sir Stanford Cade, who, I heard later, was head of cancer at the Westminster. I was beginning to get a little alarmed as to where all this was leading, and so was my wife, who had driven up with me and was waiting in the car outside. She was expecting our third child about two months later.

Sir Stanford Cade felt around the scar on my neck and, after a grunt or two, went back into the consulting room and started giving his judgment, the first words of which were the only ones I could hear. I was then ushered out to sit on a bench and wait for my own doctor to come out and let me know what was happening.

'I am afraid you are very seriously ill and we will have to remove the rest of your thyroid gland.'

'That is a pity,' I said. 'Will that mean I will have to leave the Army?'

'I know of officers who have had this operation and are still serving, but I am afraid they are in a low medical category.'

'When do you want to do this?' I said. 'You see, I want to take part in a gliding competition over Easter and I have only tomorrow to get ready for it.'

'I don't want to alarm you, but I think you should give up the idea of doing any more gliding. We'd like to operate as soon as possible, which will be the Tuesday after Easter.'

'How long will all this take?' I asked. 'And what happens then?'

'As soon as you have recovered, I want you to take a three-month course of deep X-ray treatment to prevent the spread of any malignant tissue that may have been left behind. It means, of course, that you have cancer, but, provided we operate without delay, I think we can say that you have a sporting chance.'

'What does that mean?'

'A sporting chance of living several more years yet.'

'What happens if there is some delay in doing the operation?'

'Well, your chances then are not very good, but you should last two months at least, but I should get your own personal affairs in order now.' He went on, 'I suggest you get your will made and warn your Life Insurance Company, so that there is no delay in paying up. I am sorry to have to say this, but may I repeat that you are very ill indeed.'

'Well, I don't feel it, but you have certainly shaken me. Now I'd better go and break it to my wife outside.'

I felt a little weak and stunned after this shock treatment. Thoughts and fears surged alternately through my mind in a tangled maze of frustrated hopes and ambitions, and the realization that my wife and daughters were going to be the sufferers. Perhaps she could marry again. How would she fare on a miserable widow's pension? I must check up on how much she would get. The comedy of life was turning itself into a tragedy. Anyway for my poor wife still waiting outside.

'Sorry I've been so long. They kept me waiting a hell of a time.'

'All right, darling. What did they say?'

'They said it's quite serious and they want to remove the whole thyroid after Easter.'

My wife caught her breath. She came from a medical family and had guessed what the trouble was.

'Who's going to do the operation?'

'Oh, the specialist in Millbank. He seemed to know what he was doing.'

'We must go round and see father tomorrow. He may have different ideas.'

My father-in-law had very different ideas and said he rather doubted if an operation would be necessary, but that, if it was, it would be much better done by a personal friend of his at New End Hospital, Hampstead, who specialized in thyroids. An appointment was made to see Mr Piercy the next day. He had done more than 400 such operations. He also disagreed with the previous diagnosis and said that no further operation would be necessary but that some deep X-ray was desirable to kill off any malignant tissue left behind. This would start in about two weeks.

Unknown to me, my father-in-law had not been at all satisfied with the original diagnosis and had managed to extract the section of tissue from Millbank. He took this round to another friend who was Professor of Pathology at the Middlesex. A day later back came his report that the cancer was very slow-growing indeed and had probably been removed in my operation at Aldershot over two weeks before. There was no need for deep X-ray and I was practically in the clear.

I learnt one lesson. Always have a second opinion – however expert the first one may appear to be. I only hope that a lot of other people were not operated on for something they never had.

Soon after returning from the hospital in London, I rang up Tubby Butler to put him in the picture. I had not spoken to him before about my lump.

'I thought I ought to warn you that I don't think I will be able to come in tomorrow.' I went on, 'The ruddy quacks are telling me to get my affairs in order and at worst I have only two months to live.'

For the first time in his life, Tubby was unable to say anything. After a bit he said, 'I really don't believe a word of it. How do you feel yourself?'

'Never felt better, and I really mean it. I'm going up tomorrow to see my father-in-law, who I hope will also think differently.'

Somehow the saga of my lump seemed to impress Tubby Butler, who was returning to command the Parachute Brigade the following year. He told me that, with my background, he would like me to command a Parachute Battalion, but that first I must get a positive recommendation for promotion after commanding a company. After much thought I decided to go along with this advice and, at the end of my Staff College stint, I was posted to command a company in 1st Parachute Battalion. Almost immediately the battalion was sent to Cyprus to reinforce the British troops already there.

Fortunately, in December, 1955, we had just bought our first house, Copse End, in Church Crookham, with some of the royalties from *Return Ticket.* It was a nice detached house in half an acre of garden with four bedrooms and two bathrooms. We paid only £3500 for it, but at least it provided a roof over my family's heads, now increased to two daughters aged 10 and 11, one aged 6 months, and another one due in about 8 months.

Cyprus was in turmoil, with terrorist activities stirred up by EOKA, which was encouraged by a grossly inept government in Athens. Archbishop Makarios, dressed in his black surplice and circular black hat with its rim at the top, held both political and spiritual sway over the Greek Cypriots. He was, however, the only person with whom the Governor, Sir John Harding, or the Secretary of State, Alan Lennox-Boyd, could negotiate. After many months of fruitless argument, when the Archbishop refused to abandon terrorism or even denounce violence in pursuit of his political aims, he and three other clerics were deported to the Seychelles on 9 March.

In the meantime the Battalion did its stuff on operations and my Company with it. We searched all forms of dwellings, clean and filthy, occupied and unoccupied, ancient and modern. We marched many miles by day and by night to cordon off an area and search it for suspects. We used mules, donkeys and even dilapidated oriental buses. Police dogs helped us, as did mine detectors, crowbars or sheer persuasion, to find the culprits. We scaled the Troodos Mountains to locate terrorist caves after an approach march of some six miles at top speed in the middle of the night. We found the caves but the birds had flown. After all this the Company needed a rest and we had a few days off at Snake Island on the north coast near Kyrenia and it was an opportunity for the troops to relax and bathe if they wished.

The next part of our programme was to do some live firing on a barren moonlike area in the centre of the island. Together with Sergeants Winter and Carter, I set off in a Land-Rover to drive through Kyrenia on the way to Nicosia. The news about Makarios being shipped off to the Seychelles had been on the radio that morning and, as we turned a corner in Kyrenia, large numbers of Greek yobbos came out from behind the houses and started pelting the Land-Rover with stones or anything else they could get hold of. I told the driver to speed up and at that moment a stone came right through the windscreen and bashed me on the head. Blood was pouring out and, after applying field dressings, my NCOs drove straight to the hospital near Nicosia.

I never lost consciousness but I am sure I was concussed. Very fortunately Colonel John Watts was the senior surgeon at Nicosia and he had already established himself as one of the best in the Army. He extracted about two square inches of broken skull from the bloody mess and managed to sew me up. After coming to, I found I could hear perfectly well but I could only speak with the greatest difficulty. A second operation was necessary two days later to clear up the wound and, when I woke up, streams of visitors came in to see me. I remember getting into quite a sweat each time words would not come out. One of the doctors who saw me thought he should warn my wife by letter that she must expect a personality change. Luckily, after ten days and just before I was due to fly back to UK, I woke up one morning feeling perfectly all right. It really was a miracle.

My poor wife had now received the letter and expected to see a disabled goon unable to answer simple questions. I was soon able to put her mind at rest and we had a good laugh about the letter she had received. She, poor thing, had had considerable difficulty with our fourth child, due about 5 months later. She had to go to hospital soon after I came back to prevent it being aborted. In the event our fourth daughter arrived in June, three months early and weighing only just over two lbs. The baby had to stay in hospital for over three months until she could come home at five lbs. She turned out to be the cleverest academically of all our four daughters and, thirty-four years later, is a very fit young lady.

I was now officially downgraded medically and was warned that a further operation would be needed in about six months to fill up the hole in my head. I was advised not to do any more flying until this was done and I was upgraded. Whether I really would be upgraded again after this second operation depended on my progress, but it might be another year at least before I would be A1. I thought that all this delay was ridiculous, but no amount of argument could persuade the doctors otherwise.

I did not tell Evie about the ban on flying and took part in a week's gliding rally a month later over Whitsun, 1956, when a number of top pilots were competing. I managed to come second. My log book shows that I covered nearly 400 miles flying cross-country taking a total of about fifteen hours. I was well on my way to recovery and physically I never looked back.

Five years later a tiny lump in my neck did grow again. This time it was removed by Mr Piercy in London and I have had no trouble ever since.

* 19 *

GLIDING

I could do nothing about my low medical category or indeed the rather pathetic Army jobs that I was given which were thought suitable for those recovering from broken heads. The doctors advised taking up gardening or golf. They would have had a fit if they had realized that competitive gliding requires a high degree of concentration and continuous decision-making in the air, if good results were to be achieved.

The fascination of gliding is sometimes difficult to appreciate. As it gave me enormous satisfaction in my spare time for some thirty years after the Second World War, it deserves explanation. Like skiing, sailing boats or riding horses, there is no particular use in gliding except that pilots soon discover that the oceans of air all round us go up and down as well as blowing horizontally. The art is to make use of upcurrents by circling in the invisible air going up the fastest and to fly quickly through the air going down to reach the next 'up' or 'thermal'. Naturally strong thermals warrant faster speeds between them and allow pilots to discard minor upcurrents of air, except to slow down as they pass through to find the stronger stuff beyond. Even one turn in the wrong direction can lose about twenty seconds. As races over hundreds of miles can be won or lost by seconds, the accuracy of flying, the choice of the best route for upcurrents nearest to the set course, the airspeed to fly, and the judgement of the final glide back to base airfield, all require considerable concentration and not a little nerve. Most of the gliding which I did made use of gliders whose performance when flying at about 70 mph produced a 'gliding angle' of about 1 in 25 or 30; that is, from a mile up or about 5000 ft, it should go 30 miles in still air. The best modern gliders, built nowadays entirely in fibreglass (or carbon fibre), have gliding angles of 1 in 60 or better and at higher airspeeds. This has revolutionized crosscountry flying. Very rarely is it necessary to fly blind in the clouds; indeed to do so may add to the time taken to fly round a course.

My own 'lift off' in gliding could not take place until 1956 and 1957 when the Army insisted that I needed lots of holiday or 'light duty' while my head was mending. I did, however, write some accounts of flights I had made in 1954 and 1955 when I was an instructor at the Staff College. These were to give me preparation for the better things to come. In contrast to the modern techniques of avoiding cloud flying, these flights showed an earlier need to compensate for the relatively poor performance of the glider by gaining extra height in the clouds. They may also show why gliding became such an absorbing and stimulating passion to me and many of my friends for many wonderful years.

It was during my time as an instructor at Sandhurst and later at the Staff College between 1950-1955 that I found myself building up an immense background of gliding experience which was destined to become invaluable later on. General 'Hughie' Stockwell was the Commandant at Sandhurst. He had heard that I had been amusing myself going over to Redhill in 1950 to fly the rather nice gliders belonging to the Surrey Gliding Club. He had 'persuaded' the RAF instructor at Sandhurst to set up and run a gliding Club at RAF Odiham for cadets based entirely on solo training and with no good performance gliders for anyone to fly. This did not amuse me and nor did the methods being employed to teach the cadets. I kept well away until, unfortunately, a cadet was killed. The General had me in and told me to take over the club and put it on a sound basis. A two-seater glider was purchased and gradually other solo aircraft were bought to provide logical extensions to dual training. A professional instructor, John Free, was hired and I found myself going over to Odiham (and then Lasham nearby) every Wednesday afternoon, every Saturday afternoon and all day Sunday. I found myself doing a great deal of two-seater instruction in conjunction with John Free. The best glider we had was the Olympia and we also had two other intermediate gliders which were relatively easy to fly. A number of other enthusiasts became members and over the next few years the newly named Army Gliding Club began to establish itself as a well-run club offering cheap flying to all ranks as well as to cadets.

Evie was no shrinking violet. Nor would she willingly become a gliding widow. She started gliding in June, 1951, and by August had gone solo after fifty-five flights in the two-seater. A year later and after a lot more flights in intermediate gliders, she was 'passed out' to fly the Olympia and almost immediately climbed up in thermals to over 5000 feet from a car launch. Another year went by and she stayed up for over five hours in thermals and went crosscountry landing near Poole in Dorset. This qualified her for a Silver C badge.

In 1954 she flew 76 miles to Tewkesbury and won a prize for the longest distance flown by a lady in England, which she repeated two years later with a 154-mile flight down to St Ives in Cornwall, reaching 9600 feet in cloud on the way, and beating the British ladies' record. Our two youngest daughters were born in June, 1955, and June, 1956, which put a brake on her aeronautical activities and left us with memories of feeding babies and changing nappies in open glider trailers! She could not have provided more support to my own gliding efforts and in the process had a great deal of fun herself. We both talked the same language.

★ ★ ★

Saturday, 14 May, 1955 was the scene of much activity at Lasham. Goals as far away as Germany and Belgium were freely tossed around as pilots busied themselves with barographs and laid out maps all the way to Central Germany.

I was no exception, although I was fourth on the aero-tow list, a launch was not available until 11.20, after Lorne Welch and Wally Kahn had both been seen disappearing eastwards about half an hour before. I declared Brussels just before Derek Piggott towed me off.

A strong 20 mph wind was blowing and, straight upwind, a line of not very hopeful cumulus was building up after a wide gap of blue sky. Unfortunately 2000 feet was reached before getting to the cumulus and rather stupidly I released in a very poor area. I soon realized that the Olympia could not reach the upwind edge of the clouds, where I could expect to find some upcurrents. There was nothing for it but to go back to Lasham. With a curse I turned downwind back to the airfield, which I reached with 700 feet to spare. It was not a very good start.

A lucky thermal on the airfield boundary took me to just over 6000 feet and I was off. I did not find conditions particularly easy and quite a lot of side-stepping between clouds was necessary to keep aloft. In spite of this the Ashford-Lympne area was reached in just over two hours, or an average of about 40 mph. I spent the next half-hour in the area north of Hythe trying to find a respectable-sized cumulus as a stepping-stone across the Channel, but unfortunately none were to be seen, and it was only with some difficulty that I remained airborne.

About 2.15 pm, after reaching nearly 5000 feet, I saw from a plume of smoke from a bonfire that the wind had backed to west-south-west, and I decided that the Channel was off. The problem was now to shorten the road retrieve to my landing place, and so I decided to fly back along my original course as far as possible.

The wind was so strong that my best hope was to make use of the line of the North Downs which stretched most of the way from Hythe to Chatham. By now the wind had backed even more to south-west and, although the ridge is quite low, it provided sufficient lift in combination with numerous small thermals to reach the end of the hill near Rochester by 2.50 pm.

The thermals had been getting weaker and weaker, which completely ruled out any idea of making much headway against the strong wind. On the other hand, in the distance across a wide blue patch of sky, I could see a long line of black clouds approaching from the west. The tops of the clouds disappeared into a very high level stratus and snow or rain could be seen falling from the blacker parts.

It was an artist's dream. The clear, freshly washed air made the clouds look much closer than they really were as they rolled over the tops of the Kentish towns of Sevenoaks and Tonbridge. The sunlight on the ground between lit up the flowering orchards and the patchwork of tiny fields, which fitted into a maze of roads and tracks like a gigantic jigsaw puzzle.

I decided to make use of any height I could get in a cloud, but unfortunately I was now in the outer London Airway Control Zone in which cloud flying was prohibited. I had to fly back along the hill parallel to the advancing line of clouds to get to the nearest uncontrolled area, which was about 15 miles to the south-east. Half-way back, I began to get a smooth lift from the advancing front, which took me without further trouble to a very large black cloud, which had formed ahead of the main line like an outrider to the Valkyries of the clouds beyond.

Cloud base closed in round me just downwind of the little village of Charing on the Pilgrim's Way. I felt a bit like a pilgrim at that moment, except that I was looking for upcurrents rather that plodding my weary way to Canterbury.

The upcurrent was fairly strong to begin with, and pushed me up at 600-1000 ft per minute, but after climbing a thousand feet or so it started to peter out. It was clear that I had not reached the main core of the storm, and so I straightened up the Olympia on a westerly course and flew straight for six or seven minutes. This represents about five miles through the air and gives some idea of the extent of the up and downcurrents of air.

At 4,200 feet I came into very strong, smooth lift which only required a few 'figure of eights' towards the strongest surges to send both variometers off the clock.

Seven minutes later, 18,500 feet was reached giving an average rate of climb for 14,300 feet of 2000 ft per minute or 33 ft per second. Lift then stopped quite suddenly, which answered a little gremlin who had been talking into my ear about lack of oxygen after we passed the 15,000 ft level. Steering due west, I quickly sank down to 18,000 feet when more very strong lift was encountered. Lack of oxygen was now the problem and meant that I must get down as quickly as possible. I opened the dive brakes to the fullest extent and increased airspeed to 60 mph. Still I went up and reached a maximum height of 19,000 feet before getting to a vast area of rapidly sinking air which in about two minutes brought me down to 17,000 feet. Almost as suddenly I broke cloud a long way above all the other peaks of minor cumulus in sight.

If below cloud I had been shown the artist's dream, I must now be in paradise. Over to the north-east lay London, half-covered by a level layer of cloud out of which rose isolated pinnacles of dazzling whiteness like Grecian columns set haphazardly in a sea of concrete. Underneath the cloud the blue-grey buildings were set in a smoky haze with the Thames winding its way eastwards and dividing the city into two. Behind me lay the cloud out of which I had flown, standing, like Mount Everest, majestic and overpowering. I could see that I had come out of one of the lesser peaks which went to make up the mountain range.

Right down below was the Isle of Sheppey with its multicoloured fields standing out from the brown-looking water of the Thames Estuary. The country looked wet after the storm and sparkled in the afternoon sunshine. To the south lay the coast with Dover, Folkestone and the sharp beak of Dungeness until it was lost in the distance towards Hastings.

I was poised almost motionless in a wide bank of blue sky that had followed the line of clouds in which I had done my climb. I was still flying westwards at 60 mph, and right out in front another long line of clouds could be seen approaching, although this time the edges were no longer crisp and inviting. It was time to come down, after I had taken some colour photographs to remind me of that heavenly sight.

Rather north of west I could just see the runway of West Malling which I decided to land on rather than risk a field. From 15,000 feet or so I came in flying straight like an airliner to land outside flying control at 4.30 after one of the most exhilarating flights of my life.

It had been so cold that freezing level was only 4000 feet and at 19,000 ft the temperature was down to -25°F. Yet inside the tiny cockpit it had been comparatively warm. The gain of height registered on my barograph was 17,900 feet, and gave me a 'Diamond' to the Gold C qualification.

★ ★ ★

I was lucky to be able to spend so much time gliding during the spring and summer of 1956. In addition to giving a considerable amount of two-seater instruction to club members, my log book shows about 800 miles of cross-country flying in the Skylark 3. This glider was made by the pre-war firm of Slingsby's of Kirkbymoorside and was a good design with an 18-metre wingspan (or 59 ft). My Skylark was the original prototype with an extended nose and which I bought for £700. Like all other gliders of this period it was made of plywood with a fixed wheel. Its finish was good – particularly after a lot of hand waxing and loving care. It would be another 10-15 years before the explosion of fibre glass and carbon fibre in glider construction would lift performances by at least 25% and outdate previous methods.

Once again it was the Germans who led the way and persuaded all other countries that 100% fibre-glass construction was not only strong enough but also produced a superb finish accurate to fractions of a millimetre. It was also lighter.

1957 started with a bang. On 6 April I declared Land's End Airfield as my goal 218 miles away and I landed there four hours later. Clouds had formed themselves into long 'Streets' running east and west with a visibility of more than 50 miles. Cloud base was up to 5000 feet above sea level and only occasionally was it necessary to pause and circle up in a really strong thermal. On that day it was a pity that England was so small

Two weeks later in a light northerly wind I was able to fly a 300 km triangle with turning points at Kingham Junction and Castle Cary. This was the first time that this had ever been done in UK with turning points confirmed by photography. In a few more weeks I was able to notch up record times for the 100 km triangle, the 200 km triangle and an out-and-return flight to Kidderminster. These flights were in preparation for the British National Championships held at Lasham at the beginning of August, 1957. This was an occasion when some forty pilots came from all over the country to compete against each other. The following year a British Team would be entered for the World Gliding Championships to be held in Poland. Provided I did well at Lasham, I thought I might have a good chance to be selected.

There were six competition days ending on the last day with a pilot-selected goal. On the first five days I had been 2nd, 1st, 2nd, 5th and 3rd. As there was a light SE wind blowing, I selected Hawarden Airfield near Chester for my goal. Conditions were not easy with only weak thermals. The majority of competitors landed within 100 miles of Lasham. By circling continuously in lift which barely kept me airborne Hawarden came into view at 1000 feet, 163 miles from Lasham. I won that day, and also the championships.

Later in 1957 The Royal Aero Club was kind enough to award me their Silver Medal for the contribution I had made to soaring flight in that year. In October I was upgraded medically and in November given command of 22 SAS, then in Malaya. As I had also been selected to fly in the World Gliding Championships in Poland in 1958, the Army was very cooperative and arranged for my return to UK for a short course and a month's leave in May, 1958.

Four British pilots competed and I was to fly the new Olympia 419. This had a span of 19 metres and was markedly more efficient than my Skylark 3. My team consisted of my wife and John Archer*, who helped to rig the glider and tow the long trailer over many thousands of miles. John was a delightful and witty companion on this journey which was particularly

* Now General Sir John Archer.

necessary when we discovered that the whole British Team was to be housed in one large tent at Leszno in Western Poland. We survived that, and the interesting Polish food which included items like a raw egg broken into raw mince for breakfast, and accompanied by cocoa. The pilots were also given food for consumption during the flight and on one occasion tins of sardines were handed out with no means of opening them.

The championships started with races round 100, 200 and 300 km triangles and with two days of free distance or distance along a set line. I was first on two of the days, but overall I came seventh. Not too spectacular but the whole occasion was enormous fun. It was a great opportunity to see and fly over Eastern Europe and put up with an appalling telephone service. While waiting for my retrieving crew at Chelm (305 miles from Leszno) I was entertained by a schoolteacher and his librarian wife. They both talked at once in German and in French, but no English. They had a common loathing of the Russians only a few miles away across the River Bug. 'Why,' they asked, 'could Poland not be like England and not be invaded every twenty-five years, with all the misery of moving frontiers, starvation and refugees?' I had no answer.

Selection for subsequent World Championships was based on the performance in the previous British nationals. We were a little handicapped at this time because Philip Wills, then Chairman of the British Gliding Association, thought that we should fly British-made gliders, although there were many examples of foreign gliders which were at least 20% more efficient. Unfortunately the factories at Kirkbymoorside and at Newbury did not keep up to date and over the next six to ten years their products became totally outclassed. The British team continued to fly their gliders but the results showed that, even if we had top-class pilots, we also needed comparable gliders to gain the prizes. Since 1968 the policy was changed and British pilots have frequently been top or near the top ever since.

I was fortunate to be selected to fly in the British Team in West Germany in 1960, in Argentina in February, 1963, and in Britain in 1965. Although the results were quite creditable for the gliders we flew, they did not compare with our international competitors. We had fun and we made good friends, but increasingly we were outclassed. This became obvious to everybody at the World Championships held at South Cerney near Cirencester, in 1965. Soon after, the rules were changed.

At the end of 1966 I bought a Ka6E glider. This had a 15-metre (49ft) span and was an updated Olympia with about a 20% improvement in performance. It was a 'standard' class glider and relatively light and easy to put together. The larger span gliders became the 'open' class with no holds barred for innovative designs or expense.

The British Championships were held that year in May and once again were based at Lasham. Unfortunately the weather was very wet and only four days counted. On the last day a triangular race was set with turning points at Bicester airfield, South Marston airfield near Swindon and return. A 25 mph SW wind was blowing, with very large clouds developing, but in between there were nice patches of blue sky. Occasionally violent storms developed and the wet ground effectively stopped all thermals for an hour or two. It was quite a challenge to get round the course, let alone make a race of it.

We carried small Pye Bantam transceivers and were able to talk to our crews back at base up to about 50-75 miles away. During competitions and when flying blind in cloud, the rule was to announce your position and height on a common frequency so that any other glider would keep at least 500 feet clear vertically. Unfortunately the RAF Soaring Association did not agree because it would give away how far along the course their pilots had flown. They managed to arrange special frequencies with the Air Ministry which did not include the officially approved civilian glider channels.

On the first leg of the triangle to Bicester, I was climbing quite fast in cloud at 8000 feet just south-east of Oxford and calling my position and height when I received an almighty and deafening bang. Obviously I had been hit, but the glider continued to fly quite nicely and I steered out of cloud towards Bicester. From the cockpit, looking along the wing, I could see that part of the wing outboard of the aileron horn had been broken off. This was another handicap to my performance on a day when no handicaps were needed. I was furious. I wanted to win. It never even crossed my mind to land at Bicester or that if the cockpit had been hit I might not be here to tell the tale.

After rounding Bicester airfield I steered towards another large cloud to the West. Over Blenheim Park strong lift in cloud took me to 14,000 feet; I reckoned I would need every foot of extra height to get round South Marston and get back to Lasham.

Unfortunately the cloud I had been in had already deposited a lot of rain over an area about 15-20 miles round South Marston. As I had a broken wing and although I had about 2000 feet of height, I landed at the turning point. I was really angry, partly because of the accident but mainly because I might have had a good chance of getting back to Lasham and even winning the day with a bust glider. That would have been a nice bit of theatre with which to end the competition.

The broken wing was more serious than I had suspected; approximately 6 feet of wingtip had been knocked off and by the Chairman of the RAF Soaring Association, Paddy Kearon, who had been calling his heights on his special RAF frequency. As I was Chairman of the Army Gliding Association a certain amount of fairly amicable interservice argument developed. The

RAF needed no more encouragement to give up their special frequencies after this event – or at least not to use them in cloud. Paddy Kearon landed at Bicester. Apparently my wing had hit him half way along his wing and he was worried that this had weakened the structure.

In mid-1966 the Army gave me command of 3rd Division with Headquarters at Bulford on Salisbury Plain. This was a super job, but there was precious little time left over for gliding. Although I took part in the Championships each year, my lack of practice was not helping me produce good results. In 1967 I was 3rd in the Standard Class; in 1968 I only managed 5th at Dunstable. In 1969 I sold the Ka6E and ordered a new German glider, the LSI, with David Ince as partner. This was a beautiful-looking glider made of fibre glass with retracting wheel and a T tail. It had a performance which was much better than the Ka6E, but the writing was on the wall. In addition to lack of proper competitive practice, the younger pilots were getting more skilled. My main interest in gliding had always been concerned with competitions; if I was no longer able to come out in the top half-dozen, it might be better to call it a day.

My last competitions were the so-called Regional Championships held at Booker near High Wycombe in 1974. There were six scoring days and on one of these a 130-mile triangle with the Northampton Reservoir-Cambridge and return to Booker, my instruments became disconnected near Northampton when I flew through a massive downdraught. There was not time to go back to Booker; I had to carry on round the triangle with no instruments working except the altimeter. I found I could cope quite well without rate of climb indicators, but adjustment of airspeed was a problem. There was not much difference in the background whisper of air flowing past the cockpit between quite wide margins of air speed. It was a beautiful English summer day with a blue sky and a light wind, but no clouds to help mark the thermals. The maximum height I could get was about 4000 feet and I managed to fly the next two legs of the triangle keeping an eye on my competitors. If I saw one climbing extra fast, I went over to join him. I was fifth that day out of twenty-four. As someone remarked when I arrived back at Booker, 'There is life in the old dog yet'. When all the scores were added up I only came fifth in the Regionals. As this was a local competition with only the best qualified going up to the Nationals the results were not good enough to satisfy my ego. This was the last serious gliding that I did.

* 20 *

THE SAS

We were losing height fast on our way down into Kuala Lumpur airfield on the short flight from Singapore in a Malaysian Airways Dakota. Only four weeks before, I had been upgraded medically to A1 and two weeks ago I had been given command of 22 SAS Regiment. The rush was on because George Lea, my predecessor, was needed urgently for another job and I had to take over within a few days.

The origins of the SAS lay in the Second World War. Apart from the raid into Italy in which I had taken part nearly seventeen years earlier, under the banner of the 11th SAS, David Stirling's idea of small parties operating behind the lines only took root in the Western Desert in '41/42. More aeroplanes were blown up on enemy airfields by him and his patrols than were ever shot down by the RAF. Other SAS patrols raided ammunition and supply dumps far in the enemy's rear. In Italy, Yugoslavia and France they organized resistance movements, provided them with military stores and gave them training. Communications were also laid on to control operations, which were to give real tactical and strategical support to regular units fighting on the European Front.

More by chance than good judgement, a Squadron of SAS arrived in Malaya in 1950 after being diverted from going to Korea to join the United Nations force fighting the North Koreans and the Chinese. After many trials and initial failure, a regiment of soldiers was gradually built up in which the old Second World War techniques in the resistance movement were used in reverse. It was a case of setting a thief to catch a thief and much credit was due to my predecessor, George Lea, and those who had gone before him. They had set the standards and demanded results. George Lea, in particular, I had known before (he was brother to Christopher Lea, my friend in Italy). He combined a sunny temperament with firm discipline. A sound foundation had been laid which I was fortunate to take over.

The aim of the communist terrorists in Malaya was to take over the whole country, to oust the British or later the Malayan Government, and to seize the enormously wealthy and efficiently run rubber estates and tin mines. Behind the hundreds of terrorist groups all operating from what had been a safe base in the virgin jungle was a complete organization of District and Committee Secretaries, food suppliers and couriers, all leading back to Chin Peng, OBE, who lived in the jungles of Thailand, just clear of the Malayan border. Chin Peng had been decorated by the King after the war for his work in Malaya fighting the Japs, but almost as soon as he arrived back, he returned to the jungle to organize his own 10,000-strong rebel army.

Chin Peng was a convinced and intelligent communist. He believed in the Leninist dogma that revolution and war were inevitable and he set out to prove the point in Malaya. If there were people he hated more than the Japanese, they were the British. He had the withdrawal of Britain from Palestine and India always in mind to give him hope for the future. But he did not understand British politics and neither did Lenin.

Even while the fight was still on, the Malayans were given their independence in 1956. This had been proposed to the British Government by Gerald Templer, Commander-in-Chief and Director of Operations in Malaya. HMG agreed and asked him to put it into effect. This supremely simple transfer of power spiked the main aims of the communist terrorists 'to oust the British so that the sons of Malaya could run their own country'. From that moment on, surrenders of the weaker members increased dramatically, aided by an efficient Police Special Branch and chivvied out of their lairs by the British, Australian, New Zealand and Gurkha battalions.

The job of the Special Air Service Regiment was to go where normal units would not be effective; to go into the deep jungle and live there in small parties for three months at a time; to befriend the near-pygmy aborigines whose home it was, and to find out by patience and observation if they had any news of their communist friends; to follow up tracks, to find the camps and if possible to go in and kill the utterly ruthless terrorists inside. It was a desperate job, in which a page was taken out of the communists' own tactics and adopted for use by the SAS. The C.T.s never moved in large groups; it would leave too many tracks; they never cut their way through the jungle because it blazed a trail for even the most stupid white soldier to follow. The SAS did likewise. The patrol was rarely more than four men and the leading scout frequently carried as a weapon a repeating shotgun with deadly nine-ball ammunition. His life would depend on the speed and accuracy of shooting at a maximum killing range of 10 - 20 yards, which was also about as far as one could see, except along tracks.

Much ingenuity was used to devise different ways of getting into the jungle with the object of surprising the CTs who were living there. Sometimes helicopters were used, but they were noisy and gave away the entry. Parachuting into the treetops had also been tried and it solved many of the problems, but there could be no guarantee that a man might not be hurt in the process. If he was, a helicopter had to come and get him out and so nullify any advantage. Lastly, we could march. Although the most painful from a physical point of view, it was frequently the best way of reaching a new base for operations.

Each troop was divided into three patrols of three or four men. Nominally it was commanded by a subaltern, but because of the shortage of officers, sergeants or even corporals frequently had to take on the task. Even at this early stage, there was no shortage of volunteers among the soldiers. A tradition had been established that, regardless of the rank they had achieved in their own regiment, all new arrivals in Malaya came in as troopers and on troopers' rates of pay. Four out of five had already been weeded out in the selection process at Brecon and even then some new recruits could not take the strain of long operations in the deep jungle. They were sent back to their regiments.

Sometimes the SAS were given a swamp area in which to operate. The efficiency of normal units dropped a lot in such ghastly conditions and reliefs had to be carried out frequently. The SAS stood it for three months and were by no means exhausted. Tracks in the swamps could not be covered and even footmarks on treetrunks lying in the water left signs where the bark had been bruised. Swamp tracking was easy compared with the jungle, but to be effective it was necessary to keep at it for at least two months at a time. The essential continuity that this provided had led to success in the past and no doubt would do so in future.

So much for George Lea's briefing on current operations and my own background reading. The only fly in the ointment which was nagging away at me was a discussion I had had before I left with a senior officer in the War Office recently returned from Malaya. In a slightly condescending tone he told me that my future Regiment had already lost two attached SAS squadrons from the Parachute Regiment, and from New Zealand, who both had gone home, leaving only three operational 'sabre' squadrons. This had been a direct result of Gerald Templer's initiative in handing over the country to the Malayan Government, and signalled the start of the end of the Malayan War. 'It will last out your tour of duty all right, but don't ask me to forecast what will then happen. At the moment you are in the long term order of battle, but do not ask me to predict what will happen when the next financial squeeze comes along. Your chaps have been quite superb in the jungle but I can't see a task for them away from the trees.'

I thanked him for his comments and kept them to myself. When money and equipment are tight, as they always will be in peacetime, the Army cannot afford to have outfits that can only fight in jungles, however nice it might be to have a corps d'elite of specialists. Every new unit has to fight for its life and prove its worth every year or else the traditional conservatism of the rest of the Army will gather together to destroy it or deny it the men to make it effective. New units in a small Army must prove their value in all sorts of conditions to earn them a place on the roll of honour, which is as it should be. My long-term task must be to take up any opportunity to show the Regiment's worth in non-jungle situations. But for the moment I had to find out just how good this new outfit really was.

* 21 *

THE JUNGLE IS NEUTRAL

The rhythmic beat of the helicopter blades above us appeared to change gear as we slowed down to come into a V-shaped clearing halfway up a 5000-foot mountain in the deep virgin jungle 20 miles east of Ipoh. I had been in Kuala Lumpur nearly a month and was on my way to see D Squadron which was half way through their three months' operation. Information had been received that a terrorist gang was somewhere in the area and the task was to find them and, if possible, to kill them. A year or two before, a patrol from D Squadron had killed the notorious Ah Tuck in the same area and this time a successor had murdered three rubber tappers on estates near Ipoh.

As we dropped lower down, the immense trees, as high as church steeples on each side, disappeared far above us. A trooper with arms outstretched was bringing the helicopter in slowly until it hovered over a near horizontal platform made from giant bamboo and fallen branches. A further signal allowed the helicopter to rest on the platform and, after testing it for strength, the pilot let it settle, allowing me to jump out with my Bergen rucksack and FN rifle to meet John Watts for the first time. In the meantime the helicopter rose up a few feet, turned round over the platform and flew back out of the clearing to Ipoh.

John was no beauty. Pale-faced but swarthy with his tattered jungle hat and dark green shirt and trousers, he saluted with a smile of welcome.

We had to move to his base which was several thousand yards from my entry point, which by now might have been pinpointed by any terrorists in the area. The plan was to spend a night with him and then move round all the troops in turn, coming back in six days' time. All new recruits to the Regiment had first to complete a three-week training operation in the jungle, but I only did one lasting two days and a night. This was a helpful introduction and let me appreciate the skills of my training team. It was also as much time as I could afford, because my main object was to meet everybody and get some appreciation of how good they really were at their job. As soon as we moved into the jungle, the sunlight was blotted out by the tops of the trees whose foliage joined together to form an impenetrable screen against the sun high above us.

The burning heat in the clearing changed to a stifling humid warmth to sap one's energy as we quickly moved off. Two men led the way in single file, followed by John, myself and two more bringing up the rear. We followed a narrow game track running along the side of a stream, and nowhere could we see more than a few yards in any direction. No words were spoken. Every few minutes we would stop and listen and look hard in every direction because it was quite easy not to notice someone standing quite still. We still had about 2000 yards to cover to reach John's base.

Insects crawled everywhere. Ants marched in single file, centipedes, beetles and spiders covered the foliage and the tree trunks. The jungle was living and dying at the same time. Everywhere it was growing up on the remains of the dead forest which had fallen down. The rotting vegetation exuded a strange scent which was wafted on the hot and humid air and enshrouded us. Only the occasional tinkle from the stream disturbed the dead silence.

We climbed up a small hillock after carefully stepping over trip flares set on all likely approaches into D Squadron's base. We had arrived. Rectangular pieces of tough green plastic to keep off the rain were sited tactically round the hillock and then the rain started. It came down in torrents as is only experienced in the tropics. Everywhere became much darker as lightning flashed above the treetops, lighting up the gloom like flash bulbs going off. Still more water seemed to pour down until suddenly it all stopped at about 5 pm and we could look at John's map and hear how he proposed to track down the C.T.s. Later on I was able to tell them all that was happening in the rest of the Regiment.

As dusk fell the whole jungle came to life with a cacophony of sound which produced an almost deafening clamour. A type of cricket made a lot of noise, but every insect and animal seemed to wait for the evening to make as much din as possible. Behind the toneless screeching, the roosting birds and devil bats screamed their greetings and even large monkeys could be heard hoo-hooing with agonizing and penetrating bellows.

Half an hour before it became dark we had to stand-to. If we were going to be attacked, this was the most likely time, as not even C.T.s could move through the jungle in the dark. Our bashas* were all sited tactically and the men's positions were next to them. Everybody faced outwards and remained quite still. As it grew dark, the jungle noises reduced in volume, but kept going in the background, while we strained our eyes looking and listening for any signs of movement. Half an hour after dark a single clap of hands gave the signal to stand down and soon after we all turned in. Every man had a loaded weapon by his side and could turn out at a touch if the imposs-

* *Basha* - Malay for shelter.

ible ever happened. Half an hour before dawn a double clap was enough to turn us all out to stand to again until it was light.

So went the routine and I had asked that nothing should be changed or altered because of my visit. I went on to visit all four troops spaced about 10,000 yards apart round the area, coming back to the entry point after six days and via John's base. I was delighted with what I had found. These were intelligent professionals quite determined to produce results. One troop, commanded by Sergeant Ross, had mounted an ambush on a C.T. track 3000 yards from the troop base and had so far kept it up for twenty-one days. He was a dour individual, but had become a superb tracker with needle-sharp reflexes to fire the first shot before the C.T. could shoot back. All ranks knew him as Gloom Ross except to his face. But he produced results as I was to hear when back in K.L. After thirty-two days two C.T.s were killed as they went into the ambush. Both carried loaded and cocked shotguns and were carrying letters to their leader. I sent off many strawberries to D Squadron and Sergeant Ross.

Back in Kuala Lumpur I had plenty to do. Harry Thompson and B Squadron had just come out of the jungle and were due for two weeks' leave. Over six foot tall with red curly hair, he had dedicated his life to the SAS and was on his second tour of duty. He did not want to serve anywhere else, and did not suffer fools gladly. He was in his element running an independent jungle operation where his squadron was entirely responsible. Although they had drawn a blank on the last operation, confirmation had been received that the C.T.s had recently abandoned the area of jungle where they had been. Harry was quite sure it was because the C.T.s had become scared of the SAS. They had found several old C.T. camps and tracks all over his area.

'Don't worry, Harry,' I told him. 'Intelligence reports a complete C.T. gang in your next area of jungle. Enjoy your leave and I will tell you all about it when you get back.' I think he rather wanted to know more about it straightaway, but he thought better of it and took his wife and family off to Penang for a week.

Our job was to mount operations anywhere in Malaya and, as such, we came directly under the Commander-in-Chief for orders. He was now General Jim Cassels. He had taken over from General Bourne and I was delighted. We knew each other from Palestine days when he had commanded 6 Airborne Division only 10 years before. He congratulated me on my new command and told me to let him know personally if anything was worrying me. He also said he would like to come and see the Regiment when it was convenient.

Every trooper in the SAS was a potential NCO and many of them had dropped rank in their parent regiment to join the SAS. Back in barracks we kept the highest standards, certainly far higher than the infantry battalions doing a tour of duty in Malaya. Our soldiers were more mature and, when put to it, enjoyed showing that their drill and turnout was better than anybody else. So it was when Jim Cassels came round the Regiment. 'Well done Tony,' he said. 'Your chaps are quite the best I have seen in Malaya, not only in the jungle where they are superb, but also here in K.L.' He went on, 'I was impressed by your smart guard. I also enjoyed hearing how your operations were proceeding in the Ops room.' A nice strawberry for the Regiment which was much appreciated by everybody.

* 22 *

THE HUNT FOR AH HOI

Harry Thompson was briefing his Squadron of about seventy strong and I came in to hear how he did it. His face was tanned after three weeks out of the jungle and his red hair was short and well brushed. Everything about him exuded knowledge and efficiency, and his eyes twinkled as he talked. I listened intently as he unfolded details of the plan.

'The Malayan Government are getting worried,' he said. 'All C.T.s have been eliminated from a wide area around K.L. except for an enormous jungle-covered swamp which is only twenty miles to the north. An infantry battalion did its best a year ago and it managed to ambush some terrorists near the edge, but this lot are believed to be right in the middle.

'The difficulty is to get to the middle of the swamp without leaving tracks, and to get there quickly I have chosen to go in by parachute. I am completely confident that we will pull it off where others have failed.

'First I must tell you about our enemy. The leader is a very senior member of the Communist Party by the name of Ah Hoi. He has some delightful habits and he is know as the Baby-Killer by paddy planters on the coast from whom he has been extorting food and money.

'He achieved this infamous nickname in a remarkable way. He heard that a man had passed some information about him to the police and so decided to make an example of his wife. Secretly he arrived at a village near the coast and called a meeting of all the inhabitants, including the informer and his wife who was now pregnant. He could do this quite easily by threatening murder or torture if they did not attend.

'He pulled the frightened woman out of the audience and said he was going to make an example of her in front of them all. With a flash of his parang* he had her belly cut wide open and, reaching in, he pulled out her unborn babe and flung it on the ground.'

A gasp went round the squadron. These tough men, well used to every sort of horror, found this description quite enough, even for them.

'So you see we have a pretty poisonous and diabolical character and we

* Parang – Heavy-bladed knife about 18 inches long.

must try and get him within the period of our three months' operation.'

Pointing to a large-scale map pinned to the blackboard, he said,

'This small river, winding its way through the middle of the swamp, must provide a focal spot for all who live there. I am sure that we shall find tracks and C.T. camp-sites if we follow it to the coast. We will land in the trees near its headwaters in a week's time and then I want you to move as follows.'

He then described the action to be taken by the different parts of the Squadron after landing, and the thousand and one minor things which must be remembered and planned in an operation like this.

We all knew that the Regiment had not used the parachute entry method for a long time because of the risk of casualties. Harry had, however, made up his mind that the chance was worth taking and it would certainly get him there quickly. He also rather relished the spectacular. This op was certainly dramatic. If it came off, it would add to the prestige of his Squadron. I hoped he would be right.

The drop took place at 7 am on a February morning in 1958. Two large Beverley transports each dropped thirty-five men into the middle of the swamp out of which grew the usual 200-foot-high trees with their interlocking top canopies from which an occasional giant tree pushed up a further 20 or 30 feet. We all knew it would be some time before everybody could be gathered together and radios opened up to give us the news. Unfortunately one man had been badly hurt. His parachute had caught up in the branches of a monster tree and just when he was preparing to slide down on his 250 ft line, the branch broke off and down he fell nearly 200 feet across some splayed-out tree roots. By rights he ought to be dead, but he was lucky, he only broke his back. Some of his ribs had been pushed into his lungs and a thin stream of blood was dribbling from his mouth.

This was what we had all feared might happen, but by a freak bit of luck, which had not shown up on air photos, there happened to be a large hole in the trees only 100 yards away, where lightning must have made a natural clearing. A marker balloon was put up as a guide. These were orange plastic balloons about 3 feet in diameter, which were inflated by gas bubbling off white powder after water was poured in. The neck was then tied with thin string which was paid out to allow the balloon to float above the tallest trees. Against all the rules, the helicopter pilot let down into the hole almost vertically, first to drop the doctor and later to come back and take them both out. The blades clipped the leaves all round which were sucked in by the rush of air. As it rose up vertically, the helicopter appeared to pass through the pieces of jungle foliage flying everywhere, but at last it was clear of the trees and on the way to K.L. hospital. The man took a year to recover before the doctors pronounced him completely fit.

With the chopper gone, and sixty-nine out of seventy men on the ground,

Harry was able to get on with the job. It was tough going. The first task was to get into squadron and troop bases near the River Tengi. From there he would start his patrols as they moved downstream towards the coast.

The water became deeper as they pushed slowly forwards. From only about 6 inches, it rose up to a foot or 18 inches as they climbed up, down or through the tangled debris of thousands of years. The stench rising from the stagnant water was overpowering as they climbed over the trash, now mostly hidden below water. Sometimes a freak hole would drop someone up to his armpits, but most of the time it was not more than knee-deep over the roots. Humidity remained at about 100% for the duration of the operation. Tropical storms came most afternoons, crashing through the treetops and soaking everybody to their skins. Clothes were perpetually sodden from either sweat or rain and did not dry out for the whole time they were in the swamp.

By the end of the first day, after covering only 1000-1200 yards from the drop point, they came across the river. The squadron and troop bases were all separated to allow small patrols to operate and therefore leave few tracks. Every evening radio reports of progress were sent through to the Squadron and another one direct to base in K.L., with an encoded signal for necessary supplies. Every morning the radios would open up for a minute or two, to check that the instructions received the previous evening were still valid. Patrols would then start.

After three days Peter de la Billière, commanding one of the troops on his first operation, reported C.T. tracks near the river. Under the water the print of C.T. hockey boots could clearly be seen and also where they had cut tunnels through 10-foot-high sword-grass. Old C.T. campsites were found where they had left piles of turtle shells. Spikes from sword-grass were tearing the clothes to pieces. Some of the men's boots fell to pieces; they had to go on practically barefoot until the next resupply.

Harry was getting more and more optimistic that he was getting closer to Ah Hoi and his gang of twenty-one C.T.s. His appreciation that they would be somewhere near the River Tengi in the middle of the swamp was looking quite accurate.

Sergeant Sandilands, commanding another troop, suddenly saw two terrorists not 75 yards away across the river. They had their rifles by their sides and were intent on tying fishhooks to a line. Carefully moving up behind a log floated out into the river and up to his shoulders in water, he killed one terrorist and the other one dived off and escaped. The next few days they tracked the terrorists for 8000 yards and found their camp-site, but they had gone.

Although conditions were quite ghastly, the men's health remained good. Only one man had to be evacuated by chopper from the whole of B Squadron in the course of three months. The swamp was a challenge to the whole Regiment; it was a bit of an honour to survive in it. It was a disgrace to succumb. Every troop had its medic. These were volunteers from among the soldiers and were given a month's course, followed by two or three months understudying an experienced man. They realized they were the 'doctors' to the whole troop and they enjoyed the responsibility. One problem in the swamp was the water. This was pale brown and had to be boiled before drinking it in tea or using it for curry. Swamp water was quite likely to be infected with a killing disease called leptospirosis, or lepto for short. Unfortunately the virus could also enter the body wherever the skin was punctured and leech bites frequently provided the opportunity. These developed into ulcers which took weeks to heal up and needed twice daily treatment with antiseptic ointment to stop the lepto virus getting a hold. The medics all carried a roneoed pamphlet which made them carry out a diagnosis in a routine manner on anybody who felt sick. The results were reduced to a code, which was sent back to base, where the doctor interpreted the signal and either advised treatment or ordered evacuation. The system was similar to that used in the outback of Australia and produced excellent results.

Harry now had his tail up in spite of his legs which were covered in ulcers. He hoped to squeeze Ah Hoi between the patrols carried out by his different troops and thus force him and his gang into the open. The three troops were given a large area of jungle swamp to ring, within which the baby-killer's camp should be located. Along one edge of the jungle there was a canal controlling the irrigation to the paddy fields with a village on the far side.

It now seemed likely, as a result of patrolling, that the main camps were much nearer the jungle edge than anyone had suspected. Harry moved his base to be with the local police at a post in the paddy near the jungle edge. The first phase of the operation was now over. We had a net to close over a huge area of swamp with the lines of patrols forming the strings. Harry knew that if the patrols were not carried out efficiently, the gaps in the meshes would allow the C.T.s to pass through and the whole operation would be ruined.

I joined Harry at his post and in conjunction with the police arranged night curfews on the villagers. A barbed-wire fence was next put up parallel with the canal and 100 yards into the paddy fields. The squeeze was now on the terrorists to stop them picking up food from the village. At the same time surrender leaflets were printed and dropped from the air all over the area where we thought they must be. Even a voice aircraft came along, barking its message into the swamp.

At the same time Harry intensified all patrols and the pattern of tracks and old camps became clearer every day. The C.T.s on this occasion had a charmed life and none were bumped. The ground was so mixed up with rotting timber and thick vegetation that a patrol could have passed within a few yards and not known that C.T.s were near.

A local battalion was moved up to the outside of the jungle to make quite certain that no contact could possibly take place between the terrorists and the villagers. This was done after one of the villagers complained to the Police the day after he had been visited by a C.T. and had been forced to give him food.

At last the break came. Out of some undergrowth beside one of the paddy fields stepped a girl barely four foot, six inches tall. She was taken straight to the Chinese Special Branch Police Officer, who had been expecting something like this to happen. Speaking rapidly in Chinese, she said her name was Ah Niet, and she had Ah Hoi's terms for surrender. This would be £3500 for each terrorist, to be paid to Ah Hoi, and an amnesty for all those already in jail.

The cheek of the girl was astonishing. She really thought she was in a position to dictate terms. Although Ah Hoi had been a prize catch a few months ago, he was now in a corner and was talking about surrender.

All the terrorists appeared to know about the terms of surrender then on offer. These were that individuals would be helped to take up civilian employment provided they had committed no civil crime or alternatively they would be shipped back to China.

The cheeky Ah Niet said Ah Hoi would never agree to terms like these, but I told her that the Air Force would start bombing all their camps within 48 hours if they did not surrender. This, of course, was part bluff, because we still did not know exactly where they were, but she believed it all right and went back with the message.

That evening she returned. For our part, we agreed not to patrol her entry and exit points. She then said she would go back and bring out the whole gang. Back she went again.

This was Harry's war and I left him to take the surrender. I could do no more. He waited patiently in the fields while Ah Niet did her stuff.

By now it was pitch dark. Lights could be seen coming out of the jungle. An incredibly bedraggled and miserable line of seven terrorists including Ah Niet wound their way towards the post. One of them had on a woman's blue silk jacket complete with a large straw hat to match. This was the man himself. Ah Hoi had been dressed as a woman, which perhaps explained how he had been able to move about. Even at this stage of anti-climax he ranted on and said that the communists would win in the end. Like all bullies, he was a coward and had surrendered to save his skin.

He would not say where the missing members of his gang were hiding but Ah Niet thought she knew. The next day she led a patrol back, but when she arrived at their campsite they had gone. Her willpower at last gave out and she collapsed. The doctors said she was suffering from extreme vitamin deficiency or beri-beri.

Two days later the remainder came out when they found their leader had gone. So ended the operation, almost exactly three months after the original drop.

Unfortunately Ah Hoi's civil crime could not be proved. Even now witnesses would not dare come forward and he chose to go back to China. The Police told us later that at the last minute he changed his mind and wanted to remain in Malaya, but regulations were quoted and he was given no option. The story does not relate what sort of reception he received back in China.

★ ★ ★

At the end of each squadron operation a number of cross-postings always took place to fill vacancies in other squadrons or as instructors in the TA SAS Regiments in UK and also to relieve individuals who were running out of steam. Rather to my surprise Harry did not want to keep Peter de la Billière. Peter was intelligent and determined, but he had a quiet and self-effacing personality which was the complete opposite of his Squadron Commander. Sometimes opposites gel, but this one hadn't, so I moved him to be my Operations Officer at Headquarters. He was quite excellent, but, as soon as John Watts and D Squadron came out of the jungle, I posted him to his new Squadron where he was to perform brilliantly in the Oman, and, as far as I can discover, in every job since then.

★ ★ ★

By the summer of 1958 it was becoming increasingly clear that most of the C.T.s in Southern Malaya had either surrendered or were thinking about it. There was one area in the mountains to the east of K.L. that still had a few, but the majority were now operating in the north of the country along the borders with Thailand.

A Squadron had been given the area to the east of K.L. about a month before and had not so far been able to catch any terrorists, although they had turned up a lot of old camps and signs where C.T.s had been. Johnny Cooper, the Squadron Commander, was an old-time SAS soldier. He had been a Lance-Corporal radio operator with David Stirling in the Desert War of 1941/42 and this was his second tour in Malaya. He set high standards and, like the other Squadron Commanders, he knew most of the wrinkles and the answers to them.

We received the bare details of A Squadron's op back at base, but I needed to go in and see for myself. The Squadron Headquarters was near the top of a 5000-foot hill and nearby was an old clearing for helicopters that had been refurbished. At the last moment a Royal Navy Admiral visiting Force Headquarters in K.L. asked if he could come too and see how the SAS did their stuff. As we were coming back the same day, I was delighted to show the Senior Service how we did things: or at least how a squadron base organized patrols. The RAF provided a small Sycamore helicopter with four seats and the pilot. As we would be coming out of a clearing at 5000 feet in hot and humid conditions, no more than two passengers could be taken. It was near the operating limits of this piston-engined chopper.

We arrived in our usual style and let down on to a bamboo platform. The pilot turned it round and switched off. He too was interested to see the now legendary SAS and find out what made them tick. Johnny was in good order and brimming over with enthusiasm. His patrols were quartering the jungle as efficiently as ever, but so far only quite old tracks and campsites had been found. Unless he found signs of more recent occupation in the next two weeks, it would be better to withdraw the Squadron after only two months. Police Special Branch were reporting increased C.T. activity up near the border with Thailand and this would be the scene of their next operation.

The time came to leave and, with the Admiral in the front seat, we took off and paused for a moment, hovering only about 2 feet above the platform. The pilot nosed the chopper slightly down and pulled up the collective pitch, which was the normal procedure to fly out of the clearing. Unfortunately something went wrong and we did not fly up and away but sank into the tree canopy a few hundred yards below the clearing. I saw sweat pouring down the pilot's neck as we sank into the trees. First the main rotor blades broke off, leaving only short stubs; then the tail crashed into a monster tree as we dropped down. The engine was racing flat out and may have helped reduce the force of the crash into deep leaf-mould between two trees. The torque from the flaying engine immediately turned the fuselage over on its side. I was able to lean forward and switch it off; the pilot was so shocked he did not seem to know what to do. We were lucky there was no fire.

The Squadron sent off an emergency signal and an hour later a large helicopter came in to see what had happened and take us all out. I never heard any more from the Admiral, who was unhurt. The pilot was slightly concussed and I had a stiff neck. We had all been fantastically lucky. The RAF eventually decided it was fluke wind or downcurrent that had caused the crash. The only thing recovered was the battery, and to this day I am not quite sure why.

In September, 1958, I heard that the Regiment would be returning to the UK in the Spring of 1959 and must be prepared to reduce its size to a minimum. Major Dare Newall was our representative in the Ministry of Defence and, apart from being heavily committed in the running of the selection process at Brecon for all ranks, he kept me informed on what ideas were being discussed on the size of 22 SAS when back in the UK and what their future role might be. His reports were quite invaluable, but did not make cheery reading. In addition to 22 SAS there were two TA SAS Regiments. We had to show that the Regular Army needed a Regular SAS Regiment and that there were a lot of vital tasks away from the jungle which could not be tackled by infantry battalions. We had to make a case for what was a genuine corps d'élite – without ever mentioning this phrase – which had the ability to operate in small parties in any country anywhere and in complete security. The advent of instant television and radio coverage made this last requirement essential and one which normal army units could never achieve in peacetime.

Just when it was needed we had a stroke of luck. On 20 October, 1958, I was invited to go down to Singapore to discuss with the Chief of Staff of Far East Land Forces whether a 'few SAS volunteers' could be used to oust rebels from the Jebel Akhdar in Oman, over 4000 miles away. Two days later I was on my way to Bahrein and Oman, dressed in civilian clothes to see what was involved; to meet the personalities and discuss how the SAS might be employed. It could not have come at a more opportune moment.

* 23 *

OIL IN OMAN

The control of operations in the whole of the Persian Gulf, including Oman, was in the hands of Air Vice-Marshal Heath at Aden. At the time there was a considerable weight of opinion that the domination of the many unruly tribes scattered over thousands of miles in Arabia could best be done from the air with occasional support from the Army. This view was probably based on pre-war experience when the Bedouin tribes in the Jordan-Iraq-Kuwait area had been made to keep the peace as a result of similar troubles affecting the oil pipeline from Iraq to the Mediterranean.

My first date was with the Air Marshal who had his Brigadier with him as deputy. Also present was Major Frank Kitson* from the planning branch in the War Office. He would be able to take back any request from me on the deployment of the SAS, but this would first need both political and military support, all down the line, from Aden to Bahrein, and finally from Colonel Smiley who was Commander of the Sultan's Armed Forces in Oman.

I had read summaries of what was happening in Oman, but I was not prepared for the Air Marshal when he asked me straightaway how I thought the SAS might be able to help.

I told him that my first requirement was to have a close look at the Jebel Akhdar and see how SAS patrols might be deployed. 'With a bit of luck,' I told him, 'I think there might be a good chance of killing the leaders of the rebellion before the hot weather starts in April. If we do not kill them, I think we could give the rebels a lot of bloody noses, and this could allow successful negotiations to take place.'

Frank Kitson was then asked for his opinion from the point of view of the War Office. He said that the original idea was for a few SAS to provide protection for small patrols who would be led by guides to where the leaders of the rebellion were located. (This idea was based on his own experiences in Kenya when he used to dress up as a Kikuyu and infiltrate the Mau Mau gangs. This quite brilliant and very brave effort on his part led him to believe that a similar operation could be mounted in Oman.)

* Later General Sir Frank Kitson.

A general discussion then took place. Frank Kitson's ideas were received with considerable scepticism, although they might well have to be tried out in the long term if the SAS had not been given the task. My plan was strongly favoured by all those present. We were told to travel to Muscat and Bahrein, have a look at the mountain and then come up with proposals.

I realized that part of my problem was to convince Frank Kitson that a squadron of SAS was necessary. I also had to persuade him that his idea of small 'killer squads' was unlikely to work in the time available, even if reliable guides could be found. His knowledge of the Whitehall machine would be invaluable when the time came for him to return home. Frank not only had a number of original and interesting ideas, he had also studied the subject in considerable depth.

Later on that week, when I was looking in more detail round the Jebel Akhdar, Frank left me and went off with Major Malcolm Dennison. He was the resident Intelligence Officer in Oman and was bi-lingual in Arabic. Once again Frank put forward his own ideas, but they did not match up with local conditions. There was little cover compared with the jungle in Kenya and there were certainly no British officers who could be passed off as Omanis. Even locals could not do it. One agent, who had been engaged in great secrecy and who came from the Izki area, was sent off to the Jebel where he was a frequent visitor. That night he was murdered in his own village without setting foot on the Jebel. His death made it impossible to recruit another agent from that area.

★ ★ ★

After flying all morning, with a stop to change planes at Sharjah airfield, we arrived at Bait al Faluj airstrip near Muscat on Sunday afternoon. A Land Rover came out to meet us and, not twenty-four hours after leaving Singapore, we were sitting in Colonel David Smiley's office in his white-painted Beau Geste-style fort, complete with the Red Flag of the Sultan fluttering from a flagpole on top. This was the headquarters of the Sultan's Armed Forces and was located at the tiny mud-hut village of Bait al Faluj, five miles from Muscat, in Oman. All tracks into the interior from Muscat had to pass through Bait and this had determined where the fort should be built.

Posters of Life Guards on parade in London decorated the walls and coffee was produced by a local Arab dressed in a white garment coming down to his ankles. Not long before, David Smiley had been Military Attaché in Stockholm; before that he had commanded the Blues. He had also served in the SAS and SOE in the 39/45 war. I thought to myself that this would be a great advantage when deciding how the SAS should be employed.

'Well Tony,' he said, immediately using my Christian name, 'my first job is to describe the political and military background in Oman before taking a closer look at the Jebel Akhdar or Green Mountain. I have laid on a RAF Single Pioneer aircraft which can fly you both round the mountain tomorrow and it can also land on short airstrips below the Jebel so that you can then meet the British officers running my Northern Frontier Regiment and the Muscat Regiment.

'I will ask Colonel Colin Maxwell, who has been here many years, to come in and sketch in the events to date.' A sun-tanned elderly man came in and described the background history of the Oman, its lack of money in the Treasury and the intrigues between the different factions, including the skirmishes and battles that had taken place. 'Finally the three rebel leaders, Sheikh Suleiman, the Imam Ghalib and his brother Talib had all established themselves on the Jebel Akhdar, and had taken with them their wives, their personal slaves and even some furniture.

'Current RAF opinion at the time thought that, with a few local forces on the ground, the rebellion could be snuffed out by the use of aircraft based outside Oman. We now know this to be unrealistic because there were no soldiers on the ground to describe targets, although the RAF still hankered after such a solution.

'May I now describe some of the folklore concerning the Jebel Akhdar. Local legend tells the story that the Jebel was invaded successfully on only two previous occasions out of six tries. The first was by an army of 25,000 sent by the Caliphs of Baghdad in AD 892. According to a local chronicler, they started off by beheading the Imam, they then cut off thousands of hands and ears, scooped out the eyes of the Sheikhs, destroyed the water-courses, burnt the books and utterly ravaged the whole country. The next and last successful invasion took place in AD 1265, when the Persians also used a 'vast' army to make sure of it. Once again the unruly Omani tribes of the Jebel Akhdar were holding out and they had to be defeated in battle. They climbed the north side of the mountain and, after enduring fearful losses, they stormed the mountain and won a great battle on the plateau at the top. The attractions of this Shangri La must have beckoned on the Persian warriors, with tales of wondrous lush living to be had when they won. Only 5000, it is related, of the original Persian Army of 20,000 men survived, but even after so bloody an introduction, these 5000 decided to stay on the mountain and lived happily ever afterwards. Perhaps it was this influx of Persian blood, perhaps it was the cooler, fresher climate, but the tribes of the Bani Hinna and Bani Riyam are altogether far superior to the desert bedu in the villages below. The mountain tribes seem to accept more discipline, to operate in larger groups, to shoot straighter and to have more western-type skills inherent in their make-up. They only have to be shown how to operate a mortar or a heavy machine gun to become experts, all this with an air of light-hearted enthusiasm.

'So you can see that Talib has the right material ready to hand. He has become a commander on the mountain and is a master of tactics and intrigue. Cairo radio daily carries panegyrics on his efficiency in beating back the "thousands of British soldiers who are trying to oust him from his rightful home". Our Intelligence reports state that he visits all his pickets regularly and sees to it that they know what to do in an emergency, what alternative positions they should take up, that their food and ammunition supply is adequate and conducts regular reliefs from his central reserve of Saudi-trained soldiers.

'The great man of the mountains is, however, still Suleiman bin Hamyar, paramount Sheikh of the Bani Riyam, whose word is law and on whose authority men can be executed or mutilated. He has always been noted for his ruthlessness and only on one previous occasion has he submitted to the Sultan.

'Suleiman certainly has charisma, but he is ready to sell himself to the Saudis if they will back the cause of Independent Oman. As a result he is now a rich man, by Omani standards, and can afford to give compensation to any of his tribe who suffer loss of property as a result of attacks by the RAF. Many are the tales about him, including a rather fascinating story that he has a *droit de seigneur* in his tribe. If Suleiman's walking stick is found lying across the threshold of any house, it is a sign that he is engaged with the lady who lives there and nobody can enter on pain of death.'

David then took over. 'I will now fill in what has happened since Talib arrived on the Jebel. The rebels have kept up an almost continuous harassing of our men encamped round the base of the mountain. They abduct civilians from the villages if they think they have been giving any help to the Sultan. Mortar bombs suddenly explode, bursts of light machine-gun (LMG) fire riddle a tent with a light in it and mines are laid liberally in the tracks whenever one of our platoons or companies move away from their base and go up the hillside. They are invariably repulsed by most accurate fire from one of the pickets. On one occasion, about a year ago, the Northern Frontier Regiment, supported by over 100 tribal levies, tried moving up the Kamah track which was one of the few ways up the Jebel. It ended in disaster when half-way up. They lost several killed by snipers and then morale among the levies broke down completely. The NFR were forced to withdraw to Nizwa.

'As you can appreciate, this once more reinforced the idea being muttered in all the suks* that the Jebel is impregnable. Mining increased and to date about one hundred and fifty trucks and all thirty Ferrets of the Life Guards

* suk = market.

have been blown up. Every British officer serving in the Northern Frontier Regiment has been blown up on mines at least once. You may have noticed the sandbags on the floor of our Land Rovers. These usually prevent casualties.

'The mines being laid are the small American anti-tank mines. The point has now been reached when oil company drivers are reluctant to go out unless they are protected. The need to give protection to the oil company and to increase the effectiveness of the Sultan's Armed Forces has to be counterbalanced by the adverse propaganda which Cairo will undoubtedly put out, if British troops are employed in Oman.

'In the last year the morale, efficiency, armament and tactics of the rebels have improved out of all recognition. They are now a very formidable force and make excellent use of their natural defences.

'Now I am sure you will see that nothing short of direct British intervention will put a stop to the rebellion.

'Brigadier Tinker* and I both agreed that the right way to put down the rebellion was the use of a brigade, with possibly a Parachute battalion landing on the plateau at the top, supported by a British battalion moving up from the bottom in conjunction with my own Northern Frontier Regiment. I am afraid that this was ruled out on political grounds because the employment of a force of this size would excite not only a lot of friendly nations but also the extreme left wing elements in Parliament, whose imperial education is frequently very hazy. Britain wanted to support the oil company for strategic reasons but she certainly did not want to bear the odium of another imperialist war, which is what Cairo radio would call it. She did not want to be put in the wrong at the United Nations and yet she must support the Sultan, her friend and ally for 170 years. To show real support would not only restore British prestige throughout the Sheikhdoms, some of which had been wondering if Britain was capable of doing anything positive, but it would also put the Sultan back in his saddle with much more security.

'The politicians had no difficulty in turning down our request for a brigade, but some other solution must be found. One idea was to provide a British battalion to reinforce the Northern Frontier Regiment and the two together, plus a squadron of Trucial Oman Scouts, might be strong enough to tackle the Jebel. 1st Battalion Royal Fusiliers is at Bahrein and the Commanding Officer is Terry Donnelly whom I believe you know. The Battalion is part of 24 Brigade, but the Brigadier is not at all happy. He still considers the task beyond the capabilities of a single battalion, which, in any event, would need three months' training in mountain warfare. He also doubted if adequate administrative support was available unless air resupply was avail-

* Brigadier Tinker was based in Bahrein as adviser to H.M.G.

able on a massive scale and in addition a large contingent of mule or donkey transport was on hand in case air resupply had to be cancelled due to weather or other reasons. This plan, too, was turned down for both military and political reasons; which is really why you are here.

'I have always maintained that if the three leaders could be either captured or killed, the rebellion would be over, such is the hold that personalities like these have over their followers. The War Office in London accept this argument and, as Frank Kitson knows, have suggested that a maximum of about fifty volunteers from the SAS might be given this task, operating in conjunction with the SAF. Naturally any amount of money for bribes is available; it will be now for you to see if the idea is practicable. I myself rather doubt if you will get anybody to lead you to the caves where they are based on the top, almost regardless of the amount of money available. But large amounts of cash do talk and it is certainly worth trying. Now for your questions.'

'You have given me a lot to think about and naturally I want to have a close look at this mountain before agreeing that it is a task that we could take on. Off the cuff, my initial reactions are: firstly I should like to have a whole squadron rather than fifty volunteers. A squadron is only about seventy all ranks of whom not much more than fifty would be at the sharp end up the mountain. The squadron will also need a very small base element for communications. I am afraid I must insist that we operate independently of the Sultan's Armed Forces, although, of course, we would, with your permission, like to use your camps as bases from which to operate. Lastly, I would like to know what facilities exist for surgery in the event of casualties, for helicopters for casualty evacuation and air resupply to patrols on the mountain.'

David Smiley interrupted with a laugh. 'I am afraid there are no surgical teams closer than Bahrein, 700 miles away. There are no helicopters this side of Aden, 1100 miles away, but there are, I believe, a few Valletta transport aircraft at Bahrein which could be tasked for air resupply. I do not think there should be much difficulty from our point of view about bringing in a squadron and I accept that the SAS must be given a free hand and not be tied to the SAF.'

By this time it was evening and David Smiley and his attractive wife, Moy, entertained me to supper in his bungalow nearby. They were a delightful couple and small talk developed comparing his recent lush diplomatic life as Military Attaché in Stockholm with his present position living in a hut near his fort and on a shoestring for supplies and shortage of money to do anything.

I had not had much sleep in the last 24 hours, so I excused myself early. I was looking forward to my trip on the morrow when I could see more of this famous mountain and get a feel as to whether we could do with one squadron what all local senior people thought needed a brigade. Mountain warfare with visibilities of 50 miles or more was totally different from the jungle and just what was wanted for the long-term future of the Regiment. On the other hand it would be wrong to become involved in a task which was virtually impossible. I slept well that night.

* 24 *

THE JEBEL AKHDAR

I invited Frank Kitson to join me and we were flying at about 6000 feet soon after leaving Muscat. After twenty minutes the pale blue Jebel Akhdar could be seen on the horizon. In the distance it looked enchanting, the craggy mountain shrouded in azure blue. As we flew closer, the colours became more vivid with dark blues, dark browns and black, as the mountain reared up above us from the yellow-brown desert floor below. Giant slabs of bare rock were propped up at 45° and lay against each other to form an almost continuous wall surrounding a high upland plateau some twenty miles long by ten miles wide. This wall was pierced by steep-sided wadis, gouged out of the mountain by floods of long ago, with near-vertical sides which twisted as they cut into the heart of the plateau. One wadi, called Maidan, as I learnt later, disappeared right into the middle and opened up into a giant bowl with precipitous sides thousands of feet high. The pilot was pointing again as he circled up to 9000 feet to give me a view from above. I could see in the distance the mud and stone villages of Sharaijah and Saiq grouped round the top edge of a giant amphitheatre. Below the houses an occasional streak of bright green could be seen from terraces where irrigation was still producing crops of some kind. The rebels had acquired some anti-aircraft heavy machine guns, so it was not safe to fly any closer, but I had seen enough to realize that this was not going to be any walkover. We flew on, gradually losing height, and to our right we could see how the towering slope of the mountain was formed from a whole series of sharp-pointed slabs in the shape of pyramids, all leaning against each other like buttresses to keep up the solid plateau beyond. In between each series of pyramids, more dark-shadowed wadis cut into the Jebel but none as big as the Maidan.

The Nizwa Valley was now below us, with its wide acres of dark-green date palms, irrigated by perennial water. The plane flew low over the NFR camp nearby to warn them of our arrival and touched down on a rough and stony airstrip about 250 yards long and pointing straight at the side of a hill. The valley lay between a cluster of bare jet-black mountains a few thousand feet high and a 2000-foot-high yellow limestone ridge joining up with the foothills of the Jebel.

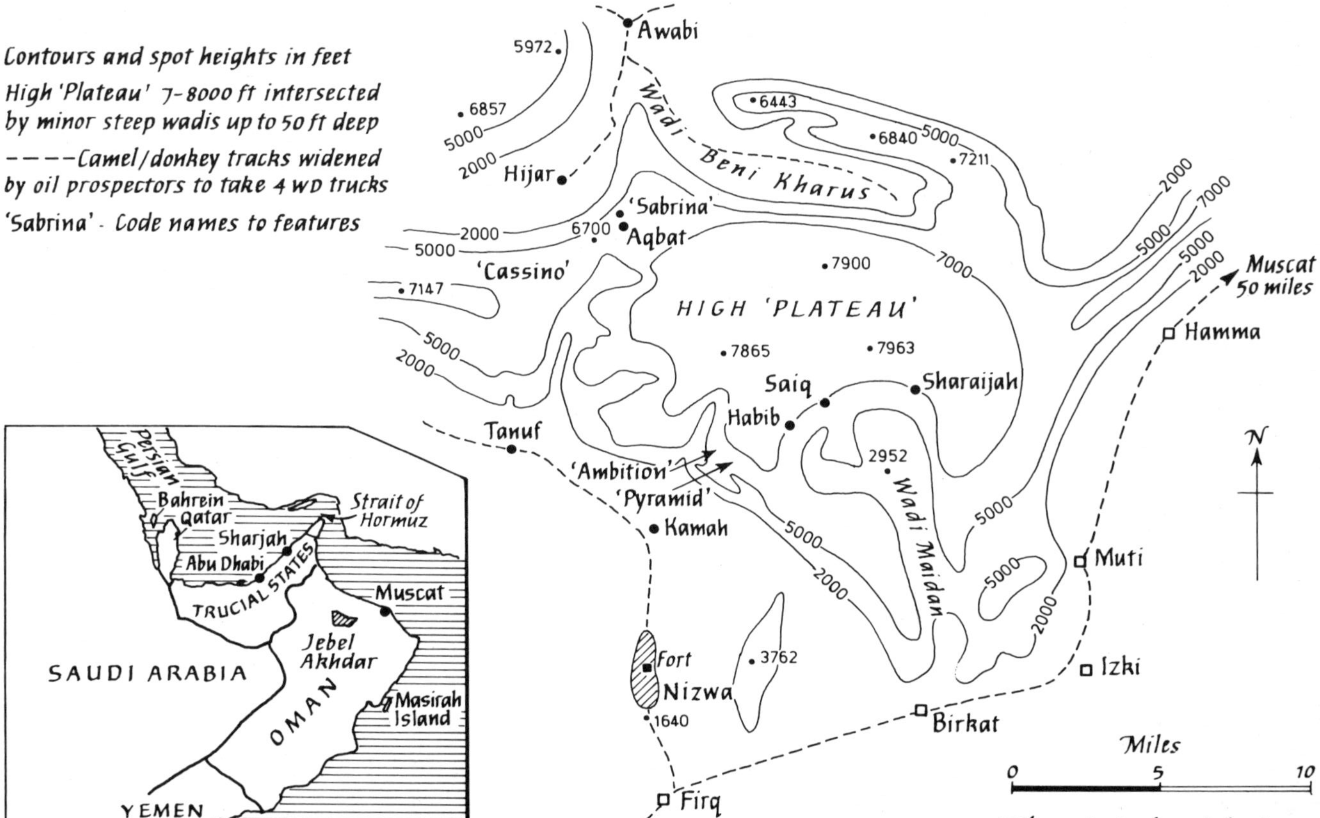

The Jebel Akhdar

As I jumped down from the plane, I had another look at the main mountain. A few cumulus clouds had formed from nowhere and floated over the highest ridges over 7000 feet above where we were standing. Somehow its grey-brown walls, with the regular dark purple splashes caused by the wadis, seemed mystical and attractive. The slab-shaped sides pointed up at the sky with the tops joined by the line of the plateau beyond.

As I stood looking upwards, a heavily sandbagged Land Rover with no windscreen drove up, followed by a cloud of dust to take us to the CO's office. Here was Lieutenant-Colonel Paul McConnel, a large man with curly black hair who had only recently taken over command of the Northern Frontier Regiment.

Paul was delighted to see us. He had been given an outline of what the SAS might be doing and had some plans of his own which he hoped would be approved. He thought that, if the SAS were given the job, this would completely change the attitude of all the local sheikhs because they would see that the British Government was really doing something about the rebellion.

'Well Tony,' he asked, 'are you bringing the whole Regiment? I'm sure you'll need it.' I quickly disillusioned him. 'Sorry. The idea at the moment is only fifty volunteers, from which patrols might be found to capture or kill off the three leaders on the top.'

'I hate to say it,' he replied, 'but the chances of your doing that are close to zero. In my view, you'll never get guides to take you to where they are, even if they were offered really enormous bribes.' He had a map covered with a transparent sheet on which were marked the ten or eleven possible tracks up to the plateau from the desert below. Seven of these tracks came from the south side and only two of these were passable to donkeys. The remainder were very steep mountain paths that he thought were just climbable on foot.

'Can you tell me all you know about the rebels on this side of the Jebel?' I asked.

'There's not a lot to say. We know that whenever we even start up the lower slopes we'll be fired at by snipers. We know that there are quite strong pickets further up all the tracks. These are tactically sited to ambush any further movement. We are still carrying out company and platoon training down here to prepare for what I have in mind in the future.'

'Can you tell me what that will be?'

'Sorry. David Smiley doesn't know about it yet and I haven't quite decided which route I should follow to get to the top of the Jebel. I'll certainly need a lot of air resupply.'

This snippet of information alarmed me. Only a year before the same Regiment, under the previous Commanding Officer, had been driven back down the Kamah track by rebel pickets. Even assuming better training, another daylight assault up one of the alternative ways would almost certainly end in disaster because the rebels now had their tails right up. All the tracks wound their way up the bottom or the side of the wadis with steep mountains on all sides. Every few hundred yards there was a suitable ambush position and it would need very well-trained troops to operate successfully under those conditions. I thought it best to make no comment.

We then had lunch, and I was interested to meet a few of his British and Pakistani officers. They were quite a mixed bunch and came from many different corps and regiments. Our plan in the afternoon was to take the plane over the mountain and land at Awabi on the north side. From there we would fly back to Muscat along the northern side of the Jebel, taking a look at any possible alternative ways up.

We took off from Nizwa, flying the twelve miles or so towards Tanuf on the south side where one of the SAF camps was located next to a wadi with running water. As we flew parallel to a giant grey slab of rock, we realized that what at first looked quite smooth was in fact a whole series of rocks of all shapes, piled higgledy-piggledy on top of the main mountain below. We then started climbing steeply and after a little while we banked over to the right, high over the mountain as we threaded our way between occasional clouds. From our bird's eye view we could see how the Wadi Tanuf cut the mountain almost in two, ending in a cliff face, the top of which was a narrow bridge connecting the high mountain on the left with the rebel-held plateau on the right. To clear the mountain we climbed to over 9000 feet and suddenly, beyond, it tumbled down in another very steep wadi which drove right through the mountain from the north. Down we came steeply to land on a strip next to the Fort at Awabi, where we were met by a formidable-looking Major with an enormous brown beard.

I learnt later that he was Group Captain Jasper Coates who had been in charge of all RAF operations in the Persian Gulf. He had become fascinated with the Arab way of life and had joined the Sultan's Armed Forces when he retired. Short and stocky, with a twinkle in his eye, he took us off to his fort to give us tea.

The Major gave us some more information about his side of the mountain.

'The wadi which leads up into the mountain from here is the Wadi Beni Kharus and, about six miles up, it divides. One part goes along the north face of the mountain through a series of villages which are more or less hostile to the Sultan, while the other branch goes on to Hijah. This village is quite friendly and it is from here that you may be able to get guides to lead you to the top. This is about as far as you can expect any guides to take you.

'You might like to know that this route is also the way the Persians are believed to have come 700 years ago, as they thought it was the only possible way up.'

The pilot wanted to get back because it was getting late, so, regretfully, we cut short our visit. Once more we took off over the little mud-walled fort with the Red Flag hanging limp from a mast which stuck out at an angle from the tower.

As we flew on back, I could see another great natural bowl on our right which cut the plateau off from a subsidiary sawtooth ridge that led back to Muscat. Even this ridge was 5000 feet high, but, compared with the real thing, it seemed to be a relatively minor obstacle.

The sun had just set as we landed back on our home strip and a Land Rover came out to take us back to the Fort. There was now no doubt in my mind that the Jebel Akhdar would provide the Regiment with a totally new environment, one completely different from the jungle. I relished the idea of coming to grips with rebel pickets which would give us opportunities for lots of real action. If we kept up the pressure, as I was sure we would, it would be bound to lower the rebels' morale and give them really bloody noses in the process. This might persuade them to talk to the Sultan's representatives, even if the rather wild idea of killing off the three leaders was shown to be impracticable.

The mountain and its plateau covered such a large area that deployment of a small SAS squadron was like pitching a tiny David against a gigantic Goliath. On the other hand some well-planned and executed battles could prepare the way for a second squadron and a small tactical HQ.

If we were to operate successfully all over the Jebel we would need administrative backup, most of which was sorely lacking in Muscat. If we had casualties we must have surgical facilities within reach. A helicopter was essential for casualty evacuation from anywhere on the mountain and air resupply must be available.

Another aspect which would only concern the squadron was security. Any publicity at home concerning our operations would immediately result in our withdrawal. In this we were helped by the Sultan who had just decreed that no reporters or photographers would be allowed in Oman. Apparently he had been annoyed by some quite accurate reporting by James Morris who had just published a book on Oman.

I sat down to write a letter to Major-General Jack Hamilton who was head of operations in the War Office at the time. He would be able to arrange the authority we needed for deployment and Frank Kitson could take the letter back.* David Smiley agreed with my letter and I told him that the earliest we could leave Malaya with one Squadron would be 15 November. The

* See copy of letter at Appendix 2.

Squadron was deployed on operations in the deep jungle and it would have to be extracted by helicopter and given about seven days of retraining to fit it for a complete change of role. My main concern was to start our patrolling as soon as possible before the hot weather arrived in April of the following year.

Provided we were given the authority, I told David Smiley that I would come back with the Squadron and start them off before going back again to Malaya. We both agreed that the task was really far too much for one Squadron. I was also concerned that the Squadron Commander might find himself side-tracked by all the different personalities on the ground and diverted from his Squadron and his fighting patrols. The key to the deployment of both Squadrons was the need for tight security and no publicity at all in the media at home as long as we were in Oman.

Our final call was in Bahrein to outline what we had in mind and get their approval. Here a three-Service committee, run by the Political Resident in the Persian Gulf, was soon convinced and suitable telegrams were sent off to the Foreign Office in London.

By the time I arrived back in Malaya late on 2 November authority had been received for the deployment of one Squadron to Oman. I also heard that a field surgical team together with a transfusion unit should be in place near Nizwa by 25 November, together with two light helicopters similar to those we had used in Malaya. We would also be able to call on the RAF Vallettas based at Bahrein for air drops. The War Office had moved fast in obtaining inter-service agreement for a small but complicated plan and I was delighted. We had got the job and it was now up to us to show that we could do it.

Some twenty years later I heard that when Frank Kitson got back to London he was asked by General Hamilton to brief the Chief of the Defence Staff, Marshal of the Royal Air Force Sir William Dickson* (He was also told that if Winston Churchill had still been Prime Minister, he would have been asked to brief him.) The Chief of the Defence Staff was soon convinced and approval from the Government quickly followed. Back in Malaya I had no idea that so many big guns were supporting our new role. Thank God they did.

John Watts and D Squadron were on operations in the deep jungle near the Thai border. Special Branch Intelligence had given us a large number of leads and his troops had already discovered unoccupied camp sites and tracks leading over the border to where Chin Peng and the terrorist high command might be located. He was astonished to get signals withdrawing the whole Squadron as quickly as possible for 'another operation'. Helicop-

* *Bunch of Five,* Frank Kitson, p.182.

ters brought everybody out by 4 November and I told John Watts where he was going next. He was astonished, as was Bob Walker-Brown, my second-in-command. Bob was a top-class infantryman who had served in the SAS before and was able to set up a crash conversion course for the new role. I told them that nobody else in the Squadron would get a briefing until they arrived in Oman. They quickly saw that the whole success of our future operations was dependent on no information getting into the newspapers.

I sent the whole Squadron on 48 hours' leave before starting retraining. Even then only seven days would be available to get everybody ready. As there had been trouble in the Sudan at this time, some maps of Khartoum and the country to the south were obtained and pinned up in the Ops room behind curtains. This would explain the need for pale brown khaki clothing and heavy boots with thick rubber soles, totally different from the relatively thin lace-up jungle boots and dark green clothing used in the jungle.

The SAS was used to hard work, but the Squadron had never worked so continuously or so energetically as they did during those seven days. The change in visibility from twenty to thirty yards in the jungle to thousands in Arabia forced a complete change of tactics. Rifles had to be shot on the ranges and a few became snipers using telescopic sights. Two teams were trained on the three-inch mortar; John Watts selected those who had been mortarmen in their own regiments. Everybody fired the 3.5-inch rocket launcher and Energa anti-tank grenade, which we thought might be useful against caves. Once more minor infantry tactics were practised to the astonishment of a battalion nearby. They could not understand why the SAS, of all people, should want to practise tactics that were nearly useless in the jungle.*

While D Squadron was still retraining, I had to get back to Arabia and see the Brigadier Commanding Land Forces Persian Gulf at Bahrein. I aimed to get to Muscat at least a day ahead of the troops, who should arrive on 19 November.

Everything went according to plan. Bob Walker-Brown laid on with the RAF an excellent deception plan in Malaya. Aircraft were tasked for Aden on the way to Khartoum with landings at Columbo and Masirah Island for fuel. At Masirah Island the aircraft were withdrawn back to Singapore for 'an emergency move' and, after they had left, two Beverleys from Aden came in to take the Squadron on to Azaibha Airstrip to the north of Muscat. I met them on arrival and told them where they were.

A line of open trucks with no windscreens and heavily sandbagged floors was waiting at the edge of the strip, driven by little brown Omani soldiers. They were soon on their way, driving like the wind and raising a long plume of white dust behind each truck. The lorries rattled and shook. Several times

* Op Instruction NO 1 issued in Malaya on 3 November, 1958.

the engines roared as the back wheels left the ground. Tarmac roads were unheard of in Oman and this was a track roughly bulldozed out of the desert by the oil company. It was one of the better roads in the country.

Our camp was in the process of erection by a small detachment of British Sappers. I had been distinctly alarmed by stories I heard in Bahrein regarding medical casualties. Apparently rather more than 100% of the few British soldiers serving in Oman had had to be evacuated each year, mainly due to gastric diseases, sunstroke or heat exhaustion. We could not afford such nonsense, and, unlike the other British who lived adjacent to the Arabs, we set up camp about half a mile away from existing tents or buildings. The Sappers had built a fly-proofed canvas cookhouse and had hired locals to dig latrine trenches more than 10 feet deep. We did not lose anybody for medical reasons the whole time we were in Oman.

After supper I had everybody together in the large tent that doubled as a mess hall and canteen. I needed to tell them what was in store.

A large map of the country had been pinned to a blackboard and showed where they were and where the rebels were holding out.

'The latest information is that there are at least 600 well-trained rebels on the Jebel Akhdar or Green Mountain. Of these, 100 received their training in Saudi Arabia, 4-500 are members of the fighting Bani Riyam tribe and about 100 are Bani Hinna. There may also be about ten foreigners from Saudi Arabia to give advice on things like 3″ mortars and possibly work wireless sets.

'The rebels are sustained and provisioned by the main villages in the middle of the plateau, the total population of which is thought to be about five thousand.

'There are three rebel leaders. One is Suleiman bin Hamyar, Paramount Sheikh of the Bani Riyam tribe who live on the greater part of the mountain. Next is Ghalib, who is an Imam or religious leader and he is from the Bani Hinna, who live in an area to the west. Lastly is Talib who has been styled General by Cairo Radio and is Ghalib's younger brother. All three are being helped with Saudi gold, arms and mines. Most of the arms, mines and ammunition come from the USA and are supplied to Saudi Arabia by their American military mission.

'The Sultan's Armed Forces consist of little more than a battalion, plus some artillery near Nizwa. So far they only hold a ring round the foot of the mountain. At the moment the rebels feel very cocky, as they always get away with it.

'The RAF have shot up what they could see with Venoms and bombed what they couldn't with Shackletons. As they have never had men on the ground to point out targets, they have wasted a lot of bombs and ammunition to not much effect. The Shackletons have dropped over one thousand tons of bombs. The pilots say that a Jebel donkey is about all they ever see wandering loose on the hillside.

'Rebel armaments include not only rifles and light machine guns, but also heavy half-inch anti-aircraft machine guns and mortars. They have been quite successful dropping salvos of 3″ mortar bombs into the Sultan's camps, usually at night.

'I have given your Squadron Commander his orders, but in outline I want you to carry out detailed reconnaissances of all possible ways up and engage any pickets you can find. The object is to establish a moral superiority over the rebels, which will give us our opportunity later on. Also, of course, it will show us the best way up.

'I am told there is no doubt that, if the leaders are killed, the rebellion will be over. When we know more about the mountain and the possible ways up, I will be in a better position to decide the next step. We may well decide to get guides to lead small parties to where the leaders are based and then try and take them prisoner or even kill them if they resist. If this is not possible or we cannot get the guides, I am sure we will need two squadrons to go up the mountain by a route you must find, not guarded by too many pickets.

'You will leave for the Jebel in four days' time, but in the meantime, I want you to study these rather poor maps but excellent air photos. I will arrange for all Troop Commanders to have a look at the whole mountain from the air and for this we can call on the use of Single Pioneer aircraft which are based here.

'There are two old Vallettas based at Bahrein 700 miles away, and you will get them when nothing else will do. It is like having the Vallettas down in Singapore and having air drops two hundred miles into Thailand, so we have to be very economical. One of the difficulties of this place is its isolation. Bahrein has a few stores, but Aden is the real stockpile and it is over 1000 miles away, or as far as Rome is from England. In practice, you are operating on a shoestring in the arse end of nowhere. A ship calls in once a month and only things with a high priority will be flown in, but, of course, if you are on the top of the mountain you must have airdrops. In case these don't work due to weather, our second line of supply is by donkey or man-pack. Donkeys are the only creatures that can get up the mountain and two hundred have just been brought here from Somalia by ship because there are not enough in the villages round the mountain. You may have to rely on them for ammunition, water and rations, so do not turn up your noses at them.'

Captain Muir Walker, John Watts' second-in-command, asked 'Under whose command are we, sir?'

'You are an independent Squadron directly under the British Colonel seconded here as Commander of the Sultan's Armed Forces. I have arranged with him that you are given the freest possible hand and that in no circumstances will part of the Squadron be put under command of any of the local troops. He is coming up tomorrow and would like to speak to you, so you will see him then.'

We drank to the future that night and the party went on until quite late. We were all excited at the prospect ahead and eager to get on with it. Before turning in I strolled out of the mess tent and stood outside looking towards Muscat over the jagged mountains silhouetted against the starlit night sky. A light breeze was blowing, which made the red flag flutter, still flying over the fort in the hollow. In the foreground our own sentry was standing by the entrance to the ring of concertina wire, which went right round our tented camp, and a light streamed out from the guardroom close by. I went back to my own tent and sat on the end of the low camp bed, unexpectedly sent up with all the rest of the camp kit from Aden. I wondered how it would all turn out. We were certainly sticking our necks out. Either we would be wildly successful, or we were letting ourselves in for big trouble. We were gambling, but the stakes for the SAS were high. The stakes for Britain with a secure source of oil in Oman were even higher.

Before I returned to Malaya, the officers of the Sultan's Armed Forces asked us all in for a drink and a meal. Also invited were the officers from the attached Squadron of Life Guards, so there was quite a big party to squeeze into their mess.

David Smiley welcomed us at the door and then we met all his officers. The Forces doctor was a Pakistani, who looked a little old and frustrated as he shook all our hands with a welcoming smile.

They were soon telling us stories about the horrors that awaited us and none of them believed we could do much good. 'After all,' one of them said, 'our men add up to nearly 800 and so far we have not achieved very much or been able to lower the rebels' morale. What we want is a brigade to come here and sort it all out for good.'

'Why the hell the War Office sends a handful of SAS to do what we know needs three battalions at least, we cannot think.'

'Nothing against you people; we're sure you are very good, but I'm sorry to say that you haven't an earthly.'

'Why not?' I asked innocently.

'Why, because of the bloody country. You will go up a few thousand feet perhaps, and you will have plenty of fighting, but you won't put down the rebellion. That is, not until you get someone to show you where Suleiman, Talib or Ghalib's caves are located. But you never will.'

'Why not?' I asked.

'Because these people are fanatical and they will never stoop so low as to show infidels where their own leaders are hiding. Even if you paid them a million pounds each they wouldn't do it; it would be against their religion and they would much rather die than commit such a sin. They are all members of the Ibadhi sect of Muslims who have an extreme code of practice determining every action. Up till only a very few years ago, a man could avoid making a pilgrimage to Mecca by murdering an infidel, which was an easy way out of a long and near-killing journey of over 1000 miles by camel. This is partly why explorers were distinctly discouraged from coming to this country. They didn't last long.'

We had a pleasant meal and did not talk any more about the country's troubles. Our hosts were kind to us, but were not quite sure what sort of people we were. By the time coffee came round, their minds were set at rest and I think we were accepted. Most of the contract officers and some of the seconded regular officers had their own reasons for serving in the Sultan's Armed Forces. For the regulars it was usually shortage of cash, or sometimes a desire for adventure, which had driven them from their sheltered regimental life.

The next day I had to return to Malaya where we still had two squadrons on operations. I was sorry to go back because I could see that success in the Oman was to be crucial to our future. But John Watts was a superb officer; I had no need to be worried.

* 25 *

JEBEL AKHDAR I

'Great things are done when men and mountains meet,
this is not done by jostling in the street.'
William Blake

I arrived back in Malaya towards the end of November and once again was able to check the progress being made with the other two squadrons. Although the war against the communist terrorists had nearly ceased in most of the country south of Ipoh, there was a lot of information from the Special Branch that the main area for us would be within thirty miles of the Thai border. Chin Peng had his headquarters in southern Thailand and SAS patrols were initially authorized to find the main routes running north-south through the jungle, to engage any C.T.s or couriers found and to build up our intelligence in the area. The main difficulty of operating at all in the north of Malaya was its inaccessibility. Very large tracts of untouched primary jungle covered not only the central spine of the country, but also nearly down to the coastline on each side of the peninsula. No doubt this was one reason why Chin Peng had decided to base himself just north of the border. He was also safe from any action we could take.

Johnny Cooper and A Squadron had just been deployed as I arrived back from Oman. He was full of hope that this new area for the Regiment would pay dividends. Reports soon came back showing results. Although no C.T.s were found, recent tracks and abandoned camp sites slowly contributed to our information which we passed on to Special Branch.

D Squadron in the meantime sent daily signals summarizing their operations on the Jebel and about once a week John Watts expanded this with a personal letter filling in what had happened. There was a lot to report.

John Watts and half his squadron had started operations in the Tanuf area and Muir Walker with the other two troops would be operating from Awabi in the north.

The journey to Tanuf had not been without incident. The oil company track led from the SAS camp at Bait al Faluj and passed through the tiny villages of Sumail, Muti, Izki, Birkat, Firq and the larger village of Nizwa. We had both seen these villages from the air before, looking like triangular splashes of green on the desert floor at the head of each wadi, where it disappeared into the heart of the Jebel. It had been much more impressive to

6 The Jebel Akhdar from near Nizwa (see map p.172) The High Plateau is on the right.

7 "The right-hand part of the Vincent slab ended in fifty-foot high cliffs up which we scrambled in and out of enormous boulders". (p.208)

8 The Great Fort at Nizwa.

9 "One Wadi, called Maidan, disappeared right into the middle and opened up into a giant bowl with precipitous sides thousands of feet high".

drive along the incredibly rough track over which the average speed was no more than 10 mph. Long plumes of white dust were put up by the trucks as they bumped and juddered their way forward. The convoy consisted of four lorries and a water truck. All of them broke down at least once and finally one of them had to end its journey on tow. All the vehicles had been provided from stockpile in Aden and were not in good shape.

The track ran straight along the valley and, when it came to a village, it wound its way in and out of the squat mud huts surrounded by date palms. The rank smell of cooking garlic and the strong stench of goats wafted over the walls as the convoy twisted between the houses. The masked women dressed in black pressed themselves and their curly-headed brown children against a wall and looked at D Squadron with interest as they rumbled through. Scrawny chickens ran out of the way of the lorries, where they had been picking at donkey or camel droppings and somewhere in every village the convoy passed over a water faluj. This was Allah's greatest gift to them; without it life would cease. The fast-flowing water came by underground conduits from a perennial spring higher up the wadi and was a relic left by the Persians 600 years ago. The rainfall on the mountain must have been quite heavy to sustain so many falujs, each one ending in a village of date palms, which varied in size according to the amount of water.

Occasionally on this journey they passed a line of laden camels led by a little man in his long dirty yellow 'nightshirt' or disdasha, with a large twisted turban on his head, dwarfing a thin bearded face. Slung over his shoulder was an incredibly ancient gun with a bandolier of ammunition round his tummy. Like most Omanis he was armed with a ½-inch smooth-bore Martini Henry, while the bullets in the cartridge belt round his middle looked equally unreliable. As I had discovered during my brief trip to Oman, after circumcision at about 15 years old, everyone carried guns to show their virility and also perhaps in self-defence. We found later on that the real mountain Arabs were incredibly accurate with their ancient pieces up to about two hundred yards and could knock over even moving targets at that range.

At last they saw Tanuf, which was already a base for a company of the NFR. After taking one look at the squalor and the fly-ridden burastis*, John set up his own camp a quarter of a mile away and upstream of the village and the NFR.

Tanuf had been chosen because it was the western limit of the rebel-held area. The wadi wound its way into the mountain with precipitous cliffs on both sides nearly joining up with another wadi coming from the north. The

* Shelter made from the fronds of woven date palms.

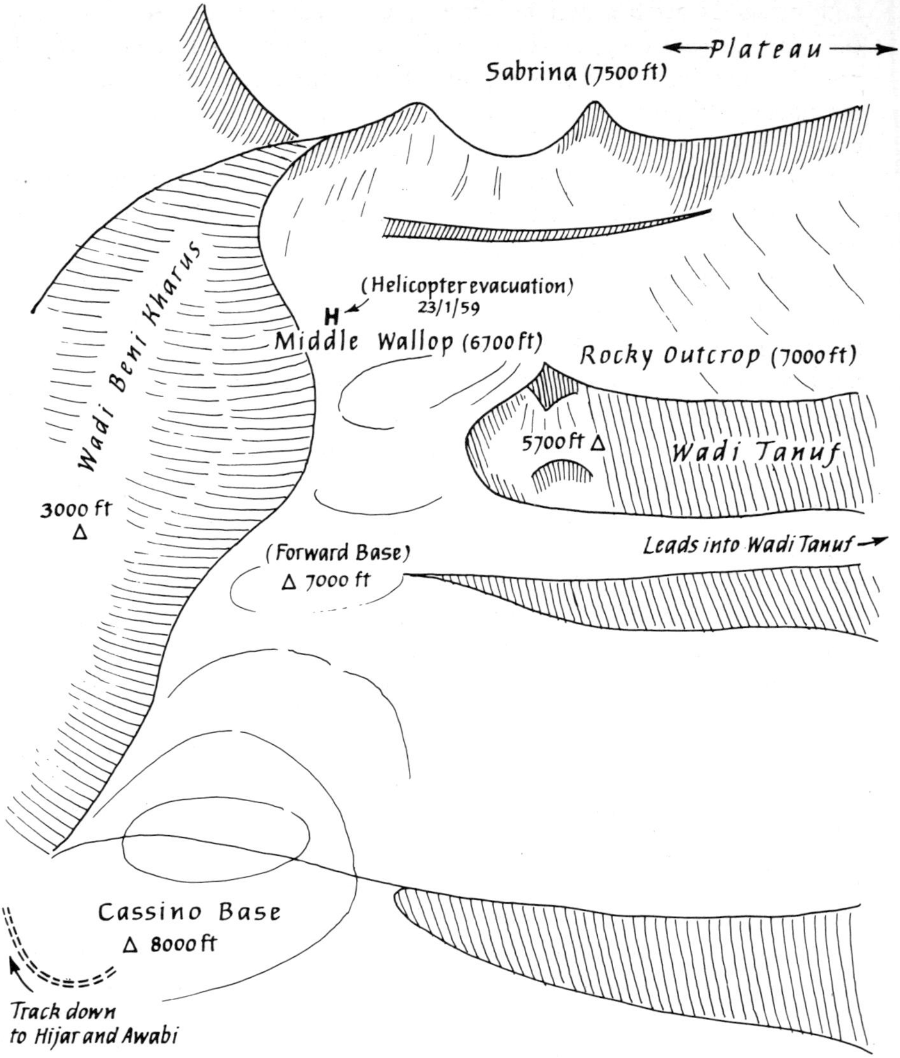

Shaded areas – near vertical cliffs
Distances – Cassino Base – Sabrina approx 2000 yards
Rocky Outcrop – Sabrina approx 800 yards
Heights (Δ) are approximate

The Aqbat

high bridge in between was known as the Aqbat-al-Dhafur and was nearly 8000 feet above Tanuf, but in a straight line was only eight miles away. It was here that the other half of the Squadron coming from Awabi would start their operations, treading the same path as the Persian conquerors 700 years earlier.

Such meagre intelligence as had been provided suggested that the redoubtable Talib bin Ali operated from a cave an hour and a half's march up the wadi. It was as good a place to start as any other.

Liaison with the NFR Company painted a depressing picture. The company had two British officers, one of them a Royal Marine instructor on short-term loan. The night before the Squadron had arrived, the rebels had mortared the camp rather inaccurately and followed this up by firing several bursts of LMG right into the burastis where lights could be seen. As the Company were all below ground, there were no casualties, but it was clear that the rebels had the initiative. Apparently the Company had tried going a short way up the shoulders of the wadi by day, but each time they were engaged by pickets and forced to fall back. They had had three casualties a week ago from accurate rebel shooting, and there was not much fire left in their bellies. They had also lost two men when firing at rebels over open sights with their 3.75-inch howitzer. The muzzle had been depressed so low that a shell exploded on the parapet round the gun pit.

John decided he would move by night into suitable positions up the mountain from which to observe rebel movement the following day. They would then come back to camp the second night.

In the meantime Muir Walker and the other two Troops had arrived at Awabi. He used his initiative and decided to move immediately up the wadi going south, as it wound its way between near-vertical 3000-foot cliffs barely fifty yards apart in some places. Where the wadi closed in, the scoring of flood water could be seen fifty feet up the sides and would make this approach impossible when the stream was in spate. Pressing on through Hijar, they climbed right to the top of the Aqbat, over 7000 feet up, which was quickly nicknamed Cassino. It was an incredibly steep climb and at one point the track went up a narrow six-foot-wide cleft in a cliff of solid rock where eighty steps had been chipped out by the Persians. It was a piece of luck that this particular route was not defended, but it was not until he was on top that Walker realized why.

Although this mountain was the highest piece of ground in the area by a few hundred feet, it was connected to the main rebel-held plateau by a narrow 'bridge' of land only one hundred yards wide in places and about a mile long. On either side of this 'bridge' great yawning cliffs dropped down into the Wadi Beni Kharus up which he had come on the left and into the head of the Wadi Tanuf a mere two thousand feet lower down on the right.

Unfortunately the 'bridge' was by no means smooth and on the far side of the lowest point, marked by a minor ravine, were two small hills about six hundred feet high. The most economical place for the rebels to defend the plateau from a manpower point of view was at the narrowest point and included the hills. These he had nicknamed Sabrina, after the well-developed lady of that name. It was possible to outflank the cleft up the cliff, but it was not possible to get round Sabrina.

Muir realized the tremendous lift to the morale of the locals if he could hold on to Cassino and so his first concern was to ferry up sleeping bags, ammunition and rations to make his position secure. He protected his position by putting out Sergeant Hawkins with five men and an LMG about 1500 yards away on the forward slope looking at Sabrina.

Gales usually blew at 7000 feet and the evening of December was no exception when the rebels attacked. It was not until Sergeant Hawkins and his men turned up at about 8 pm that Muir even knew that a battle had taken place less than a mile away, but downwind.

Sergeant Hawkins reported that he had seen forty to fifty rebels moving down the slope in front of Sabrina. The time was about 4.30 pm and he lost sight of them as they dropped down into the ravine. They used every fold in the ground to work their way forward to where the patrol was located and dropped off their LMGs on a hillock above the ravine. A rebel in a white turban appeared to do the controlling and when they had moved up to only two hundred yards from the patrol, their LMGs opened up with the main body using fire and movement in a classic infantry advance. Sergeant Hawkins held his fire until the rebels were within 150 yards and good targets presented themselves. He was certain that five were killed and he may have wounded several more. This did not stop the rebel advance because they started to work round his flank and get on a hill above him. By this time it was dark, which allowed the gallant Hawkins to pull out, also using fire and movement with Corporal Cunningham manning his own LMG in a quite brilliant manner. There had been no casualties on our side except cuts from bullets breaking off rocks nearby. About a week later confirmation was received that between nine and twelve rebels had died on the Aqbat*.

After this Muir decided to move up closer so that he could at least hear when a firefight was going on. Next morning before first light he sent out another strong patrol to check on the position. The rebels had gone. They had been shattered by our fierce opposition and they retired to their positions behind Sabrina to lick their wounds. It had been a most savage and well-organised attack that might have come off had it not been for Hawkins'

* Daily signals received in Malaya.

cool head. Muir realized he had taken far too great a risk with his own security. He must not be caught out again.

While Sergeant Hawkins had been having his fight on Cassino, John Watts had also been busy. Moving up the mountain by night two days after he had arrived at Tanuf, he put out four separate patrols to observe the rebel-held mountain by day from well-concealed positions. Some rebel movement was spotted by one of the patrols and later on a hardcore tribesman with a modern rifle started to climb up the wadi towards Corporal Smith. He was shot down and his rifle and bandolier recovered; one of the bullets from the FN rifle actually tore off the rebel's left arm. Sergeant Davidson was commanding the right-hand patrol and when he heard the firing about 600 yards to his left he started to move over to give help. Unfortunately Corporal Swindells MM stood up on the crest of the hill and was immediately shot dead by a rebel sniper concealed in the rocks two hundred yards below them. The patrol immediately returned fire, dropping the rebel who was dragged into cover by a companion. Both patrols then came under very heavy and quite accurate sniping for half an hour, together with some inaccurate mortar fire. The rebels eventually withdrew and both patrols came back down the hillside bringing with them Corporal Swindells' body. This was our first casualty. He was later buried with full military honours at Muscat. Poor Corporal Swindells, he was a really dedicated hard-working soldier, who knew the jungle backwards. He could be relied on to set a fantastic example, too high a standard for many. In the jungle it did not matter standing on a crest, visibility was just the same, but here it was different. If he had to die, he went out the way he would have wished; the army was his whole life and he would not have enjoyed being a civilian.

The other part of D Squadron at Tanuf was commanded by Peter de la Billière. His patrols were to cover a part of the Jebel a few thousand yards back towards Nizwa. They too moved by night; by day they observed an extensive cave system with much rebel movement going on about 900 yards in front of the position. They all returned that night and John decided to mount a major operation with two troops to blast the cave area with the help of our own mortars and close air support from four RAF Venoms based at Sharjah.

John Watts, together with the reserve Troop and a small radio to talk to the Venoms, would move up by night and get into a position on the cliff edge well before dawn and about 300 yards from the caves. Peter de la Billière would take his Troop and move silently to a position below the cliff and only 200 yards away from the caves. He would have with him a 3.5 inch rocket-launcher and two LMGs. All the remainder would have their semi-automatic rifles. There were still two hours to wait until dawn and no alarm had been given.

Soon after dawn one man came out of the cave and stretched. He started a small fire to make coffee. Half a hour later three more came out and sat huddled round quite a respectable bonfire. By 7.25 three more came out and the time had come. Peter's Troop gave the signal to open fire and all hell broke loose, with brens, mortars and rifles all aiming at the rebels. This did not deter them. They immediately started to fire back and a little later joined in with their own mortars. The rocket launcher scored a direct hit into the cave mouth and the Venoms came in with accurate cannon fire. Not only did they shoot up the cave but also obliterated the rebel mortar position. It was the first time that the Venoms had had such targets and they were delighted. A total of eight rebels were thought to have been killed, but a week later a report came back that a total of twenty had died in the cave attack. A further piece of information came in and John was told that he had been lucky actually to choose Talib's cave. Included in those killed were his cousin, his servant, his head mortarman and his head heavy machine-gun man. Unfortunately their master had been away. Talib turned up later and his confidence was badly shaken when he saw the mess. He sent a message to Suleiman asking for immediate reinforcements to replace his heavy losses. On this occasion, so the story went, Suleiman was unsympathetic and gave a point-blank refusal.

After the war was over it turned out that the numbers killed were an exaggeration. Not more than four were killed (plus an unknown number wounded), including the Sheikh in charge of the cave and his wife. He was the first senior rebel to be killed and was a cousin of both Ghalib and Talib. The cave was full of rations, much of which were destroyed, together with fifty goats. Talib was shocked by the death of his cousin and the loss of rations which the rebels could ill afford. The war on the ground had suddenly taken a turn for the worse.

John Watts also reported that he had been blown up on a mine, as had another truck, when going back to Nizwa to see Paul McConnel. Fortunately nobody had been hurt, but he had been shaken up and the trucks were a write-off. In the next two months, half the Squadron's vehicles went up on mines and one driver went up three times.

The Squadron had won rounds one and two on each side of the Jebel, but Muir would need reinforcing if he was to hang on to his exposed position up on the Aqbat. John flew down to Muscat to see David Smiley and find out what could be done. Two days later a platoon from the NFR, together with four teams from the Life Guards, with their own air-cooled Browning MMGs, joined the SAS on the mountain. These provided real security for the base and thus allowed the SAS to move out on patrol and plan future offensive action.

While Muir Walker was establishing and reinforcing his firm base at 7000 feet, John Watts decided to probe another part of the Jebel beyond Nizwa. The SAF had a company near Muti and this appeared to be a suitable base from which to operate.

Back in Malaya on 8 December, I was becoming concerned. There was no doubt that D Squadron was doing magnificently and was in the process of establishing a moral superiority over the rebels, but both David Smiley and John Watts were advising in separate messages that a second squadron and small tactical HQ were becoming essential. The SAS was the only effective offensive force operating and the savage nature of the fighting had been putting a strain on all ranks. This meant that the Squadron had to be pulled out every few weeks for rest and retraining and inevitably this would take the pressure off the rebels. Small SAS patrols could lie up and report enemy activity by day, provided they were not detected, but any subsequent battles which were planned could only be carried out using normal infantry tactics. Whole SAS troops, or even pairs of troops, had to be employed to make certain that success would be achieved without having casualties ourselves, or, if we had, could extricate our own dead and wounded successfully.

Three days later, on 12 December, I was able to have a long discussion with General Jim Cassels and describe our operations to date. He was most sympathetic and suggested I should go straight down to Singapore and see the Chief of Staff at Far East Land Forces. The Chief of Staff also agreed and sent off messages to the War Office on 13 December recommending that a second squadron plus a small HQ should be released to Oman.

David Smiley was also able to persuade the British political advisers based in Muscat and Bahrein that, in view of D Squadron's successes, and bearing in mind that no information had leaked out into British newspapers, a reinforcement of D Squadron by a further Squadron was essential if the rebellion was to be put down before the advent of hot weather the following April.

I was also able to fill in the gaps in bare messages with a letter of explanation to Colonel Hunter in the Planning Branch in the War Office. He did not get this until 17 December. By the time the Foreign Office had given approval – and I fancy the Christmas holiday had taken its toll – we did not receive the go-ahead until 29 December. The War Office now accepted that SAS operations in Muscat took absolute priority over Malaya and that I was free to produce such reinforcements of men and equipment as I thought necessary. This was terrific. A Squadron was in the jungle and once again we had to get them out for 'another operation'. Unfortunately, just at this moment all helicopters were grounded for technical reasons and they had to get out in the best way possible. There was quite a large river flowing through their area. Johnnie Cooper soon had the Squadron making rafts from giant bamboos to float out down the fast-flowing water. In spite of no helicopters being available, the Squadron was only 24 hours later than normal in extracting themselves from the jungle.

The same procedure applied as for D Squadron, with only seven days' retraining for the change of rôle. I was able to go on ahead and get to Oman by 1 January, 1959, and size up the situation on the ground, but in the meantime D Squadron had had some more battles – and had worn out their boots.

Boots. Boots. Boots. They wore out fast. Only five to ten days of hard patrolling over the hillside was enough to wear the thick rubber soles down to the leather. As these boots were not normal issue at the time, the War Office could not understand how seventy-five men could use up three issues of boots in twenty-one days. Rather unwisely, some well-meaning officer turned the request down and asked for 'reasons in writing' to be forwarded 'through the normal channels'. I even heard about it in Malaya and was able to unstick it with some flash messages. The boots left England by special aircraft twenty-four hours later. I heard that the War Office thought we must be selling boots to the locals. Little did they realize that Omani Arabs always went barefoot. Under English conditions these boots could not be worn out, but in the Oman they only lasted five to ten days. Such is the difference between Salisbury Plain and the Jebel Akhdar.

The men were in good spirits, but they found the new life mentally and physically tiring. Although Malaya had made the ultimate demand on physical stamina, battles were rare and only lasted seconds. Movement could only take place by day, and nights in the deep jungle were completely secure for rest and cooking large meals of curry and rice. Demands on physical endurance in Oman were just as heavy, and movement could only take place by night, which in some way increased the mental strain on everybody taking part.

I continued to get messages and letters from Oman while I was still in Malaya in the last half of December, 1958. I was on a plane within an hour of getting War Office authority and left it to Bob Walker-Brown to brief Johnnie Cooper and arrange the retraining of A Squadron. It was almost becoming routine but it was all done superbly. A Squadron arrived in Oman on 12 January, rekitted. retrained and ready for battle.

On arrival in Oman on 1 January, 1959, my immediate concern was to set up a small organization to control the two Squadrons and if possible to make the best use of the Life Guards, dismounted from their Ferrets, the Sultan's Armed Forces and Trucial Oman Scouts. David Smiley was soon converted to this idea which fitted in well with his own plans. He believed that his main task was to reorganize his base at Bait al Faluj and ensure that not only the equipment but also the dress of the Sultan's Armed Forces be brought up to scratch. He appointed me to be Deputy Field Commander of all forces in Oman with the task of putting down the rebellion as soon as possible. This was excellent, but privately he told me that he rather doubted if we could do it. In practice I was now the Field Commander of all operational troops and this was the first step towards the defeat of the rebels. Among other things it resulted in the production of the first ever plan for the assault on the Jebel and coordinated the actions of ground troops and aircraft.*

Some attempt was also made to disseminate and distribute intelligence. The troops now under command looked impressive. We had

Two SAS Squadrons.
Assault troop of D Squadron, Life Guards.
Section of British Sappers.
Two Squadrons of Trucial Oman Scouts.
The Northern Frontier Regiment.
200 Abriyeen Tribal Levies.
400 Bani Ruwaha Tribal Levies.

Aircraft on Call
12 Venoms from Sharjah.
6 Shackletons from Masirah
6 Valettas from Bahrein.
2 Light Helicopters based at Nizwa.
Artillery
2, 5.5″ guns, 2, 3.5 Screw Guns, 2, 3.75″ Howitzers,
2, 4.2″ mortars, all well served by Pakistani gun crews.

Field Surgical Team and associated transfusion unit.

Our tiny Tactical Headquarters was set up at Nizwa on 3 January, 1959. Captain John Spreull had come with me from Malaya as Operations Officer and he was in charge. It was inadequately staffed, housed and equipped by the standards of the day, but it just managed to do the job.

Soon after arrival in Oman I had to get up to date with operations and fill in the gaps in the messages I had received in Malaya. John Watts had decided to relieve Muir Walker and his two troops on Cassino by Peter de la Billière and his troop. There was now a whole squadron of Trucial Oman Scouts, plus the Life Guards, on top to protect the base, but Peter had to be in position before Muir could be withdrawn. The TOS was not prepared to be there without the SAS.

Muir and his two Troops had arrived back in Bait only the day before and

* Operation Order No 1 dated 5 January, 1959, signed by me as 'Deputy Field Commander all troops Oman'.

I had already heard that he had had a highly successful battle and had suffered no casualties.

He was still wildly excited and was reliving the fight he had had only 48 hours before. Six foot tall and hard as nails, with curly ginger hair, he had come from an English county regiment. He even played the bagpipes when not too many others were around. His face was still the colour of unpolished copper, with split lips and large areas of forehead and chin peeling from sun and wind at 7-8000 feet. He was bubbling over with enthusiasm as he described what had happened. I told him I had heard all about Sergeant Hawkins' battle, so he could go on from there.

'Soon after Sergeant Hawkins' battle, I had to reorganize the base on Cassino. The rebels were in strength on Sabrina and I could not afford to take any risks with security.

'I was countering an aggressive fifty-strong enemy working from well-sited positions behind the natural features of Sabrina. By day or by night, the rebels sent out fighting patrols and I have no doubt that there were plenty more that could be called up from central reserves in an emergency. I was after all using the same historical entrance to the plateau as did the Persians, and Talib was well aware of it.

'My orders required both Troops to carry forward a hell of a lot of ammunition for the Brownings and LMGs. Their job would be to fire on Sabrina from positions between 300 and 1000 yards away.

'One Troop and myself would have to get up the right tit by rope. Our patrols had discovered it was much steeper than it looked from back on our base. Our job was to capture it, with the other Troop giving supporting fire.

'I considered that we did not have enough men to capture the whole of Sabrina, so the plan was to carry out a major raid and then withdraw back to our main base. This would give the rebels a really bloody nose and hopefully help lower their morale and raise ours.

'We started to move up just before last light at 5.15 pm and the LMGs and Brownings gave covering fire whilst we moved forward to the base of the right-hand tit. Here I put out a Troop on our left to cover us as we clambered in and out of a small wadi immediately short of the feature. From there we had to use ropes to get up the near-vertical cliff. We managed to scramble up the rocks until we could see rebels only twenty feet beyond and across a deep wadi. The rebels knew the SAS were there and taunted us by calling out, "Come on Johnnie". While waiting for a way to be found round this deep wadi, the SAS sang in reply, "Why are we waiting, O, why are we waiting", to the tune of the carol. It was Christmas after all!

'Once on top with the whole Troop, we loosed off two magazines into a rebel sangar only fifty yards away. We had captured the whole of the right-hand tit.

'As it was only a raid, I gave orders to withdraw at 2 am and by 8 am we were back in the main ravine below the hill. We took no chances and the two troops and mortars continued to give each other support. Astonishing though it may seem, we had no casualties. We must have had a charmed life.

'We definitely hit four rebels whom we saw drop down. We heard a few days later that the rebels had lost nine killed. We also heard that they had taken fright and had withdrawn to the next hill in their rear.

'We were back in our main base by 11 am and handed over to Peter who had watched the battle from it. The next day we dropped down the mountain and arrived back here yesterday morning.'

My next task was to get up to date with what John Watts had been doing. He had just come back to Bait with both Troops for rest and retraining. The only SAS left on operations at that moment was Peter de la Billière on Cassino.

John, too, was nearly black from the sun but he was now full of confidence after he had heard about A Squadron. He rapidly brought me up to date with more battles he had had with rebel pickets above Kamah and Sumait.

'It's not quite the end of what we did. I had been promised help from two Ibex hunters and together with Peter de la Billière and three volunteers, went out with them after the rest of the troops had returned to Bait. We took three SAS with us in case of treachery by the Ibex hunters.

'We picked them up at Izki on the way through and they looked a tough pair, as they gripped the muzzles of their rifles which rested on their shoulders. We had warned them to come prepared for two days and all they had with them was a bag of dates and a skin of water. Like the rebels, their dirty brown galabias and turbans would make them almost impossible to see against the hillside.

'In the morning we had a wonderful view from our crazy perch half-way up a big slab of rock and we could see where it led on up to the top. We had crossed the worst bit and so our object was achieved. We did not anticipate any difficulty once we were on the plateau, which at that point was only about three miles from the main villages of Saiq and Sharaijah.

'We then decided to go down again that night and dropped off our wiry and footsore little friends back in their village.

'Then we came on ourselves back to Bait and here we are. I think that covers everything that we have done.'

'That all sounds like a first class reconnaissance,' I said. 'You deserve a good rest not only to refresh yourself but also because you have had the mental responsibility for all our operations in Oman. In a few days' time, after we are properly set up near Nizwa, I must climb up to Cassino and see Peter. A Squadron should get here on the 22nd and we must have a discussion on how best they can be given what really amounts to a training operation to get them tuned in to the mountains.'

'Many thanks, Sir. Before I go off I think you ought to meet Sayyid Tarik who is the Sultan's Personal Representative in the Interior at Nizwa. He has been quite invaluable as our link with the locals.'

Sheikh Sayyid Tarik was the Sultan's half-brother and an enormous man. He was dressed simply in a homespun galabia round which he had the usual belt of ammunition for the .303 rifle which he carried. In his belt was stuck a highly ornate and curved Omani dagger in a sheath of worked silver made from melted-down Maria Theresa dollars. Round the handle was strapped a gold Longines watch, it being thought effeminate to wear a watch on the wrist like a girl's bangle.

He had been educated in Turkey and Germany and spoke English with very little accent. We greeted each other and he immediately asked me if we would take coffee with him in his house in Nizwa 'just round the corner'.

He had obviously laid it all on, so, with John Spreull, we drove round to his house. He led us up a few steps to a large room with carpets on the floor, where he introduced us to two Omanis.

'My friends are Sheikhs in the area but they cannot speak English. They have said they would like to meet you.'

We all squatted on the floor and tiny white cups with no handles were passed round, followed by a black Arab servant holding an Omani coffee pot with a long curved spout ending in a little V. Each in turn was given coffee, with the spout starting close to the cup and then swept back a couple of feet as the coffee filled up in a thin stream and then sweeping back before stopping a quarter of an inch from the top.

Sayyid Tarik started, 'We are very pleased to meet you and see how you can help defeat the rebellion against the Sultan.'

This was my cue.

'I too am delighted to be here and hope to be successful in the next two or three months.'

Sayyid Tarik went on, ' "He who holds the Fort at Nizwa holds Oman" is a true saying but I am afraid this does not allow for Suleiman on top of the Jebel. As you know, there is another saying repeated in all the suks, "The Jebel is impregnable". This is based on history and I hope you will be able to prove it wrong.'

Some more coffee was passed round, together with some dark brown sticky confection in a bowl. A servant carefully swept off the flies before passing it round to each of us in turn and we used the fingers in our right hand to scoop out a little sweetmeat. It tasted very nice – if one forgot the flies. Another bowl of water followed in which to wash our fingers.

Rocking the cup sideways indicated we had had enough coffee and the time had come to say goodbye. I thanked Sayyid Tarik and told him I hoped he would give us help when the time came to attack the Jebel. We would certainly need all the assistance he could muster.

I spent the next three days based at Nizwa with our Tactical HQ. All the information produced by John Watts indicated that our main attack, with all the troops we could get hold of, would have to climb Ambition in one night and get on to the plateau before first light at about 6.45 am. The problem was to get rid of all Talib's pickets guarding this approach by deception. I also wanted to force him to remove the pickets from any of the tracks within reach and so thwart any reinforcement plan he might have. I had to get to the top, if possible, without any casualties. Our Operation Order went out on 5 January for an attack due to start on the 25th. We were on our way.

* 26 *

JEBEL AKHDAR II

Our plan for assaulting the Jebel Akhdar took shape between 2 and 4 January, 1959. Somehow I had to get Talib to move his pickets well away from the route up the mountain we had chosen which was on the high ground on the face of the Jebel between Kamah and Sumait. We would then move up on a moonlit night with all the SAS we could muster to seize prominent features on the edge of the plateau by first light. At this point we planned to take an air resupply drop after giving smoke signals. The dismounted troop of Life Guards and a company from the Northern Frontier Regiment would follow up behind and take over the features we had captured. This would release the SAS for more offensive operations with close air support from twelve Vampires and bombing support from the Shackletons.

We knew that Talib was very sensitive about any approach from the Aqbat and he was also worried that we might come up the track from Tanuf. He had kept his own end up with his pickets between Kamah and Sumait, although we had given him several bloody noses. On the other hand we had not pressed home our advantage and the way up was very steep. With any luck we might persuade him to move the fifty to sixty pickets within striking distance of our route to reinforce either the Aqbat or Tanuf. All our diversionary operations were designed with this in mind to save casualties.

D Squadron, now resting at Bait and less its troop on the Aqbat, would move to Tanuf and operate offensively up the Jebel between 8 and 22 January. 25 January was the full moon and sufficient moonlight was essential for the very difficult climb.

A Squadron was due to arrive in Oman on 12 January and would need a few days at Bait to sort themselves out. Their first task would be to move up to the Aqbat on 17 January and take over from the troop of D Squadron, who would then return to its squadron at Tanuf. A Squadron would carry out reconnaissance and offensive operations against Sabrina up to 22 January. They too would then rejoin D Squadron at the Tanuf base camp.

At last light on 25 January both A and D Squadrons would move by truck from Tanuf to the base of the mountain between Kamah and Sumait to start the climb up at 8.30 pm. Each Squadron had objectives to seize on the rim

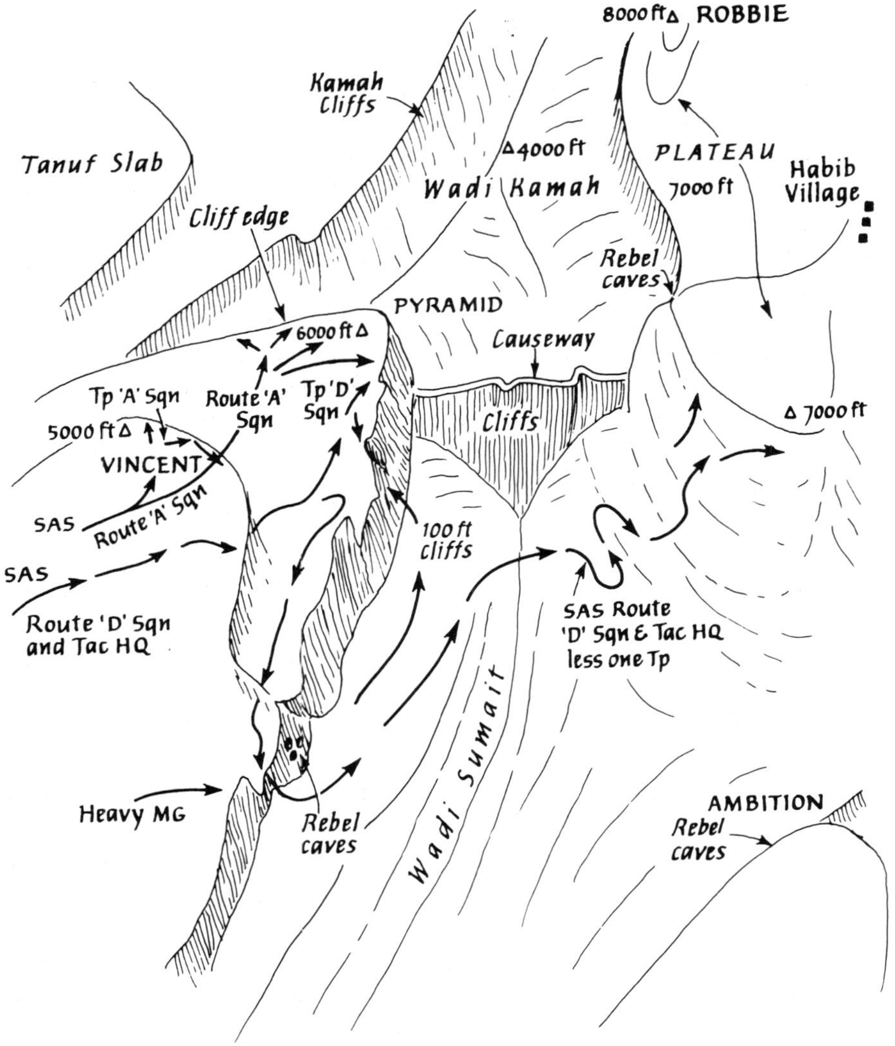

Δ Heights above sea level are approximate

Assault up the Jebel Akhdar

of the plateau by first light. My own Tactical HQ, together with John Spreull and a very fit RAF officer to talk to the aircraft, would climb up with us behind D Squadron.

Right behind the SAS but starting at 2.45 a.m. on the 26th would come the dismounted troop of the Life Guards and the company from the Northern Frontier Regiment. Their task would be to take over from the SAS on top.

The Venoms would contribute to the deception by concentrating close air support on the Aqbat and Tanuf until last light on the 25th. Likewise the bombers would initially drop on targets in the Aqbat area up to the 22nd, and from the 23rd to the 25th concentrate on Tanuf.

I now had a few days spare before A Squadron arrived and decided to visit Peter de la Billière and his troop on the Aqbat. I took the same route from Awabi and Hijar and arrived on top at about 3 pm after a very steep climb up a well-worn donkey track. I was now at about double the height of Ben Nevis in Scotland and it felt like it.

Peter took me round the different groups of men as they were beginning to cook up their evening meals. They all looked weatherbeaten and most of them had peeling faces. But every group exuded the bonhomie of troops who know what they are doing and are quietly confident they could tackle almost anything. I was most encouraged. A thirty-minute scramble took us forward and we found a good spot from which to see all the key places.

Peter then described what had happened.

'I decided to set a trap for the rebels on Rocky Outcrop. I could see this feature very clearly through my binoculars. Almost triangular in shape, it stuck up a few hundred feet and about 800 yards this side of Sabrina.

'We moved out there on the morning of New Year's Day and made sure that the rebels saw us. During the afternoon we did a little more sniping at rebels we saw on Sabrina. As soon as it was really dark, we pulled everybody out and went back to another small hill which looked down on Rocky Outcrop about 400 yards away across a small wadi.

'Sure enough as soon as the moon rose at about 11 pm, we could see the rebels moving down to attack Rocky Outcrop. We waited till they were quite bunched up and just short of the feature, when we gave them everything we had. The mortars fired rapid, all the nine Life Guards Teams joined in as well as our own, and our LMGs filled in the gaps. The rebel mortars and LMGs fairly walloped it in reply and we were glad we were not there.

'We could not see if any of them had been hit but I heard yesterday that there had been ten rebel casualties of whom six had been killed.

'The whole Troop liked that one, especially when rebel mortars wasted thirty bombs on an empty position. They never pressed home their attack when we brought down our heavy fire, but they continued to blast at the position with their weapons, presumably believing we were still there.'

My driver had come with me up the mountain. He was a Scottish soldier of the very best sort and always had a fund of stories. By now there was little doubt that he would have passed on all the latest soldiers' gossip from Malaya. He was also quite a good cook and would have some food ready. The SAS never had batmen. Not only would it have been a waste of a highly selected soldier, it would have been morally quite wrong.

The rim of the sun was just showing as it dipped below the horizon. The valleys far below looked black in comparison with a sky which was a kaleidoscope of colour. Brilliant orange flames streamed from the sunset and lit up the high clouds with a deep red light. Further over, the spectrum changed imperceptibly and deep mauves and dark blues shaded the clouds high up above us as I watched. Glorious sunsets seen from the top of high mountains always appear to be more spectacular than when seen from below. But, my word, it became cold. The temperature dropped to well below freezing and the wind had a bite in it which penetrated all three pullovers and my smock.

The Troop were sitting round a huge bonfire when I came over after my meal. 'Before I start on our plans for January, I want to explain my own position. Quite obviously all operations will revolve around the employment of the SAS squadrons, and in order to simplify the command set-up, I have been made Field Commander of all the operational troops in Oman. This will allow me to issue orders direct to all units and will free the SAF Commander to get on with his reorganization back at Muscat. I have already set up a tiny Tactical Headquarters at Nizwa with Captain John Spreull as Operations Officer.

'As you know, the full moon period falls around the 25th of the month. I hope we will finish off this rebellion within a week of that date, given reasonable luck. I have been back in this country a week and everybody now knows what we propose to do.

'Now you people know only too well that the slopes of Ambition include a large number of rebel pickets. So, up to the day before, we will carry out diversionary operations to try to deceive the rebels which way we are coming. I hope my friend Suleiman or maybe Talib will react by taking away his pickets from the route we want to use. Then all we have to do is to climb up.

'You will stay here until the 19th and hand over as detailed a recce as possible to A Squadron who should arrive here on the 18th. The task I have given them is to attack and capture the whole of Sabrina on the night of the 22nd/23rd, which I think you will agree should be as good a training operation as any to get them used to mountain warfare.' I could see the men smiling.

'When you finish here, you and the Life Guards will walk down the hill to Tanuf during the night of the 19th. From the 19th to the 24th you will have off.

'After A Squadron's attack, they too will withdraw the following night, but leaving one troop with the TOS on this hill. A Squadron, less its Troop, will then move down to Tanuf on the night of the 23rd.

'Whilst these operations are going on, the rest of your Squadron will push up the mountain at Tanuf and get as far as they can. If they can find an enemy picket they will have a go at it.

'So you see, all the SAS except one troop of A Squadron up here will be down at Tanuf. We will rest there for 24 hours and at last light on the 25th we will move by lorry to the foot of Ambition, from where we will climb up to the plateau. A Squadron behind you will hold Pyramid and the side of the mountain as a firm base. Coming up behind the SAS will be the Life Guards and a company of NFR who should take over from A Squadron by midday on the 26th. A Squadron will then move up to the top and join you. Tac HQ will move up just behind your Squadron and once on top we will play it off the cuff. Most certainly I will want patrols to go out that night and probe the rebel positions.

'I am asking the remainder of the NFR to do what they can by attacking at Tanuf and Izki on the 25th/26th, as will the Troop of A Squadron left up here.

'So you see, I hope that the rebels will be deceived by the major attack of A on Sabrina up here and by your Squadron from Tanuf. I also hope they will think that this place is a diversion for Tanuf where they will see you all concentrated to attack. Finally, we quickly sidestep and in at their back window via Ambition.

'The RAF will parachute in all our ammo, food and water at dawn on the 26th on the plateau opposite Ambition. They are also laying on the maximum effort they can with the Venoms and even Shackletons.

'Just before we start up the mountain, I propose to ask Sayyid Tarik if he can mobilize all the able-bodied men of the Abryeen tribe, which is said to number 300, to try and come up the north side of the Jebel. Likewise 200 men of the Bani Ruwaha tribe are going to be coaxed up the south side of the Jebel after we are on top. I am not very happy about the control of these characters but I expect we will work out something.'

We now had to put our deception plan into operation. Provided security was tight I was confident that it would work. The rebels had become jumpy and had been turned from a self-confident and aggressive enemy into something a lot less daunting. Our own forceful patrols were beginning to pay off. We had to keep Talib on the hop and with a bit of luck we could do the job without suffering too many casualties ourselves.

But my own confidence was not shared outside SAS circles. 'Jebilitis' or 'the Jebel is impregnable' was the usual comment at this time among quite senior people. Their genuinely-held belief was that at least two battalions of troops trained in mountain warfare would be needed to put down the rebellion. They acknowledged that we had done very well so far, but this did not alter their considered military opinion.

We would have to prove them all wrong.

* 27 *

JEBEL AKHDAR III

A Squadron touched down at Azaibha on 12 January and I was there to meet them. Back at Bait I was able to tell them a little bit about the country and what their task was going to be. Johnny Cooper and A Squadron were in good form and 'Rarin' to go'. After giving them some background on Oman and why we were there, I sketched in our outline plan of deception with the help of maps and air photographs. I ended with a few words of warning.

'Do not underestimate the rebels. In the last six weeks patrols and whole troops from D Squadron have killed more than forty rebels and may have wounded a lot more. Their minor tactics and use of ground are both excellent. They possess 3-inch mortars, ½-inch heavy machine guns, normal light machine guns, and the so-called 'hard core' are all armed with .303 rifles. As you may know, we have so far been very lucky and have only lost Corporal Swindells. And he would still be with us if he had not stood up on a crest.'

Back in Nizwa I was brought up to date on Peter's activities on the Aqbat. Every night he had sent out patrols, usually going with one of them himself. They found out more and more about the slopes leading up to Sabrina, the cliffs on each side of it and the siting of the rebel pickets in the rocks. One of the difficulties was the distance separating the two main hills and the difficult ground in between. By 18 January they knew every rock, every bush and even every blade of grass round the enemy position. Astonishing though it might seem in Oman which was mostly a bone dry desert, violent storms broke out between 15 and 18 January and all the dry wadis became rushing, roaring torrents of water. This would also delay A Squadron's move to Awabi. On three occasions the desert track had to cross erstwhile dry wadis and each time the Squadron was held up for over three hours to allow the water to subside. Only then could the trucks get through water nearly four feet deep in places which came up level with the floorboards.

Peter had taken the precaution a week before of checking the route down to Tanuf from the Aqbat. It had not been used before by the SAS and it took him eight hours to scramble down the side of the wadi until at last he reached base camp at 8 pm. It was much tougher than anyone had expected but his reconnaissance would be quite invaluable when the whole of his Troop came down at night on the 19th. He was able in the morning to describe a successful patrol he had carried out two nights before.

'One of our best patrols took place on 10 January and reached right round the left tit of Sabrina. This gave me a good look at the back of the rebel position. We were quite lucky that night, as the rebel sentry on this particular approach must have been asleep. He suddenly woke up when we were lying on the ground in his rear, and only then did he open up. All hell was let loose and our own Brownings and mortars gave us covering fire to withdraw as we had already arranged. That night rebel fire went on continuously from 4 to 6 am. Their mortars then took over and peppered our base on the hillside for the next two hours.

'The rebels on Sabrina fought back well and also used two mortars to give harassing fire. They copied our own techniques and mortar bombs were liable to come down at any hour; surely a sign that some of our own bombs had hurt.'

Meanwhile the rest of D Squadron had been pushing up the slab above Tanuf and had established a forward base on the first false crest about 1000 feet up. From here patrols were sent up the main mountain. Rebel mortars had also been active and the men of the Squadron had become champion sangar builders in the shortest time after reaching a new position. If it was built properly, a sangar provided near 100% protection. The only unlikely eventuality was a rebel bomb or grenade actually landing inside the protecting walls. Luckily it never happened. John Watts continued the story:

'The rebels were meanwhile carrying out a constant campaign of sniping throughout the daylight hours, no doubt hoping to force us to withdraw. But it didn't. The rebels reinforced their own position which is exactly what was wanted. We discovered numerous sangars and caves on the hillside. Unfortunately many of the caves were down a steep cliff, but the sangars provided good target practice whenever a rebel face could be seen through binoculars.

'On one occasion a rebel heavy machine gun, firing armour-piercing half-inch bullets, opened up on a helicopter making recces for suitable landing areas from which to evacuate casualties. Fortunately nothing vital was hit, but I am sure the pilot had a mild fright. That same night the rebels moved their own patrols down the hill into positions about 200 yards from our own, and belted into us with their rifles and LMGs for ten minutes. During this time, ten rebels crept up to within twenty yards and threw in five hand grenades which fortunately landed just outside our sangars. We congratulated our sangar-builders for their efficiency. One patrol could not see any rebel targets, so did not waste any ammunition on them. Instead, some countermortaring was laid on which appeared to be quite effective.

'The next night I sent out two strong patrols to give battle but unfortunately did not find anything, except the mortar base plate from the rebel left-hand mortar which was brought back.

'Last night we did the same but we were lucky. The patrol on the right clashed with ten to twelve rebels in a chance contact. Our Malayan training came to our aid and our normal drill went into operation in a split second. The range was only fifty yards and we dropped three of them before the remainder had leaped behind cover. Our Browning with the patrol then proved most effective and a Very light signal brought mortar fire down on the target. We then withdrew to our camp, using fire and movement to get us back.

'We came out of our sangars on the mountain at 4 am and now the whole squadron is back in our base at Tanuf.'

Then it rained and rained and rained. The heavens opened and down came buckets of water, which on top of the Aqbat was driven by a sixty-mile-an-hour gale. Cloud enveloped the upper part of the mountain on the 22nd, so I had to postpone all our attacks by 24 hours. The forecast for the following few days was good and so it turned out to be.

The next day by 11 am the storms in Arabia moved out over the Indian Ocean and left a bright blue sky which was soon studded with cumulus from horizon to horizon. The air smelt clean and our spirits went right up.

Towards evening the clouds disappeared and the rising moon gave near daylight conditions most of the night. We heard A Squadron going into the attack on Sabrina. I was confident they would do it, and without too many casualties. Johnny Cooper was able to describe his battle when he came down to Tanuf two days later.

'We started out from our position about 0200 hours on the 24th. Our orders were to take Sabrina but not to become involved in a long firefight or exploit more than 200 yards from the hill.

'It took us an hour and a half to get to our start line in a small wadi just below Sabrina itself. Our heavier support was provided by our own mortars, together with two MMGs of the Muscat Regiment back at our firm base half-way between Sabrina and Cassino. Further forward and just behind the start line we had our own LMGs, together with a section of TOS. My plan was to creep up the left tit, and when that was firm in our hands to take on the right. We hoped to get to the top of the left one without a shot being fired, but all our fire support was laid on in case it was necessary.

'It took forty minutes for Tony Jeapes' Troop to reach the top. The Troop on his left had a much more difficult climb and took twice as long. Luckily the enemy did not wake up until we had been on top for five minutes. Eight weeks of effort by D Squadron, the TOS, the Life Guards and the Venoms had forced the rebels to abandon their positions on the forward slope. They were now ensconced in their sangars behind the hill and they started shooting back at us at fifty yards' range. We cleared them out with hand grenades and energa bombs fired at point-blank range. Three rebels were dropped and a fourth took a death leap over a fifty-foot-high cliff. The remainder stuck to their positions and fired back. They even threw hand grenades until the last one was silenced. It was here that Trooper Wright was wounded by a grenade splinter.

'We then faced right and from the top we supported the attack by Ian Patterson and his troop on to the right tit. He also discovered that all the rebel positions were behind the hill, but by this time the rebels had had enough and they had withdrawn a few hundred yards to the next line of hills to the rear.

'There was no moon now, so I gave orders to hold on to what we had captured and do the final clearing-up at first light. We were now in unknown territory and we did not know how the enemy defences were laid out.

'At first light we swept forward and only found one rebel dead in a sangar, but there was plenty of blood scattered about in at least five other places where they had been. What we had not realized in the dark was that another little wadi connected up the rear of the sangars and had provided cover for the rebels to get out unobserved, no doubt carrying their wounded and dying with them. We stayed on Sabrina until 11 am when we thinned out except for one troop who was to remain in possession until nightfall.

'By 2 pm my headquarters and three troops were back on Cassino ready for the move down to Tanuf that night. At about the same time Ian Patterson brought back his troop from Sabrina because there was little doubt that the rebels would have a go at seizing Sabrina again and one troop by itself could be easily overrun.

'Our one casualty was evacuated by helicopter later that afternoon and I have just heard that his wounds are not too bad. I understand he should be fit again in a few weeks.

'Our march down to Tanuf was mighty tough. We brought some of the spare donkeys down with us and it took over eight hours. At one point the wretched animals were baffled by an eight-foot drop and we had to lift them and their loads down one by one. We were bloody glad to get in.'

I congratulated all of them. They could not have done better. I was even more confident that Talib would now be drawn back to the Aqbat. The next day I went across to Tanuf from Nizwa and spoke to the soldiers.

'You will be glad to hear that the met men say we are in for a spell of dry weather, so there should be nothing to stop us capturing the whole of the mountain. D Squadron has pushed right up the hill above Tanuf and managed to attract a lot of attention to themselves. A Squadron has captured Sabrina at long last and I have great hopes that at least one of these attacks will be regarded as deception for the other. Some of you also know about our donkeys. This afternoon we got hold of the principal donkey drovers and, in deadly secrecy and on pain of death, we asked them about conditions for watering animals up the Wadi Tanuf. As you know, all the mokes are now concentrated at Kamah and we wanted to indicate we were not going up Kamah at all but really up Tanuf. I am told that it is quite likely that the rebels will hear about this 'secret' briefing a few hours after it is given. The object of all these diversions is to get the rebels to withdraw their pickets from the four places where we know they are sited along our climb up. I am pretty sure they will take the hint.

'My next point is really the only major change since I last spoke to you about our plans. I have had a close look at Ambition and it would have been a good place but for one snag. It is joined on to the plateau by a narrow ridge about 800 yards long. If this was defended it might hold us up and delay us expanding our bridgehead on the plateau. We will therefore go up Pyramid, which as you know is an exactly similar slab of mountain to the west of Ambition between Kamah and Sumait.* We will keep on the high ground all the way up, but we must get to the plateau and hold it by first light tomorrow. Otherwise the rebels will undoubtedly reinforce the crest with their pickets before we reach the top.

'D Squadron will start at 2030 and will get three of its four troops to the plateau by first light and its fourth troop back on the top of Pyramid in support. I and the Ops officer will be on the plateau behind you as quickly as we can. We will also have with us an RAF pilot to talk to the planes and I am sure he will prove to be quite invaluable. A Squadron will seize the cliff edge to the west of Pyramid with its fourth troop in support from Vincent.

'Starting at about 0230 the dismounted Life Guards will climb up Pyramid and aim to relieve the troop of D Squadron during the morning of the 26th. The Company of NFR will do likewise for A Squadron at Vincent.

'Your mortars will be carried up by the donkeys, but I warn you that they are scrambling up the face of the mountain where there are no tracks and you may end up humping them. The mortars, I mean, not the donkeys!

'Starting half an hour after first light the RAF are going to airdrop nine Valletta-loads of ammunition, water and food on the top, on the first day. This should provide us with sufficient supplies for our advance on the plateau. They have also laid on twelve Venoms in support, so we will not be lacking air support.

'We will then move round to Kamah tonight in trucks, leaving here at

* Operation Order No 2 dated 20 January, 1959.

1715 this evening. This should give you time to brew up a hot mug of tea at Kamah before you have to start.'

A and D Squadrons now had their midday meal at Tanuf and the men checked their weapons and the ammunition they were carrying. Bergen rucksacks were repacked against a special check list to make sure that only essentials were taken on the long climb up. They still weighed over sixty pounds.

We were now all set to go and I kept wondering if our diversions would prove effective. We knew that rebel pickets were all over the lower slopes of Ambition, Pyramid and the Wadi Sumait. Any battle we had on the way up would slow us down and stop us reaching the plateau by first light. Even if this did happen, I was confident we would be on top during the daylight hours of the 26th. We would have to see.

* 28 *

ASSAULT UP THE JEBEL

The time had come. I was surprised to see David Smiley, who had just come up from Bait. He wished me good luck and we started to move up the lower slopes. Slowly we climbed up, our bodies tipped forward to balance the Bergens on our backs, although in my case the rucksack only weighed forty pounds. In my right hand I carried an FN rifle which complied with my own rule that officers should always be armed in a similar manner to the soldiers. Likewise, badges of rank or chevrons were never worn on operations, although this was more for practical reasons than anything to do with the enemy. SAS troopers had no need for embellishments to tell them who were their officers and NCOs. They shared all discomforts together, but those in charge also had the responsibility of their rank.

Already it was midnight, but we had only just passed Vincent, which had proved to be more of an obstacle than we expected. The right-hand part of the Vincent slab ended in fifty-foot-high cliffs up which we scrambled in and out of enormous boulders.

Suddenly the loud braying of donkeys, presumably from our pack animals at the foot of the mountain, broke through the silence of the night and the rasping of our breathing. Christ, I thought, this is enough to awaken the dead, let alone the pickets. Surely our approach must be given away, but nothing more happened.

In the distance we could now hear the troop on the Aqbat putting in their diversionary attack. It was good to hear them doing their stuff. So far we had encountered no pickets, although we had just passed two empty rebel sangars.

The rocks on the hillside, which looked so smooth when flying over the top, were the main obstacle to our progress. Little wadis, barely noticeable on air photographs, showed up as ditches twenty feet deep with sheer-sided rocks on each side. Each one needed a detour to get round and time was running out fast. We knew that our route went nearly to the top of Pyramid and from there we had to traverse sideways to the right to find a way around the hundred-foot cliffs where they dropped into the left branch of the Wadi Sumait. Air photographs showed a faint track leading up to the plateau from here; the only doubt was how to get down to it from the edge of Pyramid.

We reached the cliff near the top of Pyramid at 0430 and the troop from D Squadron was soon in position. From here they could support our further advance up to the plateau and also cover us while we moved to the top of Wadi Sumait.

Slowly we clambered down and along the edge of the cliff and a few yards in where we would show ourselves in bright moonlight on the skyline. Tac HQ was moving up right behind John Watts, when the leading troop sent back word that they had discovered an unmanned heavy machine gun mounted on a tripod in the rocks. There were long belts of heavy ½-inch armour-piercing ammunition already loaded in the breech. We were in luck: the rebels had apparently abandoned their weapon, presumably because it was too heavy to carry and possibly implied that all the pickets had also been withdrawn from our route. This might also mean that our deception had worked, but unfortunately we could see no way down the cliff which disappeared into the inky blackness below us. By now all three leading troops of D Squadron and Tac HQ were bunched in the area of the machine gun. God, I was tired! Men were falling asleep in the few minutes break, dropping off where they sat. Some attached engineers, who had been included to improve the donkey track, moaned as cramp or exhaustion overcame them.

It was now 0500 hours and we only had an hour and a half to get up to the plateau by first light. I had a word with John Watts and told him to drop his Bergen rucksacks and get up to the top by 0630 come what may. Tac HQ would keep their Bergens and would get up to the plateau as soon after 0630 as we could manage.

As we could not see a way past the cliff, we had to scramble down 500 feet into Wadi Sumait and then start climbing up once again. It was terrible to have to give away height, but now the troops in front only carried their personal weapons. We were reassured by the knowledge that the troop on Pyramid was manning the cliffs right above us.

The jet-black rocks towered on each side, and little did we know we were passing just in front of the three-man crew of the machine gun as they slept in some caves immediately below where we had found the weapon.

At last we reached the top of the wadi and I could see, in front and above, SAS troops spread out as they moved up the final shoulder leading up to the plateau. Even now I could see the sky lightening in the east as D Squadron pressed on upwards in a race against time. I could just hear the sweet music of aircraft engines, and there, off to the right, were three Vallettas circling for their run in to drop supplies. The higher-pitched whine of jet aircraft could be heard as they also circled over the area where the drop had been planned. Unfortunately our smoke grenades were in the Bergens which had been left by the machine gun. The Vallettas would not drop without a smoke signal. Quickly some green bushes were pulled up by the leading troops and, after lighting some flannelette soaked in rifle oil, a column of lovely white smoke was produced. Only fifteen seconds later the first dollop of pink supply parachutes started floating down on the plateau. It was the best possible welcome we could have had and we had done it in the nick of time.

The planes made several runs to make sure that all the supplies were dropped accurately. As they turned off to the left, over the Tanuf Slab, I heard the slow bark of another heavy machine gun firing at the slow-flying transports. Every plane as it flew over one spot was given its ration, but fortunately none were hit or faltered in their flying. Even so the drop was well spread out. D Squadron was tired all right, but in spite of it the majority built sangars around some minor features on top of the plateau, while others were detailed to collect and break open the packs and distribute ammunition, rations and water.

Tac HQ arrived on top at 0700 carrying our Bergens. Once on top my exhaustion disappeared and I was able to speak to John Watts from behind a big rock looking out across the plateau. We were both looking at some hills about 1000 yards away which could become a rebel position. I wanted to get a move on. Now we had our supplies, nothing should stop us expanding the area we held, provided the rest of the SAS could close up quickly behind us.

The sun was just tipping the mountains on the horizon and quite soon we were bathed in brilliant yellow light in contrast to the rest of the troops in the shadow and still sweating their way up.

The question in all our minds was how soon could the rebels form up and attack. We had caught them unawares and had only found one small picket on the way up. If they did not turn us off our foothold soon, their days of rebellion would be numbered.

Our efforts at deception appear to have worked superbly and a week later we heard that four pickets of ten men each had been pulled off positions guarding our route to reinforce the Aqbat. I do not think any of us realized how sensitive the rebels were to this particular approach. We also heard that Talib had inspected the Aqbat and had sited the extra pickets there that they had just removed from the way up we had used. The Tanuf approach had also been reinforced by regrouping the rebel pickets into parties of twenty men each and putting them in new positions all along the line of the wadi and up the mountains on each side.

Opposite our position we could see an occasional rebel dart quickly between the low hills on the plateau, and an infrequent bullet from a sniper's rifle winged its way towards our men who were improving their sangars. The RAF pilot with me was a Rhodesian who had once served with the Rhodesian SAS squadron in Malaya five years before. He was talking to the Venoms overhead as they came swooping in from shallow dives to shoot their rockets at rebels who were now also building sangars on a hill about a thousand yards away and out of range of our weapons.

At last the third troop arrived on top at 0800, having dealt with the three rebels who had come to life soon after first light. Little did these rebels realize that about twenty men had already moved up above them, when they started a small bonfire outside their cave to boil up coffee. Two SAS had scrambled down the cliff using a fixed rope and out of sight of the caves. They had stalked the rebels by traversing along a narrow ledge while spread-eagled against the rock face. The rebels saw them when only twenty yards away and as quick as lightning managed to get two rounds off which fortunately missed. Several hand grenades were then lobbed into the sangar in front of the cave and this dealt with the rebels.

I heard John Watts giving the Troop Commander a piece of his mind for not being quicker to the top; it should not take an hour to deal with three rebels. Fortunately his late arrival made no difference because the expected attack never came.

The other reason for his late arrival, which then came out, was that rebels on Ambition had opened up on him with a LMG and riflemen. He had put in a fixed rope down a short piece of cliff for the two men stalking the rebels and bullets were spattering the rocks all round whenever anybody went near. This sniping went on all morning and it was not until 1430 that a troop from A Squadron picked off two of the rebels on Ambition with some accurate shooting with an LMG. On three occasions during the morning the Venoms had shot off rockets at these same rebels but they did not get sufficiently close or perhaps we described the wrong place.

D Squadron now sent out a patrol to a minor wadi 500 yards in front and reported they had found a number of terrified men, women and children hiding in caves. After a lot of persuasion by a Lance-Corporal who had picked up some rudimentary Arabic, he brought three of them back with him.

Our troubles were multipling fast and prisoners-of-war were obviously now included. There was a little hollow in the middle of our position and this would have to do as a prisoner-of-war 'cage', although, of course, we had no wire to go round it. We were able to give them some dates dropped for the 'tribals' who had not so far shown up. This persuaded one of the trio to go back and bring out the rest of the men. In the next two days over sixty of them dribbled into our 'cage', but most were released when Sayyid Tarik came up by helicopter and talked to them on behalf of the Sultan.

The first troop of A Squadron arrived on the plateau at midday, having handed over their position to the company of NFR. They brought sad news. I had already heard cryptic reports that three men had been wounded back at Vincent, but now we heard what had happened. Unfortunately a very unlucky bullet from a sniper had hit a grenade carried in the Bergen on the back of Trooper Carter. This had also wounded Troopers Hamer and Bembridge. All casualties were evacuated by helicopter from the saddle between Vincent and the main mountain. This was a magnificent piece of flying, carried out while mortar bombs were exploding all round and showed what the pilots could do in an emergency. Luckily the choppers were not scratched, but it was a superb evacuation, done from the only really level piece of ground on the way up. Unfortunately both Bembridge and Carter died from their wounds two days later. Hamer was luckier and he made a complete recovery in three weeks.

The Life Guards' dismounted Troop arrived on top of Pyramid at 3 pm, having taken thirteen hours to get there. These were very fit guardsmen the public never see – a general's son, dirty, sweaty, unshaven and bewildered, asking for instructions. But it relieved the troop of D Squadron who then climbed up to the plateau and reached it an hour and a half later. The Squadron was now complete and at last light they spread out along the edge and occupied a hill overlooking Wadi Kamah by midnight. I was not going to take any risks in case the rebels concentrated and put in their expected attack at first light the next day. I went up with them to have a look at the ground and returned to Tac HQ where A Squadron was now on top and had put out a patrol to have a look at some high ground above Habib. It towered a thousand feet above us and the top was just under eight thousand feet above sea level. From there the patrol looked down on the village but did not have time to see if it was clear

When the patrols returned and made their reports, it looked as though the rebels had pulled right back and the rebellion might be over. I gave out orders on 28 January to enter the three main villages of Habib, Saiq and Sharaijah as soon as physically possible. We had all been scaling cliffs and marching nearly continuously for forty-eight hours, but I knew that Suleiman had his cave near Saiq and one last effort was needed before resting our weary legs.

Just before the Squadron started off we were joined by a SAF officer, Major John Clark, with fifteen of the fifty 'tribal levies' with whom he had started. When they had come to the fixed rope leading down the mountain, all but fifteen had turned back. I remember him saying that his gallant desperadoes were really there for any loot they might pick up. His job, as he saw it, was to restrain their enthusiam. He joined up with A Squadron - much to Johnny Cooper's disgust - in the advance to Habib. I was sure that the presence of the 'tribals' was politically desirable to show that they had also taken part in the capture of the Jebel. Each man had a red armband for identification and they looked a crafty avaricious lot, all out for themselves. No doubt they had visions of loot to act as spurs to their enthusiasm. This was the way all armies in their past memory had disported themselves and they saw no reason to introduce any changes. John Clark's background was interesting. A one-time officer in the Parachute Regiment, he had fought at Arnhem and had escaped capture.

Saiq was only five miles away across what looked like a reasonably level plateau. But in practice the ground in between was broken by three minor wadis, all of them two hundred feet deep, which had been carved into the surface of the plateau. Each wadi had the usual cliffs along each edge and it took some time before a way was found down and then a way up. It took six hours to reach the village sited in a banana-shaped hollow about three-quarters of a mile long with a stream flowing through the middle. Most of the little flat-roofed houses had been damaged by bombing. Many of the terraces along each side were green with sprouting garlic. Spaced out along the terraces were orchards of pomegranate and apricot trees, with vines growing over some of the mud walls near the stream.

We now had SAS troops in the main villages and had also occupied the features overlooking them. The rebellion really was over and next day, on the 30th, David Smiley and Sayyid Tarik arrived near Habib by helicopter. I also used the helicopter to transfer Tac HQ to a new position near Saiq, much to the satisfaction of the troopers who did not have the six hours' march we had found it to be. A Squadron had a troop push on through Saiq to Sharaijah. This village was only a mile and a half further along on the edge of an enormous bowl 5000 yards wide with its floor 4000 feet below. This tapered off to a bottleneck seven miles long as the Wadi Maidan wound out of the plateau between walls over 4000 feet high and less than 300 yards across.

One of the 'tribals' who spoke English knew the location of Suleiman's cave which was just up the wadi above Saiq. This was why the village had been bombed. Together with John Watts and a six-man patrol, we used him as a guide and he had an astonishing tale to tell. He said he came from Tanganyika and had lent a large sum of money to one of Suleiman's henchmen. When he was not repaid, he had travelled over 1000 miles to the Oman to see him to get his cash. Suleiman soon made him a prisoner in his cave near Saiq. As he was an educated man he was released, provided he agreed to fight in one of the pickets. He said he had been on the Aqbat a few weeks before we arrived there in November and, choosing his moment, he had escaped and travelled down to Awabi full of his grievances against Suleiman.

Our guide led the way up a shallow wadi above Saiq. The ground was terraced up each side and leafless pomegranate and apricot trees were growing everywhere. One or two of the shattered terraces were green with sprouting garlic, but most had nothing growing because the water supply had been broken. A mud trough ran along the upper side of each terrace and I could see where mud bungs were used to control the irrigation. All the water came from a fast-flowing perennial spring higher up the wadi we were following. After a few hundred yards we arrived at a squat hole in the cliff, with the usual stone sangar built in front to protect its entrance. We all crouched down to go inside its dark and musty-smelling interior. Someone had a torch and flashed it on as we walked slowly to allow our eyes to get used to the darkness.

After a few yards it opened up into a large cave with carpets on the floor and wooden chests and trunks stacked round the edge. From this Aladdin's cave led another narrow, low tunnel. We crept through this one on our hands and knees to discover it also opened out into another cave with carpets and boxes strewn everywhere. Suleiman must have left in a hurry.

Some boxes were full of clothes, which all smelt a bit high, some were piled up with weapons, and one had a new Singer sewing machine lying on the bottom. One box had two or three old swords with inlaid silver scabbards and scattered about were brass trays, blackened bulbous coffee pots and round cauldrons which could be suspended from a tripod over a fire.

I could imagine Suleiman sitting brooding on one of his boxes, his wives and slaves all looking on, half-frightened but carrying out his every wish. No doubt his bad humour was made worse by our pressure on him every day in the last few weeks. As Edmund Spenser puts it:-

> That darksome cave they enter, where they find
> That cursed man, low sitting on the ground,
> Musing full sadly in his sullen mind.

The only trouble was that our bird had flown with all his retinue. Our job now was to try and catch him, together with the infamous Ghalib and Talib.

David Smiley was also telling me that the rebellion was by no means over yet. 'Although you are on the plateau there is some pretty fierce skirmishing going on with our troops at Muti and on the Tanuf side of Wadi Kamah. In each place, the rebels you bypassed have caused us casualties and forced us to go back to our camps.'

'We can't do much about Muti at the moment,' I said, 'but I think we may be able to help your chaps at Kamah. I think John here could send one of his troops to move right round the top of Kamah and come on the rebels from above. That should sort them out.'

We now went back to Saiq and the patrols started binging in the weapons we had found in the large number of caves in the area. Once cave produced twelve Bren LMGs and quite a lot of spare parts for mortars. I also heard from A Squadron at Sharaijah that a sizeable number of people were living

10 "Down we came steeply to land on a strip next to the Fort at Awabi" (p.174)

11 "The Wadi which leads up the mountain from here is the Wadi Beni Kharus" (p.174)

12 "Corporal Swindells stood up on the crest of a hill and was shot dead by a rebel sniper... He was buried with full military honours at Muscat" (p.187)

13 "Sheikh Sayyid Tarik (x) was the Sultan's half-brother and an enormous man" (p.194). Here he watches Lt. Peter de la Billiere demonstrate a rocket launcher.

in caves and in one, used as a prison, the fetters had been struck off fifteen prisoners. They had all been abducted by Suleiman in midnight raids some months before because they had expressed loyalty to the Sultan.

I went on down to Sharaijah to see how A Squadron was getting on. This village was by far the biggest of all the villages on the plateau. Here there were terraces all down the side of the bowl, watered by ingenious falujs which were channelled along all the upper edges. This was almost a garden of Eden, with rose bushes, apricots, pomegranates, vines and even walnuts. Frankincense and myrrh used to be made here. The rose petals were made into rose water and sold far and wide in Arabian suks as 'genuine Omani rose water', while the other products were exported by donkey to the towns in return for dates and flour. The Venoms' rockets had destroyed some of the falujs and the Sultan's artillery or the bombers had damaged most of the houses. All the inhabitants had been living in caves in the cliffs and all were bitter about Suleiman leading them into this mess, which they maintained had been none of their choosing. As one of them admitted to me through an interpreter:-

'Suleiman bin Hamyar has brought this all upon us. We have fought for him to keep the infidels out, but they broke our falujs of life-giving water with their shells and bombs. We have suffered. O Suleiman, how we have suffered. We know he wants to separate us from the Sultan's rule because he wishes to be Emir of Oman. Now he has left us to our fate and we despise him for it. A thousand curses on his soul. Never again must he rule us.'

He ended his surprising speech with a spit on the ground. I thought some sort of reply was needed so I told him:

'Peace on your soul, O wise man. We come now in peace because all fighting is over. We want you to go back to your villages and I am sure the magnanimous Sultan will forgive you and even help mend your falujs. If you hand in all the weapons you have obtained from over the seas, the Sultan will be pleased and reward you. Pass on this news and live in peace.'

I had stuck my neck out making these promises but I was sure it was the right policy and this was also backed up by Air Marshal Heath who had just touched down in a helicopter.

He was most interested to see Sharaijah and asked to speak to the men.

'I would like to speak to all the SAS but you are too spread out and this is not possible. I am sure your Commanding Officer here can pass on what I have to say to everybody.

'I want to congratulate you all most sincerely for the excellent work you have done. You have taken part in what is really an epic battle and you are now standing on soil which was last conquered by the Persians seven hundred years ago. I can see now that your easy passage to the top was the result of a really excellent plan, which could not have been carried out without the two months of aggressive patrolling you put in to prepare the way. Your action has done a great deal to restore British prestige on the Persian Gulf, which has been slipping rapidly since the last war and was accelerated by Suez a little over two years ago. Now all the Sheikhs round the Gulf can breathe more freely. For me the most astonishing feature is your small numbers and once again I congratulate every one of you.'

The Times published a main feature article on 9 April describing the action. It ended with the following:

'It had been victory at the first attempt by a numerically inferior force against an able enemy with geography on his side. The mountain itself was conquered by the astonishing physical fitness of the British troops. Within a few days of their arrival from the swamps of Malaya, the SAS troopers were operating with their usual efficiency seven thousand feet above sea level in totally novel conditions, and the dismounted troop of the Life Guards had turned themselves into first-class infantry. As for the enemy, they were conquered by surprise, not slaughter; a brilliant example of economy in the use of force.'

* 29 *

ADDING UP THE BOOTY AND THE CASUALTIES, WE RETURN TO UK

We never did catch up with Suleiman, Talib or Ghalib. Many rumours came through, but I fancy most were blinds to draw us away from the caves where they were really hiding. We mounted numerous patrols at short notice based on local gossip, but in vain. A month later we heard they had slipped out to Saudi Arabia, no doubt using the last remaining Saudi gold which they carried with them. All wadis had hundreds of caves and it was too easy to divert the attention of our small numbers while they slipped out somewhere else. We heard much later that they actually got off the Jebel by going down the Wadi Halfayn from Manaker, intimidating and bribing some local tribal levies who should have been picketing the wadi entrance to prevent such an exit. After long rides on camels, they went up north of Muscat and took a taxi (!) to the Trucial States. From there they went by dhow to Damman and exile in Saudi Arabia. The only satisfactory feature was that all three had lost face with their tribes. Even if they returned, they would no longer have the authority they had enjoyed in the past.

The booty captured included twelve LMGs, nine 3″ mortars, four ½″ heavy machine guns, twenty .303 rifles, thirty-nine mines and grenades, together with many thousands of rounds of ammunition of all sorts. The SAS had lost three killed and had four wounded. In the year from January to the end of October, 1958, when we arrived, British casualties in other units around the Jebel Akhdar including NFR, TOS, Royal Marines and Life Guards added up to ten killed and fifty-three wounded. In addition 198 trucks of all sorts were blown up and upwards of 120 tribesmen living in the villages round the base of the mountain were either killed or abducted and driven up to one of the villages on top. Between November, 1958, and January, 1959, the SAS had killed fifty-two rebels confirmed, although many more must have died from wounds with virtually no medical attention available. We at least were confident that our short three-month campaign would save similar casualties on all sides in future.

The oil company was delighted. They restarted their prospecting and in 1964 were rewarded with a large find near Fahud. This was so promising that a 36-inch pipeline was put in to carry the oil to Muscat, thus avoiding the need for tankers to sail up the Persian Gulf. The economy of Oman was to be transformed in the process, although it would be a year or two before funds started rolling in.

When we arrived in Oman in 1958 it was cut off from Saudi Arabia by the 'Empty Quarter', a wide area stretching hundreds of miles and only crossed by camels with difficulty – that is until the invention of four-wheel-drive trucks and the aeroplane. There were no roads, no modern houses, no services providing water or electricity and no schools. Little wonder that time stood still and we found a country with habits, ideas and an extreme form of religion more appropriate to the 1400s than the 1950s. Sultans, Emirs, Imams and Sheikhs were being dragged willy-nilly into the 20th century out of the romances and feudalism of 500 years ago. I was really rather sorry; with all their many faults, their old way of life had much to commend it.

David Smiley was fulsome in his thanks for what we had done. He was now convinced that no other unit of our size could have done the job. He invited me to write up my recommendations for decorations and these came through a few months later in UK. Never before had so many been awarded to a small organization operating over only a three-month period of time. Although UK newspapers had fortunately been silent during our operations, we were certainly in the public eye within the Services and we had transformed at a stroke the reputation of Britain in the Persian Gulf. I heard later when I met the Minister of Defence, Duncan Sandys, that when the news was reported to the Cabinet there was considerable satisfaction all round and he was asked to congratulate the Commanding Officer. Although the Regiment's jungle operations probably required more sweat, blood and tears over many months and years, the selection system operated in UK and confirmed in Malaya produced a type of man that could adapt to new conditions rapidly and also produce first-class results. The credit for this must go to Majors Dare Newall and Hugh Mercer, who between them ran tough selection courses in Brecon and spent many hours holding discussions and interviews weeding out most of the applicants for the Regiment. We still had a few soldiers who had done very well in the jungle but could not take the exposure and hard grind of mountain warfare. They had become passengers in an outfit where this could not be tolerated. Most were found jobs in HQ Squadron or in other non-active SAS jobs.

We at least had ensured that both from a military and political point of view the long-term future of the SAS was reasonably assured. But as Frank Kitson pointed out in his book *Bunch of Five* (page 198) there were still 'moves afoot (dating from before our action in Oman) to have the Regiment disbanded or reduced so that as few resources as possible in terms of men and money should be diverted to it from the rest of the army'. On page 201 he confirms that 'The most important effect of the campaign was that it ensured the continued existence of the Special Air Service'.

I have often been asked if an infantry or parachute battalion could have done the same job. After all, the SAS was forced by the mountains and the rebel opposition to revert to normal infantry tactics and had to move in much larger groups to ensure success without incurring casualties. Provided a whole battalion could get up to the Aqbat and be resupplied by air, it would have been a reasonable task for it to get on to the plateau after capturing Sabrina and the hills beyond. If there was still opposition it was a further ten to fifteen miles to the villages.

In order to reduce the concentration of pickets on this approach, concerted and determined attacks would have to be made on the pickets guarding the routes up the Jebel. This might have required a further two companies at least of a British battalion. The military effectiveness of the units forming part of the Sultan's Armed Forces was limited at the time we were in the Oman to that of an armed gendarmerie. Their gallant efforts against the pickets on the Jebel had never been successful.

Unfortunately the level of air resupply available, even when backed by donkey transport, could only supply the needs of the equivalent of one company on the Aqbat. Even then it took nearly a month to build up supplies for Muir Walker's attack on Sabrina and another three weeks for A Squadron's successful assault. The idea of landing a parachute battalion on the top was really a non-starter. The combination of wind and very rough ground, let alone the altitude, would have resulted in 10-20% casualties, many of them fatal. The massive increase in air resupply that would be necessary and the involvement of one and a half British battalions would have been difficult to keep out of the world's press. The tactics I was able to use relied on outstanding officers leading extremely fit and well-motivated soldiers. Although the Army has plenty of them, they are usually distributed as individuals in the battalions. I was fortunate to have such a dedicated and professional lot of men to command.

The SAS was sometimes accused of creaming off the best officers and men from Army units. This might be so, but frequently the potential of individuals might not have been recognized in their parent regiments. There was no doubt that when officers or soldiers returned, they came back better trained and with much more self-confidence. It was rare indeed for a soldier not to get immediate and rapid promotion on return, although many of them opted for a second or third continuous tour of duty. Officers in their turn had the benefit of active service under real stress. This was invaluable to the Army as a whole and not only to the SAS.

Eleven years later the SAS was to return to Oman again; not to become involved with an internal rebellion but to hold back Yemeni-inspired attacks in the Dhofar, 400 miles to the south. Little by little, over a period of six years, local tribesmen together with the Sultan's Armed Forces, were encouraged and reorganized by small SAS detachments to push the rebels back, which eventually they did. This story is well told by Tony Jeapes* who had returned to the SAS from his own Regiment, first as squadron commander under Lieutenant-Colonel John Watts, and later as Commanding Officer himself. I was delighted to see that the SAS was now 'growing its own tall timber'.

I now had to return to Malaya and complete the winding down of 22 SAS in that country. The Regiment had served continuously in the Far East for nearly ten years. I was rather sorry that the time had come to say goodbye to all our friends both military and civilian. I even had a personal message from C-in-C Far East about our operations in Oman.** As I had now come to expect, Bob Walker-Brown, my adjutant John Epplestone, and RSM Schofield had everything in shipshape order and ready to hand over with a clean sheet all round. I was delighted and so was my Quartermaster, Tom Thomas. Even our locally recruited cooks could hardly believe we were really going back to UK.

We were housed temporarily in Merebrook Camp near Malvern and had to operate within a reduced establishment allowing only three troops to each of the three squadrons. I think the powers that be wanted the Regiment to be housed within a military garrison; fortunately this idea was successfully defeated by Dare Newall. A little later we heard that a barracks near Hereford was becoming surplus at the end of 1959 after being used for a Junior Leaders' battalion. I was able to confirm that the location was ideal, was close to the Brecon training area and was sufficiently far away from Army garrisons to 'allow the SAS to breathe'.

Our experiences in the jungle and Oman gave rise to a wide-ranging training programme during the summer of 1959. We trained for the mountains, for the jungle, for the arctic and for the desert. Individual squadrons were given general guidelines, together with suitable training areas overseas, and methods of entry would be equally flexible. Tree landings, free falling, helicoptering, parachuting, even an entry using gas balloons were all tried out. (Some articles had just appeared in the Sunday newspapers describing how agents had been inserted into Poland during the 39/45 War making use of balloons inflated on a trawler in the Baltic).

At about this time General Gerald Lathbury had taken over as Director of Training in the War Office and he asked if he could come down and see us. I was delighted to show him what we were doing. When he saw the pro-

* *SAS in Oman* by Tony Jeapes, (Kimber)

** See Appendix

gramme, which was to end with a flight by balloon, he said he would like to have a ride in the basket. Naturally I went along too. When the time came for him to leave, our very well-turned-out guard presented arms to see the General, myself and the RAF 'pilot' going vertically upwards. It was quite a day.

At the end of 1959 before we moved to Hereford, I was able to hand over command of 22 SAS to my old friend Lieutenant-Colonel Dare Wilson. I was sorry to say goodbye to the Officers' and the Sergeants' Messes and to the soldiers; they were all dedicated professionals and were proud of it. Evie and I will never forget them.

* 30 *

RISING UP IN THE ARMY

Leaving the SAS was an anticlimax only softened by being promoted Colonel. My next real appointment was to be in command of 44 Parachute Brigade Group (TA) and because the job did not start until the following summer, I was sent on a NATO Defence College course in Paris. Evie decided to remain at our house near Wargrave as she could not leave the children, and she only came over to Paris for a week when we were kindly lent a flat in the middle of the city. We had quite a time seeing the shows and dining in the best places – that is until I was broke.

The student body on the course included about six representatives from each of the NATO countries. In the case of the UK, this included senior civil servants as well as those coming from the Navy, Army and the RAF. The idea was to acquaint us with the current problems of NATO and also to have an opportunity on a 'grand tour' to visit most of the countries. This provided a chance to question current policies and to hear national answers. I had the feeling sometimes that we were not expected to ask awkward questions or to put forward our own ideas. Perhaps the integration of a NATO philosophy was still in its infancy and any rocking of the boat was not welcomed. I have always tended to be a bit of a rebel when someone puts forward policies as though there were no alternatives.

About two or three weeks before the end of the course I received an official telegram through the British Embassy in Paris. This invited me to come back to London for twenty-four hours to discuss publicity, including TV Publicity, concerning my next command. I had to meet a Colonel at the Public Relations Department in the War Office and from there we would go round to BBC offices in Central London. The BBC was even providing a guide because we had to enter by a back way. The front entrance was covered in scaffolding and was unusable – or so I was told.

When I arrived at the War Office, I found not only the present commander of 44 Parachute Brigade, who was Johnny Frost (who had commanded 2 Parachute Battalion on the Arnhem Bridge), but also my future Brigade Major, Michael Walsh. Clearly this was going to be a major discussion on publicity and how this might be best put across on TV. An Army car took us by a strange route using side streets to the back of what appeared to be a large office block. Together with Michael Walsh we walked down a concrete path, blinded by powerful lights from the building. A smiling Eamonn Andrews met me at the door and said 'This is your Life'! I realized that I was then on the air and, hopefully without showing it, I was furious. Eamonn led me on to a stage and I soon discovered that the BBC had obtained a copy of my book *Return Ticket*, and was now going to relive my wartime escapes from prisoner-of-war camps. Someone also whispered in my ear that I would get £50 for my trouble which helped a little to dissipate my annoyance. Tag Pritchard, Christopher Lea, Senora Traxler-Camerana from Italy, Mr and Mrs Huisman from Holland and Lance-Corporal Turner, my driver/batman from Arnhem, were all there. Renée Nouveau in Marseilles could not come to London and she was shown talking to me on a stage screen. And finally Evie with our four lovely daughters were all on the stage together. It all ended much better than it began and we had quite a party afterwards to round it all off. Evie told me she had been warned a month before, but had been sworn to secrecy. She even had to get the elder two girls out of boarding school and get party dresses for all of them. Our village was quite agog when they heard that some of the residents were going to be on the 'telly'.

44 Independent Parachute Brigade Group (TA) was a superb job with four parachute battalions spread all over the country. One was based in London, another in Yorkshire, one in the Durham area and finally the Scottish battalion. In addition we had the usual support from parachute gunners, sappers and signals. Finally there were small units from Ordnance, RASC, REME and Medics. Most were up to strength in both officers and soldiers and some had a waiting list. There was, however, a problem with senior officers. Often the best qualified were unable to accept promotion because it would mean giving even more time to the TA.

Quite a high proportion of the Brigade carried out much more training than the minimum laid down for the TA. They were keen and enthusiastic. All new recruits had to qualify as parachutists in a similar manner to the regular Brigade. Later on, when deployed on exercises, they were surprisingly efficient. Provided the orders were clear and simple, the task would be done well. We carried out small-scale exercises all over England and Scotland and much larger ones in Germany in conjunction with NATO training in the autumn of each year. Some of these involved a parachute entry. Visiting senior officers from headquarters in Germany were very complimentary about our units. Almost without exception they were surprised that such high standards had been achieved. In many cases the results, so they said, were better than some regular British battalions and considerably more efficient than performances put up by a few of our NATO allies.

Once a year I ran battlefield tours which were designed to stretch the imagination and techniques of those who attended. Most were invited to give out suitable orders representing some of the units concerned and there then followed a critique of what had actually happened. As well as having an opportunity to see a new place, everybody had to do some work. We carried out one such tour to Crete to examine how in 1941 the Germans had only just managed to capture the island against fierce British and New Zealand resistance. Although we would have liked General Student to come and say his piece on behalf of the German Parachute force, we did have a Lieutenant-Colonel Genz who had been a German parachutist in Crete and whom I had met on the NATO course in Paris. We also found officers from Britain and New Zealand who had been there and were able to describe what happened from the Allied point of view. The RAF supplied two Hastings aircraft and we landed at Heraklion in Crete on a Friday and returned to the UK on Monday. It was the first time that an organized British party had been to Crete since the war and we were able to represent Britain at welcoming lunches held by the Mayors of Heraklion on Saturday and Khania on Sunday. I found the trip very worthwhile and it was given high marks by all those who took part.

In my last year with the Brigade we managed to arrange for everybody to go out to Cyprus for their two weeks' annual camp. Brigade HQ went out ahead and we had two battalions come out for two weeks to be replaced by the other two for the next two weeks. We ran a series of test exercises leading up to battalion attacks. A large number of visitors came out from the UK to see our exercises, and I usually managed to find an 'umpiring' job for them to do. They thus became involved and had to work for their supper. They also had to make comment on what they had seen. That is, except for my boss, General Sir Roderick McLeod.* By the end of two weeks I was quite content with results. The Brigade could have been called up almost immediately and produced a good performance. In addition to working hard we also had fun and there was time to relax and enjoy ourselves in the half-day off that most battalions gave to their men.

15 Parachute Battalion (TA) was our Scottish battalion and like all battalions from north of the border had a pride and a spirit all of its own. Living nearby on his farm was Colonel Alastair Pearson and his wife Joan. His record when commanding 1st Parachute Battalion in North Africa and Sicily had been without parallel in the British Army and his decorations included a DSO and three Bars. He had been the first Commanding Officer of 15 Parachute Battalion (TA) when it had been formed after the war and now he was Honorary Colonel. Quite rightly he was the *eminence grise* in the background, and he kept close tabs on its progress. He liked to be involved and,

* Letter at Appendix

I fancy, no serious decision could be taken in the Battalion without a nod and a wink from Alastair. He was a great man to have at one's side. He agreed or was persuaded to agree with nearly everything I thought necessary.

None of the other battalions had quite such a sensitive background as the Scots, but they all had a fierce pride either locally or in the various towns from where they had drawn their men. There was no doubt in my own mind that the TA was one of the best recruitment agencies for the regular army as well as for themselves. It was rare indeed not to find a drill hall in a town of any size throughout the whole country. The TA provided a link between a tiny Regular Army much of which was deployed overseas and a civilian population, most of whom have not had the time to give much thought to military matters. As memories of the last war recede the rôle of the TA becomes that much more important. At the very least, indoor weekend exercises can inform, instruct and debate problems of great complexity.

It was a year or two later, when I was in my next job at Sandhurst, that I heard that the War Office had decided to reorganize the TA. The men were to be used in future as individual reinforcements for regular units and for this they would be renamed Volunteer Reserves. There would be no need for TA battalions to operate as such, nor indeed for brigade or higher organizations to command them. A senior TA officer rang me up and told me, 'The War Office has cut us down to size and our morale is rock bottom. I don't know how I am going to tell my soldiers.' I cannot quite remember my reply but it was on the lines of, 'I hope you won't leave the TA as a result. I am sure that crazy policies will eventually be changed. The worm always turns in the end.'

A few years later it became fashionable in BAOR to move by battalion groups rather than brigade groups. At a stroke, the War Office abolished all Brigade HQs both regular and VR (the old TA). This clearly would save a lot of money. But once again the worm really did turn and the TA was reconstituted and Brigade HQs once more became an essential part of the Army organization. It was a pity that what was seen by the TA battalions to be a bureaucratic nightmare aimed at the TA and all its traditions was eventually put right. The need to save money was of course blamed, but the method chosen to put it across was unfortunate. Some of my TA friends called it a disaster.

My job at Sandhurst was Assistant to the Commandant. For about half my stint it was John Mogg, and when he left, he was replaced by Peter Hunt. This was an interesting time with over one thousand cadets doing a two-year course. About half the instruction was devoted to academic studies taken by a large number of lecturers under the Director of Studies, Kenneth Ingham. Theoretically, I was responsible for all military training and Kenneth Ingham for all academic studies, although in practice we worked quite closely together. The course had been running smoothly for many years and any idea of change, even quite small ones, was regarded with suspicion. In practice, Sandhurst has now become a place where short sharp military courses are run for all types of entry. At the same time every possible encouragement is given to the graduate entry including generous scholarships. Another aspect of my time at Sandhurst was concerned with interviewing some of the cadets doing very well and also those who were likely to fail the course and not be commissioned. I enjoyed talking to the good ones. Many of them were going on to a university as a result of qualifications obtained at school or at Sandhurst. One young man who said he was going to read 'Greek Mythology' at a Northern University surprised me by his choice of subject. Apparently the real reason was that his girlfriend was nearby.

The bad ones were depressing. Usually very weak on both military and academic subjects, they had crept through the original selection tests. After talking to some of them, it appeared that a surprising proportion had come from broken homes. I ran a check on all the cadets doing badly and about 80% came from this type of family. It was brought home to me that the sins of the fathers or mothers must have had a strong influence on their offspring. Although I myself had come from what is now known as a broken home, this handicap had not affected me. Perhaps I was lucky in that most of the time I was growing up was spent as a boarder at school and away from home.

In the holidays I was lucky to have my sporting Aunt Gabrielle who took the rough shooting in the winter on the whole of the Isle of Arran in the Clyde. Wild pheasants, woodcock and duck bred in large numbers and on most days a party of six guns, walking up and down the many different glens, could bring back at least forty pheasants and thirty woodcock. The island was mainly used in summer for grouse shooting over pointers and the winter shooting was let to help with overheads. A small hotel was taken over as a shooting lodge and I enjoyed the atmosphere and the company of all the guns enormously. On the other hand I also enjoyed the company of my mother in the Cotswolds, who encouraged all my different activities. She was a great friend but she could not replace a father in the house.

Towards the end of my time at Sandhurst I heard I was to be promoted and to be given command of 3rd Infantry Division based on Salisbury Plain. It had four brigades at Plymouth, Bulford, Tidworth and Colchester and the regular Parachute Brigade at Aldershot. We were the strategic reserve Division for the UK and had over forty different plans for reinforcement or insertion as battalions, brigades or a division into possible hot spots all over the world. We also had 22 SAS under command for administration as well as regiments such as the Royal Horse Guards mounted in Ferrets and based at Windsor. Their main role at this time was the protection of aeroplanes at

Heathrow in case of hijack or even guarding entrances to the airfield if terrorists attempted an armed publicity stunt.

My main job was to try and get to know the personalities in my large command, which was split all over Southern England. We trained all over the world, including Australia, Kenya and Canada, and nearer at home in West Germany, Cyprus and the Gulf States. The majority of this training was done by battalion groups and I travelled widely to see them on the job. Most of them did very well, but, as is usually the case, a few were not too good. From time to time I also reviewed the different plans which the staff kept up to date. Although the Ministry of Defence was responsible for giving us the task, it was our job to make sure that we had suitable units available and that rehearsals without notice were carried out as necessary.

The largest exercise we mounted was in West Germany and we were given the Eiffel Area. This was outside the British Zone but a highly successful inter-brigade exercise was carried out ending with a divisional attack. The troops worked hard over a three-week period and when they returned to the UK were all given two weeks' leave.

I had made very extensive use of helicopters to get round all the units and brigades in the Division. When we came back from Germany I decided to take a three-week conversion course at Middle Wallop to fly them. I thought this would be a good gimmick when visiting the troops. At least 'This General would be on the ball and not too decrepit to fly himself.'

I told the staff at Middle Wallop not to ease off on any tests they might give me just because I was a senior officer. If I could not pass in three weeks I would go no further. At least this would give me a better idea of the problems faced by the pilots.

When I first started, I began to think I had bitten off a great deal more than I could chew. Gradually one learnt to coordinate hand, feet and eyes. I was sent solo after a few days and little by little I learnt and practised flying under instruction in and out of ever smaller clearings in the woods and also landing with the engine completely throttled back. One of the most difficult exercises was done at the hover a few feet off the ground. The idea was to keep up a steady rate of turn over one spot. It was particularly difficult in a strong wind. I was already sufficiently practised in using the radio and there was no problem with navigation. My final handling test by the Chief Instructor was interesting. He certainly put me through it ending up with a descent into a tiny keyhole in a wood with the rotor blades only just clear of the leaves and the tail fitting into a small elongation. He had already criticized me in another clearing for not making use of the passenger to open the door and look back to make sure the tail was quite clear. On this occasion I made him carry out the procedure, which was good for my self-confidence because he could not have taken over the controls if anything had gone wrong. He had the last laugh, however, when we climbed up from the clearing to about 300 feet. He suddenly switched the engine off and we made a good landing just inside an airfield, while at the same time managing a Mayday call on the radio. He had already found out that I could judge height accurately, which was something I was well used to doing when landing gliders.

I was quite proud to be awarded my wings. After a few more hours without passengers, I took my ADC on most of my trips to visit battalions. I usually tried to fit in a landing with engine throttled back on my flights, I was quite determined to land without damage if ever the engine failed. I was rather sorry that it never did. The ADC's face went white as a sheet on the first few pseudo forced landings, but it soon became a part of every flight.

There was no doubt that, by using helicopters, I was able to double or treble my effectiveness as GOC, although the need to take over the aircraft and file a flight plan meant that I had some additional work to do before I started my job.

One of the Regiments I visited by helicopter was the Blues at Windsor. After carrying out a normal inspection, I was shown after lunch a book which recorded the date my father had joined the Regiment at the end of 1914. He had been quite a firebrand in his day and had visions of himself taking part in cavalry charges against the Hun. He once told me that if he ever fell off his horse in the riding school, he had to pay a sovereign to the Riding Master for 'dismounting without permission'. Later on, in France, he discovered there was to be no rôle for cavalry and transferred to the Cheshire Regiment. He ended the war commanding a machine-gun battalion by which time he had been awarded the DSO and Bar plus an MC and a *Croix de Guerre*. He was also badly wounded on two occasions.

I had never queried any posting that I had been given and when I heard about my next job in the Ministry of Defence I was suitably flattered. At the age of 51 in midsummer, 1968, I was to be the Assistant to the Chief of Defence Staff (Operations). This sounded fine but I was to discover that a high-sounding title revealed an organization that had been made to work only by good will all round. Unfortunately I joined at a time when we were withdrawing from the Far East and the Persian Gulf and there were many minor distractions in other parts of the world. There were bound to be occasions when one Service or another would have to feel the pinch. There was never any doubt in any of the Services that the Ministry of Defence had to take a global (and later a NATO) view of our requirements and had to tailor the three Services to meet them from both a political and military point of view. But each of the three Services kept large operational staffs headed by two-star officers.* Each Service had its own Chief of Staff who attended

* Major-General or equivalent in the other Services

Chiefs of Staff meetings with the Chief of Defence Staff acting as Chairman of Committee. All the Chiefs were technically equal and each had the right of direct access to the Prime Minister if they felt they were not getting their fair share, although this was practically never used.

I had an efficient three-Service staff who prepared papers in conjunction with the operation staffs of the three Services. Inevitably this required one Service or another to give up some aspect which was then used to brief their own Chief of Staff. This led to further argument at the next meeting of the Chiefs who then wanted a compromise. We wasted a lot of time.

This outdated system continued until Michael Heseltine became Minister of Defence in the early 80s. The two-star operational jobs in the three Services were abolished and this gave rise to considerable disquiet. No service would voluntarily have given up an important part of their own organization. It struck at their 'sovereignty'. But the military logic was inescapable. The central staff now had complete responsibility to prepare papers taking into account the needs of the country from a political and military point of view. The military aspects naturally included the views of the three Services. This reform was long overdue, but it did not help me in the job I was trying to do in 1969.

Officers from the three Services who worked in the Ministry of Defence were theoretically all civil servants. There were a few who kept coming back at different levels and were real experts on the organization. They knew how to get things done and probably knew personally the real civil servants who worked there. The Services probably benefited from the continuity that these officers provided. The snag was that when back in uniform many were lost and unhappy. One of my friends described them as useless in the real Army. I tended to agree. It was probably better that they returned to be 'military' civil servants.

Many other minor tasks also came my way. A tiny British island in the Caribbean called Anguilla suddenly declared independence. The character behind this declaration had assembled weapons and had announced he would defend his freedom 'on the beaches'. This required the despatch of a company from the Parachute Regiment to sort it out. Michael Stewart was the Foreign Secretary at the time and I was invited to attend the meeting with his mandarins when he went over the draft of his speech to the House of Commons, while the parachute force was still on its way. At the end of his discussion, he turned to me and asked what I thought the reaction of the Commons would be to his statement. I told him that on the assumption that there would be no casualties, the reaction of the members was likely to be that he was using a hammer to crack a nut. Which was, in fact, exactly what happened – and there were no casualties. This was one of the very few days when I may have earned my pay.

Being wise after the event, I should have turned down the appointment in the Ministry of Defence. The top end of the three Services was in such an organizational muddle that the job I was doing was fatally flawed from the start. When all three Services were deployed at full stretch there was no problem. The snags only came out when the shoe started to pinch. The small contribution I had made certainly did not justify my rank, nor did it draw on my background of experience. I had been frustrated and left my job in the Ministry of Defence after the normal two years, knowing that a fairly radical reorganization was essential at some time in the future. It was a pity it took another ten years for the penny to drop.

At about this time the Army had to cope with many riots in Northern Ireland and elsewhere. These had even erupted in the UK and were giving concern to the Army, who might then have to be called out to assist the police to restore order. The Army Chief of General Staff, General Sir George Baker, asked me to tour the world and visit any country that had had riots, see why they had them, discover how order had been restored and find out any lessons that had been learnt. Robert Mark, who was then Deputy Commissioner of Police in Scotland Yard, would accompany me and a Lieutenant-Colonel 'writer' would come along and take notes. We visited a lot of places and had most interesting discussions. France, Italy, the Netherlands, Singapore, Hong Kong, Japan, USA and Canada were all on our list. It took over six months and the arrangements in most cases were made through the embassies concerned. In Tokyo, for example, we visited the Chief of Police and had discussions with him and his senior officers before watching a demonstration of equipment. On advice from the Embassy we followed protocol by giving a large bottle of Johnnie Walker to the Chief and smaller ones to his officers. They all had to be gift-wrapped. In the evening we were invited to a Japanese dinner party in the police-owned geisha house. For this we were also carefully briefed by the Embassy that we would find three oak stairs leading up to a flat area before the stairs continued on up. On the flat area we would find 'our geisha girls' and they 'would squeal with delight when we arrived at the entrance'. This also took place exactly as described and we were led upstairs to a room where we had a meal with our three Japanese policemen hosts and accompanied by a cabaret turn consisting of rather strange squorky musical instruments. The geisha girls acted as waitresses, filled up the saki glasses and smiled sweetly on all possible occasions. As an example of ancient customs existing side by side with a brightly lit, chromium-plated city, it was fascinating.

We produced quite a lengthy report, but it did not provide us with many lessons that could be applied in the UK. Every country had its own background history and constitutional development. This led to requirements in most countries for an armed police force with some form of Army or riot police to back them up. The lessons learnt in the different countries were many and various but not too many had any relevance to the UK. There was no doubt, however, that riots did take place in all the countries we visited and were put down successfully with 'minimum force'. Sometimes 'minimum' could be interpreted in quite interesting ways. After I retired from the Army, the RUSI invited me to write a small book on *Riot Control*. This was published and quite a number were sold in the next few years.

I was given six months' notice at the end of 1970 that I would not be getting another job. This gave me an opportunity at the age of 54 to consider what I should do next. We looked at several farms of about three to four hundred acres which at this date were worth about £70,000 – 90,000. Unfortunately we did not have the capital resources both to buy the place and to run it, although we did make an offer on one place which we later withdrew. At the same time, I was applying for different jobs which were advertised nationally. One in particular asked for a Director or Chief Executive to run the Paper and Paper Products Industry Training Board. I thought I had the necessary qualifications and applied to the Management Consultant handling the advertisement. Later I discovered that over two hundred others had applied, although the consultants weeded the applications down to six and I was to be one of them. I was delighted. I then did some homework, thinking out what sort of questions I might be asked and therefore the replies I should give. As I heard that one of the applicants had a double first at Cambridge and had been running a paper mill for years, I did not think I had a chance. So I enjoyed myself. I was interviewed by the whole Board of about fifteen, who sat in a semi-circle with myself at the point of focus. It went on for over an hour and started with one of the questions I had anticipated.

'I see that you are a Major-General. Would you mind being called Mr in this job?'

I replied, 'I don't mind what I am called – as long as it is reasonably polite.' This caused a titter and the rest of the interview went well and produced only one question I had not prepared. Next day, the Chairman, Neville Whitehurst, rang up and asked to visit me at home and meet my family. This he did, and the day after, to my genuine astonishment, he offered me the job. I accepted.

* 31 *

A SECOND CAREER – TRAINING IN INDUSTRY

My job in 44 Parachute Brigade (TA) seven or eight years before had taken me far and wide. I had enjoyed meeting the officers and soldiers in hundreds of large and small towns all over the country. I was particularly keen to meet them at their civilian place of work, if time allowed, and was intrigued to find out what my officers did for a living. As much of TA training took place at weekends or in the evenings, it was not difficult to arrange visits in my spare time. Our officers came from every type of background from running supermarkets to stockbrokers, from working in insurance companies to pawnbrokers. I went into many different sorts of factories . I was entertained by farmers. I visited lots of different schools and colleges. I heard about their gripes and also their enthusiasm for their job. I felt I came to know them much better. One of the factories I visited was a pig plant. After seeing the pigs trotting in at one end and coming out as pork pies at the other, it quite put me off pork or pies for a long time.

One big lesson which emerged with crystal clarity was that the proportion of time spent on training or retraining all employees working in British Industry or in the Services sector was almost non-existent compared with the Army. I was puzzled. How did they get away with it? Naturally the professions of accountancy and law, for example, had lengthy training and experience to fit them for their specialist tasks. But most jobs, including young managers, were 'trained' by sitting next to someone else and picking it up as the months or years went by. Their qualities or lack of them were then recognized by those above, but they also acquired all the bad habits as well as the good ones. There was nothing like the Army's careful initial selection and training, followed, ten to fifteen years later, by further weeding-out for mind-stretching courses at Staff or other Colleges later on.

Might it not be possible to set up a few assessment centres and schools where selected up and coming managers could be given training, covering the important facets of management? Were the business schools in the Polys and Universities any good? Or were their lecturers or instructors already failures from business? What was the status of these schools and were they already supported by companies in the industry I was joining? What could I do about it?

With this background, I thought I was well adjusted mentally and psychologically for my next job as Director of the Paper and Paper Products Industry Training Board. Although my future task would be to encourage sensible human relations and purposeful training within the industry, the overriding difficulty faced by all of British industry was its perceived low status when observed by undergraduates or students in universities, colleges or schools all over the country. Low status inevitably produces a mediocre input, particularly for potential managers who may choose alternative careers. Of course there were those who bucked the trend and these were a superb minority. There was only one company that I could discover that deliberately paid competitive salaries to future potential managers. If, after a few months or years, they did not develop as expected, they would be out on their ears. Alternatively, this company hoped that most of their future high-fliers would come from this source. It had decided as a matter of policy that the heavy investment in time and resources would be paid back over the years. I have heard that this is in fact what happened and the company has prospered.

I joined the Board in June, 1971, and it took me a few weeks to discover how it worked. The idea of Training Boards was put forward by a Conservative administration in the late 60s and was continued by Labour in the years that followed. My Board had been in operation nearly two years. It consisted of a Chairman, Neville Whitehurst, one-time Chairman of Bowater-Scott, the tissue makers, together with members representing seven senior employers from different sectors in the industry and seven senior trade unionists. Board meetings took place every two months or so, when mainly the Director, but also the senior staff, would describe developments to date, and propose what should happen in future. Debates then took place after each item and it was rare indeed not to find an agreed way forward. Occasionally the Chairman had to bang the table, but this did not happen too frequently.

The Board's staff added up to about eighty and this number was never exceeded throughout the years I was Director. A lot of jobs changed to meet new requirements and also to recruit specialists to run the courses. In addition to the normal Board Secretary and Financial Adviser, the main thrust of the Board was through the Chief Training Adviser, Alun Davies, and his team. Training Advisers were recruited to be helpful and diplomatic but firm. They lived all over the country near where 'their' companies were located. Some of the senior non-training staff did not like the persuasive approach and thought a more legalistic line should be adopted. I did not agree. The idea of doing any training at all was such an anathema to so many companies, the only way to get progress was to convince the manager in charge to change his ways. Back in my Service days, this was known as a 'hearts and minds' campaign. The top man had to be convinced. This could only be done by persuasion and if possible by comparison with similar companies without revealing any confidences. Silk purses could not be produced from sow's ears but even the worst manager could be improved after a lot of discussion. This really added up to giving him training, although the amount either my senior staff or I could give in the time available was very limited. If he was intelligent it was worth it, otherwise it was a waste of time. Many small companies with quite high turnovers were being run in an unimaginative but conscientious manner by dullards. 'There were no bad soldiers; only bad officers.' There was certainly no leadership.

I was invited as a guest to many banquets, dinners and discussion groups run by the different sectors of the industry. These included the paper makers, with their massive investment of capital, and those who converted the paper or cardboard into thousands of separate products from cigarette cartons to corrugated cases; from wallpaper to printed wrappings for biscuits. The Stationers and the Envelope Makers also had their own excellent dinners. We included the paper agents or merchants, who provided a service between both UK and overseas mills and the customer, although only a few of the bigger companies employed more than one hundred.

These social-cum-business occasions gave me an opportunity to meet large numbers of people in the industry from Chairman to Manager. I was invited to visit many different offices housing the major groups, and countless mills and factories. My main task was, of course, to see if any help was needed on the human side of the business. My visit cost nothing, but if, as a result of my visit, I thought the company needed courses and the managing director agreed, I could lay on the necessary specialists to put them into effect. For this the firm paid.

I was quite pleased when even the poor companies were ready to allow an outsider to come in and suggest how it might be improved. In many cases this was by word of mouth from a similar company who had profited from my visit or one made by one of my senior training staff. We had a right of entry by statute but it was still up to the managing director what he did about it.

Many employers had either come into their job because it was a family concern or had become managing director or general manager by promotion from within the company. They were in charge of mills and factories which were profitable, although some were only marginally in the black. About a quarter of them were run extremely well and set a standard for the rest. In my eight years as Director I visited nearly 500 companies and well over half needed a great deal of help. We only dealt with firms employing at least one hundred people.

One rather poor factory employed about 300 and was located 'North of Watford'. It was about two-thirds of the way down my 'Swingometer scale' from excellent to disaster. The managing director had been there five years and had been trained originally as an accountant. His office was one hundred and fifty yards away from his factory. My own method was first to have a chat to him and then ask if he would take me round the plant. He excused himself from this chore and I was shown round by the production manager who, it turned out, did not even know the names of some employees. I gathered he regarded his job as mainly concerned with machinery which had to be kept working without stoppages or down time for maintenance. He saw no point in spending money on things like safety, although we were nearly decapitated when some large crates fell down in front of us. Even the loos were a disgrace. I had lunch with the managing director and we had a discussion afterwards which took over three hours. I was astonished to hear that he only went round the factory once a year before Christmas. His dealings with his employees were done mainly through his Trade Unions and tended to bypass his managers. I could see that morale was low but I was assured that sufficient cash was taken to pay all operating costs and a little left over. This was not nearly good enough and was probably why he had asked me to come in.

There was so much wrong with this factory on the human side that it was difficult to know where to start or to persuade the MD that it could be put right. He had never had any management training. Very gently I tried to indicate a priority list of things requiring attention and top of the list was himself. I suggested that a ten-minute walk round the factory every day would be useful, because he would at least get to know the names of his employees. '*Everybody* likes to be noticed,' I told him. I think I suggested he should go on the next suitable course run by the Industrial Society. We parted on the best of terms and I continued to get invitations to visit him again in the next three years, but I could never fit one in. I did, however, hear from the training staff that a turnaround did take place and that both productivity and morale improved out of all recognition. Increased productivity allowed the prices to be dropped, profits increased and the order book lengthened – or so the MD claimed.

This was a success story, but I am afraid I can only claim that this sort of improvement was achieved in rather less than a third of my visits to the poorer companies. Many were run by individuals who were sure they knew all the answers. The difficulty was to get through to them that the human dimension and the skills of the whole workforce were essential to the running of any business.

Fortunately I also visited really well-run factories which were a joy to look round. One in particular also employed about 300 and was running shifts for twenty-four hours a day. The thirty-year old manager came in most mornings early to see the night shift and note any problems that had arisen. He opened his own mail and held brief morning conferences with his managers. Morale was high and productivity excellent. Training was well done. His background was unusual because he was a graduate and his group had given him a long course in management two years before. After that he was promoted general manager to run the factory.

Large numbers of companies have gone broke or out of business because the customer is no longer content to buy a poor-quality product if a better or cheaper article is available from overseas. If the 'Widget' can no longer be made profitably in this country, lively-minded managers should be able to diversify into other products. I met many grandsons in family firms who had lost all desire to innovate or get up from behind their desks. The Institute of Personnel Management also reported in 1988 that government training grants and incentives, let alone propaganda, are not inducing firms to develop proper training facilities. A Warwick University research team says Government grants 'make no difference or only marginal difference to the training they do. The view of key people at the top is *decisive* as to whether an organization carries out training for anything other than stop-gap reasons.'

My own criticism of the training board idea was that it was essentially a 'Bottoms up' system. Train all employees, and managers will naturally arise to take over and run the enterprise. This may well happen in twenty to thirty years if schools and colleges produce much better educated and motivated people. But what is needed now are crash courses for managers and managing directors. A lot of them need it. I can foresee someone reinventing the training board or something like it to provide the organization to put this into effect. *Plus ça change!*

My contacts with other industries revealed that the Paper Industry was by no means unique. In fact, it was a good deal better than average, if the stories I heard were to be believed. The basic trouble did not lie with the training of the work force, it lay with the poor quality of the general managers or managing directors. Like any other activity, selection of the boss on the spot was crucial. All too few were first class; the majority were appalling. How has this happened? What has gone wrong with British Industry, once the pride and a source of income for the whole country?

In April, 1987, two reports by Handy and McCormick were published on managers in Britain and in other countries.* These showed that 85% of American top managers and 65% in Germany and France had degrees. This can be compared with only 25% in Britain. The way to the boardroom in Britain appears to be through accountancy. There are more than 120,000

* *The Economist,* 20-26 May, 1989 - Survey of Business in Britain.

qualified accountants in Britain compared with only 6000 in the whole of Japan. Lastly the reports show that more than 40% of American firms and most firms in Germany and Japan give more than five days off-the-job training each year to every manager. In Britain, the average was about one day, - even allowing for the massive amount of similar training given by a very few British companies. Once again the fault must lie with the poor quality of the average boss.

There is no shortage of well-qualified individuals but this disdain for business has become apocryphal. Changing this attitude will take generations. The advent of a so-called 'enterprise culture' in the last ten years may have made money-making respectable. Unemployment has shown that the alternative to growth is not a cultural idyll but poverty. There is little doubt that one way might be for the Royal Family to give the lead and promote businesses of every sort, as much as places to work, as a way to get rich. 'This would not boost profits at a stroke, but it could, in time, help encourage the best to go into business and help motivate those who are there.'*

After about seven and a half years in the job, I thought I had achieved about as much as was possible, although theoretically I could have served a further three years until I was 65. After the first six months, I had enjoyed myself and felt that I had contributed to the better working of an important industry. All our children had left home and our house near Great Missenden had become too big for us. I gave in my notice that I wished to retire for the second time the following summer. The Board was very kind and both Evie and I had quite a send-off after a meeting which was held in the Hyde Park Hotel in London. In some way I was sorry to go, but it was high time to do something else. In spite of my strictures on poor training, I could not help noticing that many companies were producing good products but made little effort to sell them. The manufacturing process was king; selling should not really be necessary. Customers should beat their way to the door to buy – an attitude, I thought, which should have gone out with the Dodo.

After we moved house down to Somerset I was determined to set up a small business and this would involve selling to customers. After seeing so many small firms being run by incompetent people, I was sure I had to do this to satisfy my ego. I knew I could do it, but I had not been tested before as an entrepreneur. What was the niche in the market I could fill and what could I persuade customers to buy?

* *Economist*, 20-26 May 1989.

* 32 *

ENTREPRENEUR IN SOMERSET AND WARWICKSHIRE

After looking at at least twenty to thirty possible and impossible houses, we eventually bought Bitwood Farm at Charlton Musgrove at the end of 1978. Only a few miles from Wincanton in Somerset, it was in an extremely run-down condition with holes in the roof and a drainage system that did not work. On the other hand it had potential. Stone-built and painted white with a pink tiled roof, it was eighty yards from the road with a tiny stream flowing through our own ten acres. Useful outbuildings included two barns to house our various activities. The stream would need to be dug out to form a small lake with an island, a bedroom would have to be converted to a second bathroom-cum-dressing-room and a utility room connected to the house would have to be newly built at the end of one of the barns. We could visualize exactly what we wanted.

As I was not due to retire from the Training Board until June 1979, this gave plenty of time for builders to carry out essential work before we moved in. Our main reason for choosing Somerset was that it was about halfway between where our two eldest married daughters were living in Devonshire, and our two youngest unmarried daughters who were more likely to be in the London or Cambridge area. Bitwood Farm was near the A303 which provided a fast road connection between the two. It also included a few acres which Evie could use for breeding ponies, after we had put up a couple of stables. She crossed her own Connemara mares with thoroughbred stallions to produce a type well in demand for teenage children.

One of the attractions of the old farmhouse was its long brick-built barn with a collapsed roof. After this was replaced and covered with old tiles, it provided exactly the sort of space I needed in which to develop a small business. Unfortunately this would require permission from the Local Authority because it was a 'change of use' – although the building was virtually derelict.

The idea that a retired Major-General should want to 'dirty his hands' in a trade surprised some of our new friends in Somerset. I was not deterred. I had to do something constructive to absorb my energies and also to satisfy that little gremlin inside which was nagging away. I had to show that not only could I do it, but I could do it successfully.

One idea was to produce handmade furniture to order. I had always been a competent carpenter and had used the hobby as a form of relaxation in the evenings at the end of a day's work. I would tackle almost anything provided time was not a factor. My output included things like oak and mahogany bedheads, an oak refectory table, Hi-Fi and TV cabinets and a new oak stairway and front door for our house at Chobham. At Bitwood we had a gap of six months while we were arguing about permission for the barn. The house needed a new staircase which this time I made in elm. We had heard rather gruesome stories about two of our predecessors who had fallen down the stairs. One of the steps dropped down an extra two inches and caused one old lady to fall and die from a heart attack. The other described a lady battle-axe who was so fed up with her husband that she pushed him down the stairs and he died with a broken neck! In addition I made four oak-panelled doors from old floorboards to replace rather nasty softwood doors which did not fit or hang properly.

The snag of being a maker of custom-built furniture was that my personal output and time was unlikely to be very profitable in cash terms. To be 'successful' in the modern idiom meant that I had to show that I could make money, although this was not really necessary at the time from a financial point of view.

Another idea we toyed with was entering the antique business. I could certainly repair anything needing it, but we had no contacts. It would also mean that we would probably have to buy a shop in Wincanton and could not use our barn except for storage. In the end we settled for setting up a centre for giving advice on woodburning stoves and then selling them.

The great plague of elm trees had hit the South of England in the 70s, resulting in vast quantities of elm wood becoming available. The normal use for elm up to this time had been for coffins or for cheap cladding on houses or sheds. There was now a gross oversupply of wood and this would make it cheap. If suitable stoves were available, it would also provide an ideal source of heat.

When we bought the house we thought it would be a good idea to supplement the central heating system with two stoves in our drawing and dining-rooms. We went round many different sources of supply and found difficulty in obtaining professional advice or service nearer than the Basingstoke area about forty miles to the east, or the New Forest about fifty miles to the south. I already knew something about the subject because we had a large Jotul No 6 stove in our Buckinghamshire house which I had installed myself. Naturally I read up all the literature and discovered the advantages and the snags. Most problems with stoves were concerned with their installation or the chimney rather than the functioning of the equipment itself.

There were quite a lot of shops selling fireplaces and sundry stoves within thirty to forty miles of Wincanton, but the advice provided was generally incompetent and sometimes dangerous. One shop demonstrated a stove with a single wall-flue pipe only an inch away from woodwork which had blackened and was steaming. Another one had just recovered from a chimney fire caused by burning green wood. I would have no difficulty at all competing against people like these.

When we applied for permission to change the use of the barn from a cowshed it was turned down flat by the District Council, who said it would affect the 'amenities in a mainly rural area'. We pointed out that both an agricultural engineer and a haulage business had been operated from Bitwood Farm in the past but to no avail. We appealed to the Department of Environment who sent down an inspector. All our neighbours supported what we wanted to do and a local Wincanton solicitor was most helpful in the preparation of our case. One question I was asked was, 'Why can't you sell your stoves from a shop in Wincanton where most people do the shopping?' I replied, amidst laughter, that stoves were expensive and could not be bought like a joint of meat. I particularly wanted to show customers how they might be installed, including those we already had in the house.

After inspecting the premises, we were given permission and costs were awarded against the Council. It was now up to us, but the controversy caused a six-month delay, which I had made use of to do the carpentry.

We decided to set up a small business which we would call 'Three Counties Woodburning Centre'. Bitwood Farm was within a few miles of Wiltshire, Avon and Somerset; the description also implied we covered the three counties – as indeed we hoped we would.

The sale of our Buckinghamshire house had left us with a little spare capital, and we 'loaned' £20,000 to the Centre to start it off. I used about two-thirds of it to buy individual stoves for display and also office equipment like a photocopier. My first year aim was a turnover of £50,000 and accordingly I set up weekly advertising based on 3½% of turnover with a splash to start it all off. I had found a small builder to instal the stoves when they had been bought, and who was reliable and happy to get the work. He ran his own business separately from mine so that he was not on my payroll. This also applied later on when we gave work to several builders and plumbers within about twenty-five miles, who could be relied upon to instal the stoves to my standards.

I aimed to provide professional advice in our showroom-barn, and, if necessary, would also make a free visit to a house of a potential customer and advise on the most suitable form of heating in their particular circumstances.

The average mark-up on stoves and fireplaces was about 30%, whilst chimneys and the equipment to go with them averaged 40–50%. As my running costs did not amount to more than about 7–8%, including the car, there was a considerable leeway to offer discounts, especially in the summer.

Our many customers came from every social class from the proverbial dukes to dustmen. Country seats often wanted more efficient fireplaces to warm up their spacious rooms without ruining themselves paying bills for expensive oil. Frequently these led to more orders in the house or with friends. Old age pensioners wanted stoves to heat small rooms and were delighted when their fuel consumption was divided by four or five. One middle-aged lady dressed in rags came in to our showroom with a complaint about a stove installed by a rival. She had bought an old house and she told me that the stove had smoked and had never worked properly. It had already been removed when I arrived to see what had happened. The place was a shambles and she wore gumboots to wade through the wet and muddy floor in her sitting room. She had already selected a nice West German stove with doors that could be opened like an open fire. Our terms were always balance of cash on delivery but I began to be suspicious. When I got back I rang up my rival who lived about twenty-five miles away. Apparently her cheque had bounced and, after checking, he had gone straight round to the house and removed his stove, keeping the deposit. When I rang her up and told her that we would deliver as soon as her cheque had been cleared, she withdrew her order. She thought she could get the use of a free stove until the winter weather had passed. She was operating like a gypsy with money she did not possess. Fortunately only one other customer (this time well-dressed) tried the same trick in our third year. He was not successful.

Most people were quite superb. They were grateful for the advice I provided, particularly on the few occasions when I advised that the installation of new stoves or fireplaces was not really economic. In almost every case this produced another sale in a friend's house. Our reputation for integrity and fair dealing spread rapidly. Our turnover for the first year was just over £60,000, an increase of 20% on our target. I was enjoying myself and getting increasing satisfaction from running our little business.

As from the second year, I only stocked stoves or fireplaces that would burn wood or coal. The snag of wood was that it had to be really dry and this meant leaving it in stacks for at least a year after splitting. Dry wood produced about half the heat of coal, although its welcoming effect could hardly be beaten in an open fire. Quite a few houses had unlimited supplies of wood and, provided they had sound chimneys, a stove would give out about four to five times the amount of heat when compared with an open fire, where most of the heat disappeared up the chimney.

I aimed usually to provide a similar stove to one on display within seven to ten days of order. During the winter I kept one alight all the time and this drew a considerable number of orders. If I had been prepared to hold large stocks of one type, I could have had higher mark-ups, but I preferred to have the stock held by the manufacturer or wholesaler who was still able to give me about 30%. If a particular type did not sell fast in the winter, I changed it for something else, provided I was satisfied about its construction.

Some customers preferred to use their own builders or plumbers or occasionally to do the work themselves. After two of them came back in our first year with complaints, I prepared a handout with recommendations on how they should be put in. We never had any complaints when the work was done by our approved builders or plumbers; such problems as occurred were invariably a result of faulty installation.

Our aim for the second year was to increase turnover by 25% to £75,000. I became more selective in the type of fireplace or stove we had on show and also I started to expand into other areas such as carved wooden fire surrounds and chimneys. Any stove, fireplace or central heating cooker had to look right in the room and then be connected to a chimney of adequate internal diameter and height. Sometimes existing large chimneys could be lined or alternatively constructed from pumice blocks or double-wall stainless steel.

British building regulations in the 70s were really only designed for coal-burning open fireplaces or for solid fuel boilers. They were not nearly so stringent as those found necessary for safety in Scandinavia and North America. I soon discovered that chimney fires could be virtually eliminated by lining a chimney with easily-laid blocks of pumice with appropriate-sized holes in the middle. This system also provided a well-insulated flue pipe which was the basis of modern practice when wood stoves were in use. Alternatively double-skin stainless steel flues could also be used, although some States in USA had banned their installation because they melted in a bad chimney fire and set light to the wood-frame house in which they were normally fitted. If wood was to be the normal fuel, I always recommended pumice linings, unless the customer already had a satisfactory chimney.

The adaptation of old inglenook fireplaces to take fireplaces or stoves became a normal feature. It was very rare indeed for my advice to be rejected after carrying out an inspection on site. Another sale was made and by the end of the second year turnover was just over £90,000. This was highly satisfactory, but I was reaching the limit of running a business on my own, although Evie provided a superb back-up by typing the letters and the price lists. She also ran the showroom when I was out. I thought a more modest target of £100,000 turnover for year three should be attainable without over-stretching either of us. We also planned to visit our youngest daughter, Celia, in Vancouver in June where she was completing a two-year post-doctoral fellowship in the University of British Columbia. One of my aims was to see if Canadian stoves were suitable for use in the UK and then to import and distribute them. Unfortunately, in my judgment, they were both ugly and relatively expensive.

In what turned out to be our last year running Three Counties Woodburning Centre I concentrated even more on quite expensive stoves made by Coalbrookdale, stoves with glass doors that could be opened up like a fireplace made by Dovre, open fireplaces with circulating air round the back made by Jetmaster and Stronglow and central-heating cookers made by Bosky of Sheffield. All these could burn coal or wood and were first class. In addition we dealt directly with over twenty different manufacturers or importing agents providing a range of equipment covering all price ranges. I would not sell any stove or cooker that was poorly designed or had features likely to give trouble in the future. This excluded quite a number of firms who had spent heavily on advertising their products. Once again we exceeded our target and turnover was just short of £120,000. Our reputation had spread far and wide. Some of our customers came from over fifty miles away. But we both worked hard.

Half-way through our third year a tragedy struck our eldest daughter, Shirley. Her second marriage had fallen apart and her only assets were half a house in the middle of North Devon and a lot of debts left by her husband whom she had divorced. Legally she was responsible for them because she had also signed the papers. He said he was unable to support her, although he was the father of her youngest daughter. Later on he provided individual and irregular cash payments which went some way to help.

We were not prepared to see Shirley go down hill, so we decided to sell Bitwood Farm and its business and move up to South Warwickshire where my sister had been living for more than twenty years. We found a large old house which could easily be divided into two, with separate stairways. Old Manor House at Halford fitted our requirements exactly. Part black and white but most of it built in stone, it dated originally from the 16th century and came with seven or eight bedrooms. Adjacent to a 12th century church on one side and with some lovely old stone cottages on the other, it was on a small hill with an unrestricted view across its own five acres of paddocks, the River Stour and farmland beyond. Shirley came with us when we first looked round. We were all captivated. This was our dream house. We thanked our lucky stars for the extra capital we has acquired from our little business in Somerset. It was to come in very handy.

Shirley and her three children would live in one half and Evie and I in the rest, which included a 'ballroom' forty-two feet long by twenty-two feet wide. I divided this into three by putting up two partitions, making a kitchen, a dining room and a morning room, from which stairs led up to our own two bedrooms and a bathroom. Evie likes warm houses so we heated 'our' part of the house by Calor gas. On Shirley's side, a new oil boiler heated the whole of 'her' house, but, as she was unlikely to be able to afford to run it, I put in a large Coalbrookdale multifuel stove in her sitting room. This worked beautifully and together with the Aga in her kitchen kept her downstairs as warm as she wanted.

The large towns of Stratford upon Avon, Warwick or Leamington Spa and Banbury were all within fifteen miles and should provide opportunities for employment for Shirley, while Evie could help with school runs. Shirley's only qualification at that time was as a secretary. So she applied for and was given a job as Secretary/PA to a consultant in Banbury hospital. She did it for two years and this gave her the idea of becoming more involved with hospitals. At the age of forty she was accepted for a three-year training course as a Registered Nurse which she completed in the Spring of 1989.

In the end we were not sorry to leave Bitwood Farm and move north. Our family came first and my sister was able to introduce us to large numbers of delightful people living near us in the lovely South Warwickshire countryside. Pretty stone-built houses with colourful gardens nestled among charming villages which were largely untouched by obscene development. That is until the new M40 motorway, opened in January, 1991, pierced the countryside in sweeping curves past Warwick and Banbury on its way to London.

It took us a year to sort out our new home. Once again it was in a rundown state and most of the bathrooms had to be scrapped. Our predecessor had had a flood from frozen pipes and this necessitated a new oak floor in our 'ballroom'. I made drawings of a new oak kitchen and had the cupboards superbly made by craftsmen from near Hereford. I then put them in and Evie says it is quite the nicest kitchen she has ever had. She also became an expert decorator and did all the tiling in the kitchen and bathrooms. On Shirley's side there was also a great deal to do. Her bathroom in the oldest part of the house, with plaster fleur de lys on the walls, and very sloping floors, had to be rebuilt with a step to climb into the bath. Some lovely old wooden panels in her sitting room were covered in at least five layers of green, black and blue paint and varnish, which took three weeks to remove. The outside of her inglenook fireplace was covered in plaster, which when removed, exposed a fine old oak beam. In this were a number of holes, into one of which had been stuffed an old bill dated 1702, listing buttons and bows adding up to fourteen shillings and two pence three farthings. We were very busy in our first year.

By this time Celia was a lecturer and research scientist up in Durham University. She was on a three-year contract and lived in digs, although she still kept on to her little house in Cambridge which she had let. While her time in Durham had not been the happiest, mainly due to academic politics in her department and being starved of funds for her research, she decided to sell her Cambridge house when she still had a year to run.

Towards the end of our first summer, we had a look at Compton Verney Lodge. Built of stone about 1850 it had already been auctioned but had been withdrawn because it had not reached the reserve price. It was derelict and under a compulsory order for demolition and removal if a buyer could not be found. Internally it was a shell and outside large quantities of stone were lying all round in overgrown weeds and shrubs. Most of the black-painted internal doors were off their hinges, all windows and frames were either broken or rotten. I thought we could tackle it if we paid the right price. After a lot of haggling by us, and after a survey, Celia bought it together with three acres of land including about an acre of 'Amenity Woodland'. She thought she might get a long-term job in either Warwick or Birmingham University.

★ ★ ★

Compton Verney Lodge had been built in the mid-19th century as a prestige lodge for the magnificent Grade I listed Compton Verney House. This had been put up in 1714 with lakes and gardens laid out by Capability Brown, who had also designed the stone chapel behind the house. The Lodge had sandstone quoins with local Lighthorne stone for the courses, and its background history was interesting. Originally designed by Mr John Gibson, the architect, it was a completely square building with decorated stone gable ends on each of its four faces. It must have looked quite delightful. Two large stone-built bay windows opened into the sitting room and traces could be seen of the original curved sash windows with curved shutters on the inside. There was, however, only space in the roof for one small room on the first floor.

Living conditions had been primitive. There was no drainage and no mains water, but electricity had been connected. In spite of all this the Lodge had been occupied until the early 50s when the tenant could stand it no longer. It was left unoccupied for fifteen to twenty years, during which time vandals got in and stole a considerable quantity of lead off the roof. This was not replaced, and over the next few years water and frost rotted the roof timbers. A large barn attached to the back of the house, providing covered access to the well, had also fallen in. But the main structure was still there and it could have been rebuilt. A few years later it would have been listed as Grade 2. By now, however, another new owner bought the estate and he decided to 'modernize' the Lodge by raising the whole roof by two feet to allow sufficient headroom for a complete first floor. In the process he vandalised the unique appearance of the Lodge with its pretty decorated gables and dumped the surplus large blocks of sandstone and building stone all round the outside. After a year or so the local authority woke up to what was happening and all further building work was stopped. The owner then lost interest and did nothing, in spite of tart letters from the Council, until the Estate was sold again to Christopher Buxton in the early 80s. The Lodge was now derelict, with water coming in through a temporary roof. The Council must have lost patience and served a demolition and removal order on the building which would only be revoked if it was brought up to minimum standards for habitation.

The officials concerned with building regulations were most helpful and soon stamped my plans as approved after being satisfied with some additional sectional drawings showing the new stairway and the garage. We were now ready to go out to tender for a builder willing to take on the work.

After much deliberation, we selected Bob Simmonds, an elderly small builder and stone mason who then lived in Wellesbourne. He started work in January, 1986, and thought it would not take him much more than five months. I would put in the windows and glaze them, the skirting boards, all the doors and the kitchen. I would also arrange separate contracts for the plumbing, electrical work and tiling the two roofs. My job was really a 'clerk of works', but I would have to make sure that none of the contractors cut corners. I knew enough about it to make sure this did not happen. I fitted the new dog-leg staircase in parana pine together with a pine balustrade and spindles. These were stained and polished to match the ground floor doors and complemented the feel of the ground floor. After the rooms were all plastered it began to look rather nice. Evie then came in and decorated the whole house and also tiled the kitchen and bathrooms. It really had now become a superb small house in which any of us could have lived very comfortably. What is more, we had both enjoyed doing the work. Then at Christmas, 1986, Celia changed her plans. Not only was she not going to Warwick or Birmingham universities, but she was thinking very seriously of giving up her career in science and joining the Church. In the meantime, Harvard had her over for a week but she did not get the job. She had been offered a place in her subject in California, but she turned it down. So she gave it all up, and this would mean selling the Lodge.

Fortunately house prices had now risen, but we were quite proud of the internal finish. It was up to a high standard. Outside, the stone-built double garage and utility room nearly doubled the length of the property and this improved the overall appearance. By the time the area round the house had been turfed and a flagstone path laid to the front door, we were quite pleased with our work, which had taken about a year. To celebrate, we had a 'topping out' party in the drawing-room and had a nice wood fire burning in the grate, surrounded by green marble together with a green marble hearth and inside an Adam-style decorated fire surround. As might be expected with my background the fire drew very well with its own air supply led in by ducts under the floor.

We sold the Lodge on Celia's behalf in the Spring, repaying the loan I had made to her and we were able to pass on some of the surplus cash to our other daughters. Most of this represented the work I had contributed to the rebuilding, so she was very ready to take advice on where help might be needed. We all celebrated a little when contracts were exchanged. We thought we had deserved our success, although we were sorry Celia would not be living there.

* 33 *

HOUSES FOR OURSELVES

Old Manor House was a lovely house in which to live and it also provided a roof over Shirley and her three children. But it was a large place with an even larger garden, and neither of us was getting any younger. Shirley was in the first year of her nursing training and she kept saying that her part of the house was too big or too awkward to keep clean. She did not want to move in the spring of her final year of training because she would be involved with exams, but she could see herself going to a more convenient house between her second and third years. This also suited us and we set about looking for our 'final resting place'. This would surely be our last major move.

We looked at a large number of houses until Elm Tree House in the High Street of Chipping Camden came on offer. It was sandwiched between Gabb's café on one side and an antique shop on the other. Like many houses in the High Street, it appeared to be an amalgamation of two old houses on to which a fine-cut stone front had been built a century or two before. We were first struck by the large white-painted semi-circular bay window that stuck out over the pavement and was adjacent to a really old front door. High up on the second floor, three stone gables provided a distinctive symmetry to the front elevation. Behind the house a long garden stretched back the full width for about forty yards to a very old square building on one side with a Cotswold stone roof. This had once been used for carriages and then as a double garage. Later it was used as a lending library for the local children. This would do fine as my future workshop. Moving on down the garden through a pair of black-painted wrought-iron gates, there was a large turning area with a timber double garage. A fifty-yard long drive led from it to a road at the back. So far it was just what we wanted.

Inside it was difficult to imagine a house less conveniently arranged or so inadequately heated. Not much maintenance had been done for forty years. The kitchen was dark and the wall on the garden side was damp and smelt of mould. This dampness was probably caused by some stone and concrete steps which had been put up on the outside of the kitchen wall to give access to the first floor from the garden. We discovered later that, earlier on this century, the house had been used as a Guild Workshop to house printing machinery. The steps must have been put in as a fire escape. Most of the dim light in the kitchen came from a modern obscured glass window which 'looked' straight into Gabb's café and through which we could hear talking and the smell of cooking.

The key to the modernization of the kitchen was clearly the removal of the steps, insertion of a new window in their place, and blocking up the existing window to stop the noise and smell coming through.

The remaining downstairs rooms were delightful with a nice inglenook fireplace in the drawing room, a good sized study and a hall with a dining room beyond. Most of the internal doors were dreadful, but this could easily be corrected.

The first thing to be sorted out had to be the kitchen. The nasty concrete steps had to be removed and a stone-mullioned window put in its place. There were signs that a window had once been there. All the electric boxes were rusted solid and a direct short in a ring main cable was discovered in one wall. The fuse had not been repaired for many years. We knew the house was 'listed', but we were not aware that when a listing takes place this includes all modern or near-modern additions that had been added in the past. Putting the window back in the kitchen was really restoring the room to what it had once been. We accepted Robert Groves' estimate for this work which was done very expertly and included changing the door into the first-floor spare bedroom back into a window.

The kitchen needed a lot of work after the new window was put in. Vertical studding was put in on the opposite wall and faced with half-inch ply. This would not only allow sound insulation from Gabb's café but also provide an air outlet to the extractor fan above the stove. We also completely refurbished the two bathrooms, and installed new and up-to-date central heating. Then just before Christmas, 1987, Shirley said that full-time nursing training in Warwick/Leamington nearly fifteen miles away, at the same time as looking after her part of the house and cooking for her children, was beginning to get her down. She had also hurt her back falling off a roundabout at the 'mop' (fair) in Stratford. She was unable to work for a month and she was worried. She felt that she could not now move in the following spring, and would have to postpone everything for two years. This became a blessing in disguise. We had come to realize that living in a town was much noisier than our peaceful and quiet life at Halford. We decided we would sell Elm Tree House in the spring, and all our moves would be put back about two years. In retrospect, this might work our rather well because not only would we all be moving house in Halford, but also our two youngest daughters were likely to be on the move that year. This would get rid of their furniture which we had stored at Old Manor House for several years.

By late February we had just about finished Elm Tree House and several agents came in and gave valuations. Because we could not guarantee to show all potential buyers round the house, we selected a local agent and I had a draft letter in hand to give to him. One day when I was putting the finishing touches to one of the front windows, a pretty girl in her 20s wearing a man's homburg hat, put her head round the corner and asked for directions to where another house was for sale in the High Street. I told her and also mentioned that this house would be coming on the market in the next week or two. Apparently she was an assistant solicitor working for a firm in Devizes, and she had been despatched to Chipping Camden to see what the houses were like and whether it was a nice town in which to live. She asked if she could pass on my address and phone number to her boss, because she had seen a lovely old door through the bay window and was sure that Elm Tree House might suit her boss's client. She said the right thing, because I had just made and hung the dining room door, which included a genuine seventeenth century panel in the middle.

To cut a long story short, Mr and Mrs Jackson eventually bought the house privately at a price which reflected the very high standard of its fittings and convenience. We also thought it compensated a little for the loving care which we had both expended on getting it right for ourselves. Having taken the decision to sell, we hoped that the new owners would enjoy living in Campden as much as we had hoped we would have done ourselves.

★ ★ ★

So ends my story. In December, 1988, we received planning permission to put up a small house for Shirley in our garden. This kept us busy during the summer and autumn of 1989. It turned out very well and melded into our delightful village with hardly a murmur. She moved in just before Christmas, 1989. We now, of course, find that living in a very large house with a large garden is rather too much for either of us to contemplate as we become older. We have just found what we hope will be the perfect answer. It is a newly built house on the edge of Little Kineton. It faces south looking over fields, with room for a conservatory, workshop and greenhouse, and there are shops and a church in the village. We hope it will turn out to be as nice as we both believe it should be.

Apart from creating a new garden, I wonder what our next projects will be?

BIBLIOGRAPHY

Allfrey	*Warlords of Oman*	Hale
Bauer	*The Battle of Arnhem*	Bauer
Brereton	*The Brereton Diaries*	Morrow
Deane-Drummond	*Return Ticket*	Collins
De Guingand	*From Brass Hat to Bowler Hat*	Hamilton
Eisenhower	*Crusade in Europe*	Doubleday
Foxall	*Guinea Pigs*	Hale
Frost	*A Drop too Many*	Cassell
Golden	*Echoes from Arnhem*	Kimber
Hinsley and others	*British Intelligence in the Second World War.* Vol. III, Part II	HMSO
Kershaw	*It Never Snows in September*	Crowood Press
Kitson	*Bunch of Five*	Faber
Montgomery	*Normandy to the Baltic*	Hutchison
Morris	*Sultan in Oman*	Faber
Ryan	*A Bridge too Far*	Hamilton
Sims	*Arnhem Spearhead*	Imperial War Museum
Smiley	*Arabian Assignment*	Cooper
Thesiger	*Arabian Sands*	Longman
Urquhart (Brian)	*A Life in Peace and War*	Wiedenfeld and Nicolson
Urquhart (Roy)	*Arnhem*	Cassell
Wilmot	*The Struggle for Europe*	Doubleday

—	*The Harvest of Ten Years* (A selection of diaries and photographs from the Battle of Arnhem)	Published in limited edition by the Airborne Museum at Oosterbeek
Public Record Office (Kew)	*Reports on Colossus 1940/41*	DEFE 2/152-3
	Report by Central Landing Establishment, Ringway '40/41	ADM 199-899
	Reports on Airborne Phase, Operation Market	WO 205/1123
	Report on Airborne Phase, Operation Market (Sept. '44)	AIR 16/1026

The members of 'X' Troop, No. 2 Commando, who took part in Operation Colossus

Major T. A. G. Pritchard
Captain C. Lea
Captain G. Daly
Lieut. A. Deane-Drummond
Second-Lieut. G. Paterson
Second-Lieut. G. Jowett
Flight-Lieut. Lucky
Sgt. P. P. Clements
Sgt. A. L. Lawley
Sgt. J. Shutt
Sgt. E. W. Durie
Sgt. J. Walker
Cpl. P. Julian
Cpl. J. E. Grice
Cpl. P. O'Brien
Cpl. D. Fletcher
L./Cpl. R. B. Watson
L./Cpl. D. H. Boulter
L./Cpl. D. E. Jones
L./Cpl. H. Pexton
L./Cpl. H. Tomlin
L./Cpl. J. E. Maher
L./Cpl. D. Henderson
Tpr. J. Nastri
Tpr. A. B. Ross
Tpr. E. Samuels
Tpr. E. Humphreys
Tpr. F. Picchi
Tpr. J. Parker
Tpr. A. Parker
Tpr. D. L. Struthers
Tpr. G. Pryor
Tpr. D. J. Phillips
Tpr. J. W. Crawford
Tpr. R. Davidson

From: Lt Col A.J. Deane-Drummond

Headquarters,
Land Forces Persian Gulf,
British Forces Post Office 63.

30 October, 1958.

I am giving this to Frank Kitson to bring back.

I have had a detailed look at the problem and it is certainly an excellent SAS task. Owing to the enormous area of mountain leading up to the plateau, it will take time to get to know it all. I think there is a good chance of killing Talib before the end of April 1959, but it will be essential to start as soon as possible. Even if we do not kill Talib I think we should be able to give his followers really bloody noses. This should condition the rebels' frame of mind to the extent where negotiations will be successful.

Success will be dependent on starting quickly and setting up an efficient system of collecting information.

You originally asked for 50 volunteers for the force. I far prefer to give the task to one squadron whose strength is about 70, but who will only be able to put about 50 up the mountain at the sharp end. Naturally we could do the job better with the whole Regiment, but I know the political and administrative snags to this one.

The entry of the squadron can be dressed up in any politically acceptable form but British administrative backing will be essential. This should include surgical facilities within reach, a helicopter for casevacs and facilities for air re-supply.

It is an ideal task for us and I do hope agreement to go ahead will be reached at your end. We can leave Malaya on 15 Nov if we get the word.

I have shown this letter to Col Smiley, who completely agrees with it.

[signature]

Major General J. Hamilton, C.B., C.B.E., D.S.O.,
The War Office (DMO),
LONDON, S.W.1.

TOP SECRET

Appendix 4

MESSAGE FORM

COMM. CEN/SIGNALS USE

PRIORITY

NUMBER

D/0138

PRECEDENCE — ACTION	PRECEDENCE — INFO	DATE — TIME GROUP	MESSAGE INSTRUCTIONS
PRIORITY	DEFERRED	070500Z	

FROM FARELF

PREFIX GR

TO 22 SAS

SECURITY CLASSIFICATION

SECRET

INFO CBAFP

ORIGINATOR'S NUMBER

CIC/9 (.)

PERSONAL FOR CO FROM CINC FARELF (.)

HAVE JUST HEARD OF SUCCESSFUL OUTCOME OF RECENT EVENTS IN YOUR AREA WHICH REFLECTS THE GREATEST CREDIT ON YOUR TROOPS OPERATING UNDER SUCH NEW AND DIFFICULT CONDITIONS (.)

PLEASE GIVE THEM MY CONGRATULATIONS AND THE BEST WISHES OF US ALL IN FARELF

CRYPTO CENTRE
7 FEB 1959
BATU SIG. TROOP

A - Paraphrase NOT required
No unclassified reply other than one of the following -

YES	NO
AGREED	NOT AGREED
APPROVED	NOT APPROVED
CONCUR	REQUEST REPLY
CONFIRMED	ACKNOWLEDGED (ACK)

of pages | REFERS TO MESSAGE CLASSIFIED YES NO | DRAFTER'S NAME | OFFICE | TEL No.

R | DATE | TIME | SYSTEM | OPERATOR | D | DATE | TIME | SYSTEM | OPERATOR | RELEASING OFFICER'S SIGNATURE | RANK

S. Ltd.—1088

From: General Sir Roderick McLeod, KCB, CBE.

TELEPHONE: HOUNSLOW 2371.

HEADQUARTERS,
EASTERN COMMAND,
HOUNSLOW,
MIDDLESEX.

22 April 1963.

My dear Tony,

I should like to go on record and to say how very pleased indeed I was with all that I saw in Cyprus last week. There is no doubt at all that your Brigade is in fine shape and that not only the Parachute Battalions, but also the minor units leave nothing to be desired.

I am quite sure that your Brigade could "run rings" round many regular brigades and given a couple of weeks training and hardening up I should be proud to take it to war under any conditions.

I was particularly glad to note the standard of saluting and of dress. I never saw a soldier deliberately turn away and pretend he hadn't seen me and I never saw a man who had not got his beret on straight and looking alert and tidy. I wish I could say the same of the majority of regular soldiers in England.

I shall be seeing the CIGS in the next few days and I propose to make quite sure that he hears all about your Exercise and how well it went.

I would be grateful if you would take whatever steps seem to you to be appropriate to let all ranks know how very pleased I was with everything that I saw in Cyprus and how proud I am to have the Brigade under my command. I hope that the second half of your training will go equally well and that you will not have any serious casualties.

Yours ever

Roddy McLeod

Brigadier A.J. Deane-Drummond, DSO, MC,
Commander
44 Independent Parachute Brigade Group (TA)
B.F.P.O. 53.

INDEX